Winston W. Crouch

Dean E. McHenry

John C. Bollens

All in the Department of
Political Science
University of California
Los Angeles

Stanley Scott

Bureau of Public
Administration
University of California
Berkeley

California

Government

and

Politics

Second Edition

Prentice-Hall, Inc.

Englewood Cliffs, N. J.

1960

PRINTED IN THE UNITED STATES OF AMERICA

11254-C

Preface

CALIFORNIA, in its second century of state-
hood, retains an aura of glamour that has been evident since its
fabulous beginnings. Mission and rancho gave way to goldseeker
and trader, who in turn yielded to farmer, laborer, and merchant.
In the twentieth century, the state has developed a remarkably
diversified economy, soundly based upon the great resources of
the west. Climate, petroleum, rich soils, water, and forests provide a firm foundation for a vast economic development. And
California has continued to attract, decade after decade, people
who both produce goods and services and who, as consumers,
provide a ready market for them.

As California has grown in population and economic strength,
so too her political power has increased. A minor influence in
national politics in the 1850's, California has now come to play
a pivotal role in the nominating conventions of both major parties.
With power comes responsibility. Californians need to know more
about their own governmental institutions and activities, not only
to be good citizens of the state, but also to make sure that the
influence of the state in national affairs is exerted according to
their will. Persons of other states may be interested in assessing
the impact of California on Washington by taking a closer look
at the government and politics of the state that has assumed
such a large measure of national leadership.

In the four years since the previous edition of this book many
major changes and developments have taken place in California
government and politics. Some are the repeal of cross-filing in

v

elections, abandonment of split sessions of the state legislature, creation of the long recommended office of auditor general, and alterations in state and local taxes. Others are the rise of the Democratic party in state politics, advocacy of state administrative reorganization, expansion of state and local activities, increased use of appointed chief administrators in cities and counties, and urban growth.

This new edition considers all these recent developments, as well as many others of importance, in the context of earlier trends. Significant new events and new research findings have been incorporated, and material of less consequence has been compressed or eliminated. To indicate the seriousness of the problems of urban concentrations, a new final chapter on metropolitan areas has been added. And we have deliberately timed the completion of this edition to be able to include the latest significant policy decisions of the state legislature.

We have attempted to make this book useful to a wide audience. In its preparation we have striven for a proper balance of politics and administration and of state and local governments. The book is intended to be concise and comprehensive. For additional details, we suggest that the reader consult other books and articles listed in the bibliographies at the end of each chapter.

In an effort to portray California government and politics accurately, interestingly, and candidly, we have drawn on our long-time firsthand experience as researchers and participants in many public affairs of state and community, as well as on the writings and observations of numerous other people.

We are grateful to a large number of the many readers of the previous edition for their helpful and encouraging comments and suggestions.

Winston W. Crouch
Dean E. McHenry
John C. Bollens
Stanley Scott

Los Angeles and Berkeley, California

Table of Contents

vii

Fourteen

METROPOLITAN AREAS (Cont'd)

One

The Challenge

of Growth

CALIFORNIA IS A STATE characterized by big-
ness and variety. Covering three-fifths of the Pacific Coast of the
United States, it has 156,803 square miles, a land area exceeded
only by that of Alaska and Texas. Included is a broad diversity of
topography, climate, soil, minerals, and plant and animal life.
Located in close proximity are Mt. Whitney and Death Valley,
the highest and lowest points, respectively, in the state. California is the land of sunshine but also the land where substantial
portions are snowbound for several months of the year.

THE EARLY PERIOD

The broad potentialities of California were largely neglected
for many years after the initial land claims by European countries. The region was discovered by the Spanish explorer Cabrillo
in 1542, but it was not until more than two centuries later, in
1769, that Spain undertook the first permanent European settlement at San Diego. During the subsequent period of active Spanish rule, a series of presidios, pueblos, and missions were created
as far north as Upper San Francisco Bay. Presidios were military
installations to protect coastal positions; pueblos were communities of farmers to supply food to soldiers; and missions were locations established to teach useful arts to Indians and to convert

1

them to Christianity. However, little more than a half-century passed before Mexico in 1822 declared her independence of Spain and took over California. This reign was weak and short-lived. It featured the return of the large land holdings of the missions to the public domain and the confirmation of many extensive private rancho grants. As early as the first years of Mexican control, settlers from the United States began arriving overland from the east. The Mexican War broke out in 1846 and California became the major prize transferred to the United States two years later at the end of the conflict.

The period of the late 1840's was dramatic and fast-moving. Early in 1848, almost simultaneously with the peace treaty, gold was discovered near Sacramento. This resulted in an onrush of population, inaugurating a trend which has not yet reached its peak more than a century later. In 1849 the population was 15,000, exclusive of Indians; by 1852 it had risen to 250,000. Almost overnight what had been leisurely, pastoral Mexican California became a bustling part of the United States. The American gold miners tapped a rich resource, but they overlooked many others—the productive valleys, the large petroleum reserves, and the thick forests, for example.

PRESENT FEATURES OF CALIFORNIA

Rapid Population Growth

Slightly more than a century of statehood has passed. Let us look at some important current characteristics of California, many of which affect and are affected by its state and local governments.* By 1960 more than fifteen million people had settled on its large and diversified land area. This total, exceeded only by New York, is all the more spectacular when viewed comparatively. During the twentieth century, the state's population has increased more than ten times while the national population has somewhat more than doubled. One migrant or baby each minute has made California his home in each of the last ten years. Most

---

* Items 1 and 8 in the "Further Reading" list at the end of this chapter are excellent inventories of many California features and problems.

of the population growth has been the result of heavy migration. In 1950, only about 39 of every 100 Californians were natives. On the other hand, approximately 51 were born in other states and 10 were foreign-born. Although there has been a rapid rise in the birth rate in the state, 1950 is the most recent year in which the number of births topped the number of migrants. Predictions are that this imbalance will still exist in 1970.

Urbanism and Metropolitanism

Most Californians are urban dwellers. During all of the present century more than one-half of the residents have lived in urban areas. Concurrently, the state has averaged a 15 per cent larger urban population than the nation as a whole. Another long-time phase of the distribution of the state's people is also extraordinary. Since 1900 more than one-half of the population has been located in the two metropolitan areas of which Los Angeles-Long Beach and San Francisco-Oakland are the major hubs of economic, social and governmental activity. Urban land which contained about one-half of the state's people in 1900 now has about nine-tenths of them. Furthermore, three-fifths of the current total population live in either the Los Angeles-Long Beach or the San Francisco-Oakland metropolitan area. Many of the other urbanites reside in one of the other fast-growing metropolitan areas whose central cities are Bakersfield, Santa Barbara, Fresno, Sacramento, San Bernardino-Riverside-Ontario, San Diego, San Jose, and Stockton. The trends toward urbanism and metropolitanism are continuing.

Diversified Land Uses

California's land area consists of about 100 million acres. On the average, of every 100 acres 25 are devoted to grazing, 22 are desert, 21 are in timber, 14 are brush land, 11 are assigned to cultivated crops, and 7 are urban and barren land. More than 7 million acres are irrigated. A relatively small total, it nevertheless accounts for more than 80 per cent of farm income derived from all agriculturally productive land. About 7 million acres have been judged by expert soil chemists to contain excellent or good soil. In comparison, a much smaller state such as Iowa has far more soil of excellent quality. California produces surpluses in fruits and vegetables, but is deficient in the production of cereals, eggs, manufactured dairy products, and meats.

This analysis of land uses shows that a substantial portion of the area is utilized for timber. Furthermore, most of it is commercial timberland. Timber products are being cut at the annual rate of about 6 billion board feet. This is twice the amount of growth. However, about one-half of the extensive supply of virgin timber remains untouched.

Fire is a perennial threat both to the forests and to the range lands. There are several thousand forest and range fires in the state each year. Two of the most ruinous recent fires occurred in Santa Barbara County in 1955 and the Cleveland National Forest in 1958; each spread over thousands of acres of forests.

Water and Power

A reasonably adequate water supply exists, but the major sources are largely located at considerable distances from the principal areas of demand. Such situations have required the execution of imaginative and competent plans. Some are concerned mainly with urban areas, involving, for example, the carrying of large amounts of water hundreds of miles to the people of such localities as the Los Angeles, San Francisco-Oakland, and San Diego metropolitan areas. Others, of which the Central Valley Project is illustrative, relate principally to strengthening agricultural productivity. In addition, ground-water basins have been more extensively tapped in California than anywhere else. In some instances basins are being overpumped.

The fundamental importance of water has frequently made it a subject of controversy or concern involving various governments. Thus, California has an interest in the Colorado river, which traverses both state and national boundaries; in the Tia Juana river, which is international; and in the Klamath and Walker rivers, which are interstate. Most places suitable for hydro-electric developments are so far from the major points of consumption that electrical energy must be transmitted over long distances.

Part of a devastating fire in Santa Barbara County that spread over thousands of acres of forest. Courtesy, Santa Barbara News-Press.

A number of sectional conflicts over the development and use of water resources within the state have also highlighted California's history. By the late 1950's, however, the pressures of population growth and agricultural and industrial needs, particularly in southern California, gave the establishment of a state-wide plan for water development and distribution a top priority. In 1959, the long-standing sectional deadlock on the problem was broken by the passage of a water program by the state legislature. The plan proposed a $1.75 billion bond issue to finance the diversion of water from the Feather River and Delta Pool in the north to southern California. This is the largest single water development project ever proposed by a state.

The Economy

California's economic life has undergone substantial modifications during the years of statehood, forming a pattern markedly

*Part of the farm lands brought into production by irriga-
tion in the Central Valley Project. Courtesy, Fresno Chamber of Commerce.*

different in some respects from that of the nation as a whole. In
the early years gold mining constituted the major activity. Subsequently, hides and wheat became important items for shipment,
and later petroleum and citrus fruits assumed significant positions. Quick growth of the automobile industry in the present
century brought on much greater demands for petroleum. These
nationwide needs were partly satisfied through numerous new
oil-field discoveries in the state. Improved rail transportation
made it possible as early as World War I for California to ship
considerably larger quantities of agricultural produce, including
processed foods.

Significant changes in the distribution of workers came about
in the late nineteenth century.* As productivity and real income
increased, people spent a smaller portion of their money on basic
essentials, most notably food, and a larger part on more elaborate

---

* These shifts are well explained by Margaret S. Gordon in her book,
Employment Expansion and Population Growth: The California Experience
(Berkeley: University of California Press, 1954).

goods and services. Simultaneously, many activities which had been traditionally performed in the home were transferred outside to factories, service establishments, hospitals, professional offices, and public entertainment locations. Also, greater agricultural productivity diminished the number of workers needed to supply an adequate amount of food. What were the results of such developments? Proportionately, agriculture greatly declined in occupational importance, and manufacturing and distributive and service trades grew.

For many years California has had a higher proportion of workers in distributive and service occupations than the nation as a whole. In 1870 one-third of its workers were so engaged; nationally the total was one-fourth. By 1958 the proportion in California had grown to more than three-fifths whereas the national figure stood at slightly more than one-half. The extensiveness of urbanization and the comparatively high real per capita income largely explain the greater emphasis in the state on these phases of employment.

Other aspects of the economic pattern also deserve consideration. As a direct response to rapid and continuing population increase, construction work engages a larger proportion of the workers in the state than throughout the nation. Although manufacturing has been historically of less relative importance in the state than in the nation, it has experienced tremendous growth in the last decade. Between 1950 and 1957 it far outstripped all other segments of the state economy with a 61.4 per cent increase. On the national level, over the same period, the state's rate of growth in factory employment was nearly twice that of Texas, the second most rapidly expanding major industrial state. However, the number of Californians engaged in manufacturing activities (22 per cent) was still below the national average of one in four in 1957.

Similarly, California has a smaller proportion of people in agricultural work than the nation on the whole. Yet agriculture is a vital part of the state's economy and has national prominence. Its continuing importance, despite the lower employment ratio, is explainable in that many California agricultural activities are highly commercialized and highly specialized. In addition, many materials for food-processing operations, a major part of manufacturing in California, are derived from local agricultural products. The number of workers in all occupations totals approximately 6 million people, or almost three-fifths of the state's population fifteen years of age or over.

Transportation

Numerous kinds of facilities to move people and goods are in operation. As a result of the extensive development of transportation, most California localities are no longer remote either from one another or from many principal centers outside of the state. According to a recent estimate, annual transportation expenditures are between 6 and 8 billion dollars.

More than one-half of this money is spent on highways and roads. For every 100 Californians there are 50 vehicles, each averaging about 10,000 miles yearly. Furthermore, the use of large-capacity trucks and trailer-truck combinations is widespread, particularly since World War II. There are approximately 14,000 miles of constructed roadway in the state highway system, 25,000 miles of streets, and 67,000 miles of county roads. It is especially impressive that there are over 1,300 miles of limited-access highways permitting consistently high speed and affording greater travel safety. Such roads, known as freeways, are far more extensive in California than in any of the other states; and, unlike many other states, there are no tolls charged. Serious deficiencies exist in various highways and roads, but on a comparative basis the California system is outstanding. Since 1956 federal aid has played an important role in California's highway program. In the 1959-60 fiscal year, over $300 million were authorized for use within the state. According to current projections, federal funds will account for more than one-fifth of the $18 billion which will be used in the state's building program between 1960 and 1980.

Air transportation occupies an increasingly important position in California's development. Since 1955, with the advent of the jet age in commercial flights, Los Angeles has advanced from fourth to third nationally in the annual total number of passengers. Together, the Los Angeles and San Francisco airports account for more than one-ninth of the total number of passengers in the nation. California leads the country in the number of licensed private planes with more than 10,000. The state is also a leader in commercial helicopter operations. Similarly, rail transportation has played a significant role since the first transcontinental line was finished in 1869. Several companies have regular interstate trains, and there is a vast network of passenger and freight rail operations between various California points. Railroad trackage has gradually declined since the 1930's, but at the same time an upswing has occurred in the number of train miles operated.

Other transportation methods should be mentioned. During recent years pipeline transportation has become an important means of carrying gas and oil over long distances. Also, inland-waterway and ocean transportation have been influential in the development of the state, with the latter having greater current impact.

Critical Problems

Population growth has been a constant challenge and stimulant to California, and, apparently, it is going to continue to be a prodding force. The prediction of various experts is that another 6 to 10 million people will be added to the state's population of more than 15 million by 1975.

Operating amid these pressures and changes, state and local governments have had to adjust many times to meet popular demands for service and regulation. The total accomplishments are impressive, but all the resulting difficulties of the past and present have not been resolved. There are critical problems that currently exist or that seemingly will increase or emerge in the immediate future. These will require imaginative responses by the state's governments, the national government, and people and organizations functioning in private capacities.

Education

One of the most critical of these problems is that the public-school facilities, especially below the college level, are already lagging far behind actual current need. Furthermore, the heavy recent birth rate coupled with the probable population influx will place unprecedented demands for teachers, buildings, and equipment upon all levels of public education. The boom in students already has been felt substantially in the elementary grades. By 1970 public high school enrollments are expected to be 134 per cent greater than in 1955. By the same year (1970) enrollment in public colleges and universities is anticipated to be well over double its 1955 level. Consequently, sound decisions will be needed on many phases of educational policy and programing.

Urban and Metropolitan Difficulties

Many of the most crucial problems are materializing in urban and metropolitan areas, where most of the state's people already live. Some of the most pressing are the depletion of local water supplies and the growing need to go longer distances for adequate sources; the increased intensity of water and air pollution with many implications for health and comfort; and the heavy investments necessary to expand sewage- and refuse-disposal operations. Others are the spread of blighted or run-down areas and the frequent inadequacy of recreation and park facilities. The urban transportation problem by itself constitutes a long series of difficulties. Even now many urban and metropolitan areas are plagued by street traffic congestion, insufficient automobile parking space, and mounting traffic accidents. All of these problems will be aggravated by population growth unless adequate solutions are found. It is imperative that consideration be given to the interrelationships of all phases of urban circulation, including mass transit (which has been declining), traffic, parking, freeways, trucking and other forms of transportation. At present, comprehensive efforts are frequently lacking. This is especially apparent in metropolitan areas where numerous governments often seek to handle matters of area-wide importance on a limited territorial basis. Extending intergovernmental cooperation or establishing a government endowed with wider areal jurisdiction are two possible solutions which are receiving increasing attention on both the state and local levels.

An elementary school in Los Angeles, one of the many needed for California's growing school population. Courtesy, Los Angeles Public Schools.

Land Uses and Natural Resources

As population increases, far-reaching judgments must be made on land use throughout the state. Residences, industries, agriculture, recreation, commercial services, highways, airports, and military installations all make competing demands for land. Communities in metropolitan areas are worried about the loss of potential recreation land and nearby dairies. Agricultural leaders are concerned about the disappearance of much productive farmland. An additional million urban dwellers may take over, for example, hundreds of thousands of rural acres for residences, business, industry, and highways. Even after decisions are made about the general type of use of certain lands, determinations frequently have to be made about the specific kind of use. In agriculture, for example, should the trend toward more land in field crops and pasture and less in fruits and vegetables be encouraged?

Fundamental decisions must also be reached regarding the development and conservation of many other natural resources. The increased requirements expected for simply one type of water use are indicative. More than a million additional acres of irrigated land will be necessary to supply food and fiber for the population increase predicted by 1975. The anticipated increased demands on water, minerals, plants, forests and ranges, and fish and wildlife call for accelerated technical progress and sound public policies. It is likely that other sources of power, probably from nuclear energy, will be needed to augment present supplies.

Housing, Employment, Social Welfare

Much new residential construction will be needed. The zoning policies, building regulations, and subdivision controls of local governments and the financial aid programs of other governments will have a profound effect. The labor supply in the state will possibly increase by several million by 1975, the result largely of the entrance into the job market of present school-age children and expected migrants. Agriculture will continue to be an important part of the state's economy, but most of the new workers will seek employment in urban areas. It is imperative that government, business, and labor concern themselves with sound industrial expansion.

Furthermore, the state's population is increasing in all age groups. Some of the immediate consequences for government of sharp rises in the younger categories have already been noted, but there are also important ones for other classes. For example, an increase in the number of people over 65 years of age has important implications for various governmental programs—public assistance, medical care, and recreational opportunities.

❋   ❋   ❋   ❋   ❋   ❋

Many matters facing the state are vital and enormous. Californians can take justifiable pride in the way certain past problems have been met, but the feeling of satisfaction should not lead to complacency. As observed at the beginning of this chapter, California is big and varied. Continuing population growth makes certain that its problems have similar qualities. Successful surmounting of difficulties will be best accomplished through broadly based citizen concern and action. "We," not "they," can most properly undertake the job. The immediate future will therefore require imaginative responses by the people of California, working through our governments at all levels, our political parties, and our private organizations.

Further Reading

Assembly Interim Committee on Conservation, Planning and Public Works, *Planning for Growth*. Sacramento: State Printing Office, 1955.

———, *Metropolitan Government in California*. Sacramento: State Printing Office, 1959.

Caughey, John W., *California*, 2nd ed. Englewood Cliffs, N.J.: Prentice-Hall, Inc., 1953.

Gordon, Margaret S., *Employment Expansion and Population Growth*. Berkeley: University of California Press, 1954.

Joint Interim Committee on Highway Problems, *Report*. Sacramento: State Printing Office, 1959.

Thompson, Warren S., *The Population of California*. Los Angeles: Haynes Foundation, 1955.

Senate Fact-finding Committee on Commerce and Economic Development, *California Statistical Abstract*. Sacramento: State Printing Office, 1958.

University of California Chancellor's Special Committee, *California Development Problems*. Berkeley: Chancellor's Office, 1954.

Two

Statehood and the Constitution

ON SEPTEMBER 9, 1850, President Millard Fillmore signed a document entitled "A Bill to Admit California as a State into the Union." The admission of California as the thirty-first state was in keeping with its fabulous reputation born of the gold rush. Omitting the usual territorial stage, California drafted a constitution and asked Congress for admission.

THE QUEST FOR STATEHOOD

California Becomes American

The roots of the American conquest of California reach far beyond the Mexican War. New England sea captains built up a lively, often illicit, trade with the Indian and Hispanic peoples during the Spanish era. Settlers from the United States began to arrive in the 1820's by land and sea. Their numbers grew larger each decade, and some took part in abortive independence movements. When, in 1846, the United States and Mexico engaged in war, Americans in California were sufficiently numerous to minimize Mexican resistance.

A period of military rule extended from 1846 to 1850. Commodore Robert F. Stockton, as commander of American armed forces on the Pacific Coast, drew up and proclaimed in December 1846 a constitution for the conquered territory of California.

14

The new government was to be headed by a governor, assisted by a legislative council of seven, all appointed by the executive; local officials were made elective, and Mexican law and procedure were to be followed. John C. Fremont became governor in January 1847, but Stockton's constitution was never put in force. In March, the governorship went to General Kearny, and in the end of May to Colonel Mason. Throughout this period, Californians were demanding some sort of civil government, but Congress failed to act even after the formal ceding of the territory by Mexico to the United States in the Treaty of Guadalupe Hidalgo in 1848.

The discovery of gold in 1848 started a wave of migration that multiplied the population of California many times over. Tremendous governmental problems arose. While California waited in vain for Congress to establish territorial government, the successive military governors continued in a sort of *de facto* capacity. After the third failure of Congress to act, Governor Riley issued a call for a constitutional convention to frame a state constitution or to draw up a plan for territorial government.

CALIFORNIA'S FIRST CONSTITUTION

The Convention of 1849

General Bennett Riley's proclamation set August 1, 1849 as election day for delegates. Originally the convention was to consist of thirty-seven delegates. Some districts, however, grew so much in population between June, when the convention was called, and August, when the election was held, that they were permitted to elect additional delegates. Forty-eight delegates, a good cross section of the population, were finally seated after the convention organized in Colton Hall, Monterey, on September 3. The interest in gold digging and the expense and inconvenience of travel made attendance very difficult. After six weeks of labor, the document was completed.

The constitution framed was rather simple, drawn largely from the fundamental laws of New York and Iowa. Several points were settled only after great controversy. There was little support for the institution of slavery, even among those from the Old South, but a conflict developed over a proposal to bar free Negroes from the state. It was voted down. After much debate, the eastern boundary line was drawn along the Colorado River and the Sierra Nevada, and proposals for division of the state into two parts were defeated.

The governor and lieutenant governor were to be elected by the people for two-year terms; the controller, treasurer, attorney general, and surveyor general also were to be elected by the people, but the secretary of state was appointed by the governor. Legislative power was vested in a senate and an assembly, meeting for annual sessions, the members of which were elected for two-year and one-year terms respectively. Judges were made elective. Constitutional amendments could be proposed by vote of the two houses in two successive sessions, and ratified by the people. Provision was also made for a constitutional convention to draft a new constitution. The bill of rights contained the usual guarantees, as well as prohibition of slavery. Universal manhood suffrage was established.

The New State and Its Constitution

This proposed constitution was put before the people at an election on November 13, 1849. At the same election the voters also chose the officers who would be required if the document was adopted and California was admitted by Congress. The constitution was adopted by a vote of 12,061 to 811. Peter H. Burnett was elected governor, other state officers were chosen, and two Congressmen were elected. The legislature convened in December and designated John C. Fremont and William M. Gwin as United States senators. The legislature, without waiting for Congress to admit, then set about the business of enacting laws. In 1850 Congress finally passed the act of admission, after a sharp fight between free and slave states. The act broke the deadlock in the Senate, bringing the number of free states to sixteen, as compared with fifteen slave states.

The new state had a population in 1850 of 92,597. Its people were concentrated in the Mother Lode and Sacramento Valley sections. An overwhelming proportion were miners; agriculture occupied less than 2 per cent of the gainfully employed men. Representation in the United States House of Representatives was set at two. Contrast this with the 1950 official Census report of 10,586,223 total population: an estimated 15 million in 1960, and a possible 58 million by 2020! Agriculture and manufacturing now far exceed mining as sources of wealth. California, for the decade of the 1950's, had 30 representatives in the House (out of 437, after the admission of Alaska and Hawaii) and possessed 32 electoral votes. In the 1960's the number of House seats will probably be 37 and the electoral votes set at 39.

The Constitution of 1849 served as the fundamental law of the state for thirty years. Only three amendments were adopted between 1849 and 1879: one clarifying the process for popular ratification of a new constitution, another substituting biennial for annual legislative sessions and doubling the term of office of senators and assemblymen, and the third limiting appropriations to two-year periods.

The Second Constitution

The Politics of Revolt

Born in a boom, the new state grew by leaps and bounds. Professor Swisher has estimated that the population increased more than seventeen times over between mid-1849 and 1879. The mines continued to pour forth their riches, but after a quarter-century mining was crowded out of first place in production value by agriculture and manufacturing. Both mining and manufacturing came, to a considerable extent, under the control of a few individuals and corporations. The average man was so busy acquiring his share of the riches that he neglected his political obligations. During the decade of the seventies, however, business failed, mining stocks collapsed, banks closed doors—and attention was turned to governmental institutions.

From the economic unrest of the period, there emerged two political movements of importance. Farmers united in an agrarian revolt against the railroads and trusts, forming California's part of the Granger movement which swept the West. The outstanding example of the politics of revolt, however, was the Working-men's Party of San Francisco. Unemployed workers turned against the Chinese, who competed with them in the labor market, and against the corporate interests, which now provided but little employment. Formed in 1877, the party soon became a major factor in state politics under the leadership of the able and aggressive young Dennis Kearney. From "sand-lot" meetings in San Francisco, the movement swept to other cities, the dual battle cry being "Out with the Chinese" and "Down with the capitalists."

The Convention of 1878-79

Several attempts had already been made to secure a convention to revise the California constitution, but each time the popular vote for the proposition lacked the necessary majority of all votes cast at the election, as required by the amending clause. In 1877, however, a proposition to call a convention was adopted by the voters. The following year the legislature enacted a law providing for the election of delegates, 120 from the forty sena-torial districts and 32 at large.

As soon as the act was passed, conservative newspapers throughout the state proclaimed that the issue on which dele-gates should be chosen was "Kearneyism." It was insisted that Republicans and Democrats unite on a nonpartisan basis to defeat the radicals. The election was held in June, and resulted in the selection of 78 nonpartisans, 57 Workingmen, 10 Demo-crats, and 11 Republicans. When the delegates came together in September, the Workingmen, being unable to elect their own candidate for convention president, shifted to another anti-cor-poration candidate, but by a narrow margin failed to elect him. Later in the convention, a cooperative arrangement was made between the Workingmen's group and other anti-corporation delegates, chiefly from rural areas. This bloc worked effectively in matters of railroad regulation, on the extension of taxation to all tangible and intangible property, and on taxation of banks and utilities. A majority was secured in favor of drastic restrictions on the Chinese, forbidding employment, discouraging immigration, and denying civil rights—virtually all of which were subsequently declared in conflict with the federal constitution.

Its work completed, the convention adjourned in March, and the document was submitted to the electorate on May 7, 1879. The campaigns for and against the new constitution were intense, but it was ratified by a vote of 77,959 to 67,134.

Form and Content

The Constitution of 1879 has now served for over eighty years. It was amended, however, over 300 times between 1879 and 1960. Its present form may be outlined as follows:

Article I. Declaration of Rights
Contains the guarantees of individual rights and civil liberties.

Article II. Right of Suffrage
Universal suffrage is established, and regulations governing primaries and elections are enumerated.

Article III. Distribution of Powers
Theory of separation of powers is enunciated.

Article IV. Legislative Department
Creates bicameral legislature composed of senate (40) and assembly (80) and establishes initiative and referendum.

Article V. Executive Department
Powers and duties of the governor and other officers of the state.

Article VI. Judicial Department
Supreme court, district courts of appeal, superior courts and their jurisdiction, the judicial council.

Article VII. The Pardoning Power
Pardons, reprieves, and commutations.

Article VIII. Militia
Legislature regulates by law; governor in command.

Article IX. Education
Covers public education and school funds, the state university, tax exemptions for private institutions.

Article X. State Institutions and Public Buildings
Prisons and penal procedures.

Article XI. Cities, Counties, and Towns
Classification, home rule charters, boundaries, powers, and special items.

Article XII. Corporations
Formation of corporations, securities, liability, utility regulation.

Article XIII. Revenue and Taxation
Defines what may be taxed, exemptions, assessment and collection.

Article XIV. Water and Water Rights

Article XV. Harbor Frontage (and Tidelands)

Article XVI. State Indebtedness
State debt limit established by amendment of 1933.

Article XVII. Land and Homestead Exemption

Article XVIII. Amending and Revising the Constitution
Proposal by Legislature, by the people through the initiative, or by constitutional convention; ratification by the electorate.

Article XX.* Miscellaneous Subjects
Contains an assortment of provisions, relating to seat of government, marriage, suits against the state, conditions of labor.

Article XXI. Boundary

Article XXII. Schedule
Process for putting this constitution to vote and into effect.

Article XXIII. Recall of Public Officers

Article XXIV. Civil Service

Article XXVI. Motor Vehicle Tax

Article XXVII. Aged and Blind Aid

Article XXXIV. Public Housing Projects

Our Bulky Constitution

This outline is enough to demonstrate that the constitution, as amended, is poorly organized; the California Constitutional Commission reported in 1930 that:

> . . . its constant amendment has produced an instrument bad in form, inconsistent in many particulars, loaded with provisions of no permanent value, and replete with matter which might more properly be contained in the statute law of the State.†

Early American state constitutions were, in the main, statements of fundamental principle. As in the national Constitution, details were left to be written into the statute law by legislative

---

* Articles XIX and XXV have been repealed; articles XXVIII through XXXIII have never been used.

† *Report*, 9.

bodies. Today, however, the constitutions of most states are loaded with minute details. This is well illustrated in a volume prepared for the New York constitutional convention in 1938. It contained the constitutions of the nation and the forty-eight states. Every state constitution was longer than the federal, which covered only eleven pages. California's was second longest (Louisiana led) with ninety-six pages; Vermont's and Rhode Island's were shortest with twelve; the average state constitution was thirty-six pages in length.

The quantitative growth of state constitutions, including California's, is caused by (1) popular distrust of the legislature; (2) popular desire to overrule judicial decisions; (3) success of pressure groups in solidifying their gains in permanent fashion; (4) expansion of state responsibilities and activities; (5) availability of the constitutional initiative for the proposal of amendments.

Many amendments to the California constitution may be explained in these terms. The initiation and adoption of the state civil service amendment in 1934 might be used as evidence of popular distrust of the legislature, and perhaps of the executive as well. In 1940 a judicial opinion was reversed when an amendment was adopted authorizing state legislative investigating committees. Evidence of the success of pressure groups may be found in the public schools amendment of 1946, adopted with the support of teacher and other school groups. Expansion of state functions is illustrated by the various relief amendments adopted in 1933, 1934, and 1938. Without the constitutional initiative, it is difficult to see how an amendment like the one adopted in 1934 permitting sale of intoxicating liquors could have passed the legislature at such an early date with the requisite two-thirds vote in each house.

What harm is there in a bulky constitution? An extensive constitution, like that of California, departs from the sound rule that only important principles and structural outlines should be contained therein. The excess is mainly statutory in nature, and, if embodied in the fundamental law, must be amended frequently if the state is to keep up with the changing times. This places a burden of huge proportions upon the voters. The electorate has been called upon to vote on as many as twenty constitutional amendments at recent general elections. In times of crisis, legislators find themselves lacking the power to act swiftly because of detailed provisions in the constitution.

In 1930 the California Constitutional Commission reported that the document then contained 65,000 words. Making little change in substance, but concentrating upon improvement of form and arrangement, the commission found it could reduce the length to 27,000 words.

CONSTITUTIONAL CHANGE

The Amending Process

Amendments to the California constitution are proposed in three ways: (1) by the legislature, (2) by the people through the initiative, and (3) by constitutional convention.

Proposal by the legislature is by far the most common method. From the adoption of the constitution in 1879 up to 1960, around 85 per cent of all amendments proposed were placed before the people by the legislature; of these, three-fifths were ratified by the electorate. Two-thirds of all the elected members of each house must vote for an amendment in order to submit it to the electorate. Constitutional amendments may be introduced in either house by one or more members; they are printed like any other proposed legislation, and are designated Senate Constitutional Amendment (SCA) or Assembly Constitutional Amendment (ACA), depending on the house of origin. The 1959 legislature had before it 87 proposed constitutional amendments, 56 in the assembly and 31 in the senate. Of these, 11 were adopted for submission to the people. The form of title for a constitutional amendment originating in the legislature may be illustrated as follows:

> Assembly Constitutional Amendment No. 6—A resolution to propose to the people of the State of California to amend Section 6 of Article IV of the State Constitution, relating to the membership of the Reapportionment Commission.

Proposal by initiative occupies second place in frequency of use. This method was added to the constitution in 1911, at the same time that direct legislation was adopted. Voters equal in number to 8 per cent of those who cast ballots in the last election for governor sign petitions requesting such action. Up to 1960, amendments proposed by initiative amounted to less than 15 per cent of the total; just over one-fourth of these were adopted. The initiative process for amendments is precisely like that for statutory acts, described at length in Chapter Five.

When an extensive overhauling of a constitution is desired, the American states often rely on an especially organized constitutional convention. The California constitution provides that whenever two-thirds of the members elected to each house deem it necessary, a proposition may be placed before the electorate. If a majority favors the proposed convention, the legislature shall, at the next session, provide by law for calling it. The convention assembles three months after the election of delegates.

Since the adoption of the Constitution of 1879, the electorate has been asked on five occasions to vote on the question of the calling of a convention to revise the organic law:

PROPOSALS FOR CONSTITUTIONAL CONVENTIONS, 1879-1960

Year	Proposition	No	Yes
1898	Shall a convention be called?	65,007	42,556
1914	Shall a convention be called?	442,687	180,111
1920	Amend constitution to provide for a constitutional convention?	428,002	203,240
1930	Amend constitution to provide for a constitutional convention?	585,089	263,683
1934	Shall a convention be called?	668,080	709,915

The 1934 vote in favor of a convention came as a surprise. The 1935 legislature failed to take the necessary action to provide the machinery and appropriation for the convention. The clear mandate of the people was not obeyed, and no sanction is held by the courts which may be used to compel a legislature to act. Consequently what was expected to result in California's third convention turned out a miscarriage, and the document of 1879 is still with us. Unquestionably the legislature's failure to act was based in part on the lack of agreement on the apportionment of delegates, but the primary obstacle to enabling legislation for the convention was fear on the part of a majority of the legislators that radical sentiment was much too strong in 1935.

MEASURES SUBMITTED TO VOTE OF VOTERS

1 FOR THE VETERANS BOND ACT OF 1958. This act provides for a bond issue of three hundred million dollars ($300,000,000) to be used by the Department of Veterans Affairs in assisting California war veterans to acquire farms and homes.

AGAINST THE VETERANS BOND ACT OF 1958. This act provides for a bond issue of three hundred million dollars ($300,000,000) to be used by the Department of Veterans Affairs in assisting California war veterans to acquire farms and homes.

2 SCHOOL BONDS. (Senate Constitutional Amendment No. 1. Directs issue and sale of $220,000,000 of state bonds to provide loans and grants to school districts for (a) school sites, construction and equipment, and (b) housing and equipment for physically handicapped or mentally retarded minors. Requires repayment of advances from Investment Fund. Authorizes legislation regulating allocations to school districts and providing for repayment of allocations by districts. Declares state policy regarding public school sites and buildings. — YES / NO

3 STATE CONSTRUCTION PROGRAM BONDS. (Assembly Constitutional Amendment No. 7. Authorizes issue and sale of $200,000,000 of state bonds to carry out building program contemplated by State Construction Program Bond Act of 1958. Said act authorizes use of the bond money, when appropriated by the Legislature, for buildings and building sites for state educational institutions, mental and correctional institutions, and other state facilities. Validates said 1958 State Construction Program Bond Act. — YES / NO

4 HARBOR DEVELOPMENT BONDS. (Assembly Constitutional Amendment No. 11. Authorizes issue and sale of $90,000,000 of state bonds in accordance with Harbor Development Bond Law of 1958. Said Law permits up to $50,000,000 of bonds to be issued for development of state harbor facilities at San Francisco and up to $10,000,000 for financing of small craft harbor development program. Bonds will be general obligations of State, but payable primarily from receipts of state treasury funds designated as San Francisco Harbor Improvement Fund and Small Craft Harbor Improvement Fund, respectively. Validates said Harbor Development Bond Law of 1958. — YES / NO

5 COMPENSATION OF LEGISLATORS. (Senate Constitutional Amendment No. 5. Permits Legislature to fix legislators salaries by statute, but not in excess of average salary of county supervisors in the five most populous counties. — YES / NO

6 STATE INDEBTEDNESS. (Senate Constitutional Amendment No. 33. Changes method of publication of proposed state bond issue laws. Deletes provision establishing Secretary of State's ballot pamphlet as the only required publication and requires that such proposals be published in at least one newspaper in each of at least 50 counties (including the five most populous counties) throughout the State for eight weeks before the election at which submitted for vote. — YES / NO

7 GOVERNMENT FUNCTIONS: WARTIME DISASTER. (Assembly Constitutional Amendment No. 5. Adds enabling provision to Constitution authorizing Legislature to adopt wartime disaster laws, providing for filling offices of legislators or governor in case of death or disabling injury of one-fifth of legislators or incumbent governor; for convening of general or extraordinary legislative sessions; for elections to fill vacant or temporarily occupied offices, and for temporary location of state capital and county seats. Modifies existing constitutional provision regarding succession to governorship. — YES / NO

8 PRESIDENTIAL VOTING (Assembly Constitutional Amendment No. 2. Authorizes legislation permitting persons to vote for President and Vice President after residing in California for 54 days but less than one year, if otherwise qualified as California electors. — YES / NO

9 GENERAL LEGISLATIVE SESSIONS. (Assembly Constitutional Amendment No. 36. Eliminates mandatory 30-day recess during general sessions of Legislature in odd-numbered years. Prevents committee hearing or passage of bills (other than Budget Bill) for 30 days after introduction at general sessions, but permits waiver by three-fourths vote. Excludes Saturdays and Sundays from 120-day limit on length of general sessions. — YES / NO

10 EMINENT DOMAIN: AIRPORTS AND SCHOOLS. (Assembly Constitutional Amendment No. 16. After commencement of condemnation action, permits court order for taking immediate possession of property to be used for airport purposes by public agency or for school purposes by school district, after 90 days' notice to the owner and after putting up money deposit as directed by the court to secure payment of just compensation to the owner. — YES / NO

11 LOCAL STREET AND ROAD BONDS. (Senate Constitutional Amendment No. 21. Authorizes laws for issuance and sale of bonds for street and road purposes by counties, cities, and separation of grade districts and providing for repayment of bonds out of distributions of gasoline tax money. Validates Street and Road Bond Act of 1957. — YES / NO

12 LEGISLATOR AS NOTARY. (Assembly Constitutional Amendment No. 72. Permits member of Legislature to become notary public. — YES / NO

13 SUPERINTENDENT OF PUBLIC INSTRUCTION. (Senate Constitutional Amendment No. 2. Makes office of Superintendent of Public Instruction appointive, instead of elective, after 1962. Confers appointing power on State Board of Education, subject to confirmation by State Senate. — YES / NO

14 COMPENSATION OF LOCAL OFFICERS. (Senate Constitutional Amendment No. 29. Eliminates prohibition against increasing compensation of county, municipal officers after their election or during their terms of office. Permits Legislature to classify counties by other factors, in addition to population, when setting salaries of supervisors, district attorneys and auditors. — YES / NO

15 BOXING MATCHES. (Repeal of Initiative.) Repeals Penal Code Section 413½, which now prohibits boxing exhibitions on Sunday and Memorial Day. — YES / NO

16 TAXATION OF SCHOOL PROPERTY OF RELIGIOUS AND OTHER NON-PROFIT ORGANIZATIONS. (Initiative Constitutional Amendment.) Amends Section 1c of Article XIII of the State Constitution by providing that the property authorized by said section to be exempted from taxation shall not include any property used or owned, directly or indirectly, in whole or in part, for any religious or other school or school purposes of less than collegiate grade, unless such property shall be used, owned and held exclusively for the blind, mentally retarded or physically handicapped. Does not affect exemptions granted by other sections of the Constitution. — YES / NO

17 STATE SALES, USE, AND INCOME TAX RATES. (Initiative.) Reduces sales and use tax rate from 3 to 2 percent. Changes income tax rates (now ranging from 1 percent on incomes under $5,000 to 6 percent on incomes over $25,000) to new range of ⅓ percent on incomes under $5,000 to 46 percent on incomes over $50,000. Legislature may lower but not increase sales and use tax rates. Income tax rates may be changed only by vote of electors. Sales and use tax rate changes effective January 1, 1959. Income tax rate changes effective December 31, 1957. — YES / NO

18 EMPLOYER-EMPLOYEE RELATIONS. (Initiative Constitutional Amendment.) Adds Section I-A to Article I, State Constitution. Prohibits employers and employee organizations from entering into collective bargaining or other agreements which establish membership in a labor organization, or payment of dues or charges of any kind thereto, as a condition of employment or continued employment. Declares unlawful certain practices relating to membership in labor organizations. Provides for injunction and damage suits against any person or group for violation or attempted violation. Preserves existing lawful contracts but applies to renewals or extensions thereof. Declares that section is self-executing. Defines "labor organization." — YES / NO

California's long constitution requires frequent amendment. On the ballot of November, 1958, thirteen of the eighteen propositions submitted to the electorate were constitutional amendments proposed by the legislature.

Revision by Legislative Committee

A new and active movement for constitutional revision was launched in the 1947 legislature. Seventy-nine members of the assembly appeared as co-authors of a bill that would have called a constitutional convention. The bill passed the assembly but did not get favorable consideration in the senate. When it became apparent that the bill would not become law, proponents introduced a concurrent resolution to create a "joint legislative committee on the revision of the State Constitution." It was adopted by both houses in the closing rush. The committee consisted of ten assemblymen and ten senators, and was empowered to "study" the facts and "prepare" a draft of a revised constitution, both as a whole and in several parts in case piecemeal revision was used. The committee reported to the 1949 legislature.

Assistance to the committee was provided by an advisory committee, to which over 250 citizens were appointed, and by the committee's own small staff. The committee was also authorized to contract with public or private agencies for aid in its task. Ten subcommittees were established; each was composed of two legislators and from twenty to forty advisory committeemen. Under the procedure adopted, changes in either form or substance of the constitution would not be made without approval of a subcommittee majority and a two-thirds majority of the committee itself.

The constitutional changes proposed by the committee were confined to eliminating obsolete matters from the constitution. At a special election held in November, 1949, the voters adopted six amendments proposed by the committee, thereby eliminating about 14,500 words. The propriety of having a legislative committee prepare a general revision of the constitution was questioned both by Governor Earl Warren and former Governor Culbert L. Olson, who argued that the legislature was obliged to call a constitutional convention under the 1934 plebiscite. The unconstitutionality of a general revision by the legislature was indicated by the state supreme court in *Livermore v. Waite* (1894):

> The Legislature is not authorized to assume the function of a constitutional convention, and propose for adoption by the people a revision of the entire Constitution under the form of an amendment, nor can it submit to their votes a proposition which if adopted, would by the very terms in which it is framed be inoperative.

Although many people may prefer to have a constitutional convention do the job, few would deny the value or propriety of having a legislative committee make the fullest study of constitutional revision. So many groups have vested interests in portions of the constitution that an extensive campaign of public education will be necessary before much change is possible.

Can a New Constitution Be Adopted?

Students of American state government have long lacked confidence in the capacity of most states to revise fully their constitutions. From 1921 until 1945 no state succeeded in securing popular ratification for a new constitution. Interest groups fought violently against any change that might deprive them of some special protection received through some clause incorporated in the constitution. In a state so large and diverse as California, such vested interests are numerous and powerful. They have an immense stake in the *status quo* and will resist vigorously any reduction of special privilege.

The general state constitutional deadlock was broken in 1945. Missouri, through the constitutional convention and popular ratification method, secured a new constitution that was concise, modern, and vastly improved. In Georgia a special commission created to renovate the constitution drafted a completely revised document that was accepted by the voters. Revision in New Jersey was defeated in 1944, but succeeded in 1947, giving that state one of the most up-to-date organic laws in the union. These three civic victories have encouraged Californians to press for a constitutional convention. Possessing the voters' mandate for a convention from the 1934 election, the legislature can, if it chooses, create one by ordinary statute. Once the decision to hold a convention is made, the chief controversy will be over its composition. The proposal before the 1947 legislature for a convention of 120 delegates, elected from assembly and senate districts, will probably prove the only acceptable arrangement. Delegates might be elected on a nonpartisan ballot at a regular election.

Even if such a convention drew up a proposed constitution that was a model of brevity and modernity, it is doubtful whether it could secure adoption in this state of government by pressure. Only a very thorough educational campaign can generate the public spirit necessary to overcome the separatist and often selfish influences of organized minority groups.

Many proponents of constitutional revision feel that the best way to secure improvement is piecemeal through the ordinary amending process. Far-reaching changes were made in 1911, when many reforms were written into the constitution. Any attempt at wholesale revision in convention, submitted as a whole to the electorate, might meet a severe defeat if any drastic changes were proposed.

Beginning in 1957, the League of Women Voters rekindled interest in constitutional revision. Workshops over the state subjected the constitution to intensive study for two years. The overwhelming verdict was that the constitution needed major revision; a majority favored revision by constitutional convention. The state league's program for 1959-60 included a state constitution item on the current agenda: "Support of measures to improve and revise the California Constitution, directed toward, but not limited to, a constitutional convention, preceded by a commission with staff and time for full preparatory work." The league further declared it would undertake to stimulate interest in constitutional revision and to secure the support of other organizations.

The Chief Justice of the Supreme Court of California once described the situation as follows:

> As a result, California, the second largest state in the country, has the questionable distinction of having the second longest constitution. It is not only much too long, but it is almost everything a constitution ought not to be. It contains much outmoded matter, some of which is so deeply imbedded in paragraphs containing sound and functioning provisions that the obsolete language cannot be excised without rewriting entire sections. Many of its provisions are inconsistent. It is burdened with unnecessary detail and encumbered with many regulations that should be embodied in the statute law of the state. Certainly the people of California are entitled to something better than this.*

These views are echoed by most students of California government, yet so many groups have vested interests in particular portions of the Constitution that it is difficult to muster sufficient sentiment for change to secure a general revision.

---

* Quoted by permission of Hon. Phil S. Gibson from address delivered November 16, 1955 at 50th anniversary celebration of the University of Southern California Law School.

CALIFORNIA IN THE UNION

Distribution of Powers

The national government has the powers specifically granted under the American Constitution. Within the scope of federal authority are the power to tax, to regulate interstate and foreign commerce, to coin and regulate money, to make treaties, and to govern territories, and several other matters.

After the delegation of specific powers to the federal government, the remaining powers, if not prohibited, are reserved for the states. The broadest authority possessed by the state comes through its "police power," which permits the state to protect the public health, safety, morals, and welfare. Some powers, often called concurrent, are shared with the nation; among these are the powers to tax and to borrow. States establish and control local governments, conduct elections, incorporate and charter concerns, establish civil and criminal law. The exercise of such authority by a state must be within the confines set by the federal constitutional guarantees of civil liberties and definitions of federal powers. In the last analysis a conflict between national and state jurisdictions is settled in the federal judiciary.

Federal-State Obligations

The national government guarantees to the states a *republican form of government*. There is little agreement on what constitutes a republican form. The courts regard this as a political question, and decline to rule when a specific state, such as Louisiana under Huey Long, is alleged to have departed from republican institutions. It remains for Congress to indicate approval or disapproval of a state's regime by acceptance of senators and representatives, or for the President to choose between contending groups by use of troops to "restore order."

The national government also assures the states of *protection against foreign invasion and domestic violence*. Invasion is easy to ascertain and is clearly a federal problem. Domestic violence, however, is normally considered as not requiring federal intervention until the state signifies through governor or legislature or both that it must have help. The federal government may intervene even without a call from a state authority. In 1941 a strike-bound aircraft plant in Los Angeles was opened by the army on the grounds that the factory had been commandeered by the federal government for defense production.

Congress plays the major role in the *admission of new states*. The normal admission procedure begins with the organization of a territorial government. California skipped this step, moving from military government of conquered territory to application to Congress for admission.

The federal Constitution also assures each state of *equal representation in the Senate*, which may not be denied without the state's consent. Since the adoption of the eleventh amendment, each state is immune from suit by individuals in the federal courts.

States are obliged to *conduct elections* to fill various federal offices. Within the broad limits imposed by the federal Constitution, the state determines who holds voting rights in the election of federal officials. States have a very important role in the *federal constitutional amending* process, for one method of proposal and both schemes of ratification require state action.

California's Obligations to Other States

The federal Constitution requires that each state give *full faith and credit* to the "public acts, records, and judicial proceedings of every other state." In practice, a state is required to accept another state's laws, pardons, charters, deeds, vital records, court decisions, and records. For example, California permits the Southern Pacific Company to operate railways under a Kentucky charter, accepts at face value a birth certificate from Massachusetts, and enforces in its courts an ordinary civil judgment of the North Dakota courts. Notable exceptions to the full faith and credit rule do exist, however. Another state's criminal court proceedings are not necessarily accepted. Divorces obtained in one state are not invariably valid in another.

Citizens of each state are entitled to all *privileges and im-*

munities of citizens of the several states. This guarantee means that citizens of California may go to other states and there have a right to protection, residence, suits in courts, property, tax equality, business and trade. There is, however, an extensive array of exceptions. For example, states may require a period of residence and citizenship before new residents can engage in certain professions. Nonresident participation in a state "proprietary function," such as taking fish and game or attending an institution of higher learning, may be restricted. A corporation is not considered a citizen under the meaning of the privileges and immunities clause.

Finally, a state is obligated by the federal Constitution to provide *extradition*—that is, to deliver up a fugitive from justice to the authorities from the state in which the crime was committed. If Illinois officers receive information that an ex-convict who failed to serve out a prison term is in this state, application for extradition is made to the governor of California, who will then have the fugitive detained and turned over to Illinois representatives. If the governor decides not to render up the fugitive, the courts will not force him to act. A new governor, however, may reconsider the case, or the fugitive may be apprehended in another state with a less lenient governor.

What a State Cannot Do

The federal Constitution contains several specific restrictions on the states. These prohibitions may be listed as follows:

1. No treaty, alliance, or confederation with a foreign nation
2. No letters of marque and reprisal to prey on commerce
3. No coinage of money, no emission of bills of credit, nor other than gold and silver coin made legal tender
4. No bills of attainder (punishment by legislature without court trial)
5. No impairment of valid contracts (neither weaken nor alter the obligation of contract)
6. No *ex post facto* laws (retroactive criminal laws)
7. No titles of nobility (except honorary colonels)
8. No state taxes on imports and exports, or on tonnage of vessels (with certain exceptions)

9. No taking of liberty or property without due process of law (includes both substantive and procedural due process)

10. No denial of equal protection of the laws

Changing Federal-State Relations

Nation-state relations have changed, over the years, through various devices of coercion and cooperation. Federal powers have been interpreted more broadly through the years, and their fuller use has altered the position of the states considerably.

Federal *grants to the states* have profoundly modified American federalism. Money is appropriated by Congress to the states for activities that are deemed to affect the national interest; if the states will accept the conditions imposed, they may receive the grant. Such a scheme makes possible the reallocation of the proceeds of federal taxes over the nation, and thereby facilitates the establishment of minimum standards over the whole country.

In 1958, California received in federal grants $547,306,000, by far the largest amount received by any state, and above the average per capita received by the several states.

The major California functions aided were:

Old age assistance	$132,969,946
Aid to dependent children	62,053,279
Highway construction	157,282,000
Employment security	31,437,372
School maintenance and operation	16,609,143
School construction and survey	13,463,109

Lesser amounts were received for school lunches, aid to the blind, hospital construction, and other services.

Another cooperative-coercive device is called *federal credits for state taxation,* or "the tax offset device." It involves the levying of a federal tax; but if a state takes action along a desired line, the United States will yield and collect only a small part of its original levy.

This scheme was used initially in estate-tax collections. In 1924 the federal government began giving up to 80 per cent credit to taxpayers who paid a state inheritance tax. States with no death taxes hastened to enact them.

Congress in 1935 used the tax offset to force states to enact unemployment-insurance laws. The Social Security Act levied a federal payroll tax on employers. However, if the state set up an approved unemployment-insurance system, the federal government waived 90 per cent of its tax, and collected only 10 per cent, which is subvented to the states for administrative expense. All the states, including California, hurried to establish unemployment-insurance schemes.

Congress also has closed *the lanes of interstate commerce* to help the states to control some situation which otherwise could not be regulated effectively. Liquor shipments into a state in violation of its laws have been banned. Movement of prison-made goods into states which forbid their sale has been forbidden. "Hot oil," petroleum produced in excess of quotas set by state law, also has been barred from interstate commerce.

Congress spends vast sums of money to provide *research and informational services* which may induce the states to undertake new programs or increase efficiency in existing ones.

Occasionally the nation and the state make *reciprocal use of officials.* Federal officials may serve states in apprehending criminals and in other ways. Sometimes joint federal-state employees are hired on some sharing arrangement.

Constitutional immunity of federal property from state and local taxation, and federal ownership of 46 per cent of California's land area, combine to necessitate some fiscal arrangements to aid state and local services.

Shared revenues are federal payments to state and local governments mainly from such sources of income as timber sales, mineral leases, and grazing fees. Varying percentages of receipts from these sources are received for schools, roads, and general purposes.

In lieu payments are federal contributions for state and local services in place of taxes. Federal laws permitting such payments vary widely, but most call for negotiation and agreement between the levels of government. In lieu payments are made for federal housing projects, Atomic Energy Commission properties, and some other national enterprises.

In two areas federal and California governments have clashed in the recent past. The longer-run point of friction involves fed-

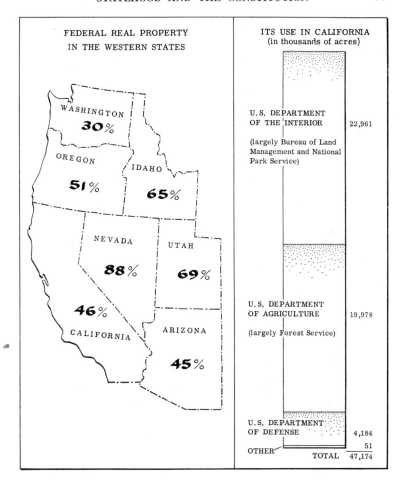

FEDERAL REAL PROPERTY
IN THE WESTERN STATES

ITS USE IN CALIFORNIA
(in thousands of acres)

WASHINGTON **30**%

OREGON **51**%

IDAHO **65**%

NEVADA **88**%

UTAH **69**%

CALIFORNIA **46**%

ARIZONA **45**%

U.S. DEPARTMENT
OF THE INTERIOR   22,961

(largely Bureau of Land
Management and National
Park Service)

U.S. DEPARTMENT
OF AGRICULTURE   19,978

(largely Forest Service)

U.S. DEPARTMENT
OF DEFENSE   4,184

OTHER   51

TOTAL   47,174

FEDERAL REAL PROPERTY

*In common with other western states, a high proportion
of California's land is under national ownership. At the
left, the percentage of land federally owned is shown for
California and her neighbors. At the right appears the
distribution of California land among federal agencies.
Most of the public domain lands are in desert or mountain
regions. Source: U.S. General Services Administration,*
Inventory Report on Federal Real Property in the United
States as of June 31, 1955. *For purposes of comparison,
all departments of California state government together
own less than one million acres.*

eral reclamation and flood control projects within the state. A more recent disagreement concerns jurisdiction over off-shore mineral and other resources.

Although the Central Valley Project began under state legislation in 1933, the federal Bureau of Reclamation has, since 1935, been the predominant element in its development. Powerful interests in the state opposed one or more of the Bureau's policies: (1) unified development of the whole basin, (2) public electric power, and (3) limitation of irrigation water to 160 acres. After the change of national administration in 1953, sentiment for state assumption of control over the project dwindled. The state water plan authorized in 1959 raises additional jurisdictional problems over new dams and aqueducts.

The so-called "tidelands" controversy was set off in 1947 when the Supreme Court held that the subsurface rights in territorial waters were subject to federal rather than state control.* After a sharp struggle in Congress, a law was passed in 1953 giving the states jurisdiction over their offshore resources. For states like California, with proven petroleum resources in the offshore areas, large sums of money were involved. The matter was far from settled, however, because Congress proceeded to pass another act claiming for the federal government the resources of the "continental shelf" beyond the territorial waters. Jurisdiction beyond the three mile limit was conceded to Texas. The two 1953 federal acts specifically limit state jurisdiction to three miles into the Pacific, but some state interests hope that California may claim as far as thirty miles offshore to and three miles beyond the "chain" of the Santa Barbara Islands.

Interstate Cooperation and Competition

California has played a role in the changing relations among the American states.

One aspect of the new interdependence of the states lies in *interstate compacts,* which require the consent of Congress. California has used the compact solution less than have other states, largely because of its lack of boundary disputes and the absence of joint waterways (except the Colorado River). California par-

---

* *United States v. California,* 67 U.S. 1658 (1947).

ticipates actively, however, in the Colorado River agreement. The Crime Compact of 1934, which provides for interstate supervision of parolees and probationers, was ratified by California along with most other states. Through the Western Regional Education Compact California joined in 1956 with sister states of the region in the work of the Western Interstate Commission for Higher Education.

Since 1927 the commission on *uniform state laws* has represented California at the National Conference of Commissioners of Uniform State Laws. The state commission is composed of three members appointed by the governor, and the legislative counsel, ex officio. The statute directs the commission to bring about the passage of uniform acts. California has adopted about one-half of the acts recommended by the national conference.

And *uniform action* may also be secured in the field of administration, through national and regional meetings of various state administrative officers and by bilateral negotiation. Such agreements made by state executive officers are not ordinarily enforceable in courts, and may be altered by successors. But they have some advantages over uniform laws because the latter are difficult to get adopted without amendment and may be enforced and interpreted irregularly even after acceptance.

California has both sinned and been sinned against in the matter of *state trade barriers,* the troublesome and dangerous walls which hamper the free movement of goods between states. Utilizing its police and tax powers, the state has required inspection and quarantine of plant and animal life, checking of equipment on trucks, grading of agricultural products, and the like. The border control stations operated by California in order to control agricultural diseases and pests have been a major source of irritation for travelers, but they may be justified on the grounds of the pest interceptions.

Although California has now established a general state agency for development, local governments are permitted to spend money for "exploitation," or advertising. During the last two decades agricultural marketing laws have authorized advertising expenditures from money collected in fees and assessments from producers or processors of certain farm commodities.

Unsuccessful attempts have been made to control the *migration of persons* to California from other states. Faced with a relief burden of alarming proportions, the legislature in 1937 enacted a law making it a crime to transport an indigent person into the state. In the case of *Edwards* v. *California* (1941), the federal supreme court unanimously declared unconstitutional the state law, popularly known as the "Anti-Okie Law." Even without statutory provision, Los Angeles police were stationed at state border posts to turn back indigent migrants during the depth of the depression in the 1930's.

California participates in the work of the *Council of State Governments.* Representation in its organizations is achieved through the commission on interstate cooperation. Created in 1939, it is now composed of five members of the administration named by the governor, seven senators, and seven assemblymen. The constitutionality of this joint effort of the two branches of government was tested before the state supreme court in *Parker* v. *Riley* (1941). The court decided that the legislator-members of the commission received no "office" in the prohibited sense, nor was the principle of the separation of powers violated.

Further Reading

Book of the States. Chicago: Council of State Governments. Published biennially with supplements.

California, Constitutional Convention, *Report of the Debates in the Convention of California on the Formation of the State Constitution, 1849.* Washington, D.C.: Towers, 1850.

California, Constitutional Convention, *Debates and Proceedings of the Constitutional Convention . . . 1878.* 3 vols. Sacramento: State Printing Office, 1880.

California, Constitutional Commission, *Report . . . 1930.* Sacramento: State Printing Office, 1931.

California, Legislature, Joint Interim Committee on Legislative Constitutional Revision, "Coordinated Draft of a Revised Constitution" and miscellaneous working drafts, proposals, and statements. Sacramento: The Committee, 1947-49.

Constitution of the State of California, Annotated, 1946, Comp. Paul Mason. Sacramento: State Printing Office, 1946.

Coy, Owen C., and Herbert C. Jones, *California's Constitution.* Los Angeles: Wolcott, 1930.

Crouch, Winston W., and Dean E. McHenry, *California Government: Politics and Administration*, chaps. i and ii. Berkeley and Los Angeles: University of California Press, 2d ed., 1949.

Goodwin, Cardinal, *The Establishment of State Government in California*. New York: The Macmillan Company, 1914.

Hunt, Rockwell D., *The Genesis of California's First Constitution*. Baltimore: Johns Hopkins Press, 1895.

League of Women Voters of California, *Constitution Kit*, Pasadena: The League, 1957. (A plan of study and workshop guide).

———, *Briefs on a Long Constitution*, Pasadena: The League, n.d.

Swisher, Carl B., *Motivation and Political Technique in the California Constitutional Convention, 1878-1879*. Claremont: Pomona College, 1930.

United States, Commission on Intergovernmental Relations, *Report* . . . Washington, D.C.: Government Printing Office, 1955. Fifteen staff and study committee reports also were published.

Three

The Electoral

Process

THE RIGHT TO VOTE and the ways and means of making the vote effective are vital to the democratic process. California adopted universal manhood suffrage, with few exceptions, when the Constitution of 1849 came into force. The state grants broad responsibility directly to its electorate, not only in voting on candidates, but also in the legislative process (through the initiative and referendum), in the constituent function (through popular ratification of constitutional amendments), and in cutting short the terms of elective officers (through the recall).

THE RIGHT TO VOTE

National Constitutional Provisions

The primary responsibility for defining the electorate is placed upon the states by the Constitution of the United States. Article I, section 2, states that in the selection of members of the House of Representatives, ". . . the electors in each state shall have the qualifications requisite for electors in the most numerous branch of the State Legislature." The same definition of the electorate, as applied to the election of a senator, is given in the seventeenth amendment. Two other amendments, however, impose restrictions on the freedom of the states in designating who may vote; in both instances the prohibitions set forth apply to elections of both state and federal officers. The fifteenth amendment forbids either state or federal government to deny or abridge the right of citizens to vote because of race, color, or previous condition of servitude. Discrimination because of sex is prohibited in identical terms in the nineteenth amendment. Outside of these federal constitutional limitations, the states are free to define who may vote.

Provisions in the California Constitution

Article II of the California constitution is devoted entirely to "Right of Suffrage." It gives the vote to citizens born or naturalized in the United States, if twenty-one years of age and residents of the state for one year, of the county for ninety days, and of the precinct for fifty-four days. Beginning in 1960 new residents of the state who are otherwise qualified were able to vote in presidential elections after fifty-four days in California. Among those excluded are aliens ineligible for citizenship, idiots, the insane, infamous criminals, embezzlers and misappropriators of public funds, duelers, and illiterates.

Registration

Registration is not a constitutional requirement for voting, but the courts have held that it may be imposed by the legislature as a reasonable "regulation" to ascertain who are qualified voters. California, along with most other states, has a permanent registration system. Once a person registers to vote, his name remains on the rolls until he moves, dies, becomes ineligible, or has failed to vote at a regular state general election held in even numbered years.

The registration process is relatively simple. The would-be voter appears before the county clerk or registrar of voters, or a deputy. An affidavit of registration is filled out, giving full name, address, occupation, citizenship, and height. He may or may not indicate the party of his preference; if he "declines to state," however, he cannot participate in a party primary election. The new voter is given a receipt containing the description of himself and indicating the election precinct in which he lives and in which he may vote. If he moves, or is dropped for failure to vote, it is necessary to reregister.

The California election code permits absentee registration as well as absentee voting. If a voter claims residence in a California county, but is absent for some reason during the registration period, he may secure the registration form and fill it out before a judge, notary public, or American foreign-service official.

Permanent registration was proposed as an initiative law and was adopted by the electorate in 1930. It was sponsored by the Commonwealth Club of California. The permanent system went into effect in January 1932. During the heated Sinclair-Merriam campaign of 1934, many charges were made concerning fraudulent registrations by "floaters" and "deadwood." Criticism of permanent registration mounted, and the legislature of 1935 took two drastic steps. It passed a law canceling existing registration and requiring a general reregistration in 1936. It submitted to the electorate a constitutional amendment specifically authorizing permanent registration but also providing that the legislature might repeal it. The Commonwealth Club opposed the proposed amendment vigorously, and the decisive defeat of the proposition may be taken as evidence of popular support of the permanent system.

NOMINATIONS

End of the Convention System

When California entered the union she adopted the delegate convention method of nominating candidates of political parties. Soon, however, factional struggles developed within the parties; the most violent came during and after the Civil War between the "long-hair" and "short-hair" groups in the Union party. The legislation passed in 1866 to remedy the situation, "An Act to Protect the Elections of Voluntary Associations and to Punish Frauds Therein," has been called the first primary law in any state. The law was *optional*, extending only to the party or group which sought its application, and consisted largely of provisions to assure due notice, orderly conduct, and supervised election.

In 1908 the people adopted a constitutional amendment that authorized a *mandatory* direct primary. This amendment still stands as Article II, section 2½. The Legislature of 1909 proceeded to enact the first *direct* primary election law; although profusely amended, the act is still the basis for our direct primary today. The 1909 law ended the convention system, which even under state regulation bore a deserved reputation for shady deals and machine control.

The Partisan Direct Primary

A partisan direct primary election involves the polling of party members to select the party's nominees for elective public offices. In California the direct primary election is conducted with most of the rules which apply to general elections. All fifty states now use the direct primary in some form. In broad features, California's scheme, as in most other states, is both (1) mandatory (not optional, but must be used by the parties) and (2) closed (party membership tests are applied; only those registered with a party may vote in that party's primary). The nonpartisan primary, examined below, is used in California for the selection of all judges, county, municipal, and school district officers. The partisan primary applies to the nomination of candidates for governor and other state executive officers, members of the legislature, and United States senators and representatives.

A party may qualify to participate in a California primary by any one of three methods: (1) any one of its candidates for a statewide office at the last state general election polled 2 per cent of the vote cast; or (2) the party has a strength in registered voters equal to 1 per cent of the total vote at the last election; or (3) voters equal to 10 per cent of the ballots cast at the last election sign a "petition to participate in the primary election," which is filed with the secretary of state. A party is disqualified if its registration drops below one-fifteenth of one per cent of the total state registration.

In mid-March of even years (seventy-five days before the primary election) the secretary of state compiles the information furnished by county officials and his staff, and issues a "notice" stating the offices for which candidates are to be nominated and the names of political parties qualified to participate. County officers then have this information published in local papers.

Candidates for party nominations must file a "declaration of candidacy" by the first week in April (sixty to ninety days before the election). The signatures of a nominal number of supporters must be filed on a "sponsor's certificate." Filing fees are required at the time of declaration of candidacy: for each party nomination sought by an aspirant for United States senator and most state executive offices the fee is 2 per cent of the first year's salary; for representative in Congress and minor state offices, 1 per cent of one year's salary; for state senator or assemblyman, twenty dollars. After the filing period is closed and the county officials have reported to Sacramento, the secretary of state issues a "certified list of candidates for nomination." The county clerks then publish the list of candidates and the notice of election in their counties.

The person who receives the highest number of votes at a primary election as a party's candidate for an office becomes the nominee of that party at the general election. The primary election is conducted like a general election. All ballots are printed at public expense; polling district officers are publicly paid and directed. The day of the election is by law the first Tuesday in June. When the returns are completed, the secretary of state issues a certificate showing candidates nominated at the primary election and publishes the election results in a pamphlet entitled *Statement of Vote*.

Party membership tests for voters are based on registration records of preference. In this matter, California follows the majority of states in allowing a voter to participate only in the primary of the party with which he is registered. Voters may change their party registration up to fifty-four days before a primary, a liberal provision for those who wish freedom in voting. Eight states, however, allow greater flexibility in permitting voters to choose at the polls the party primary in which they wish to vote. This "open" variety of primary makes possible interference in one party's primary by voters of another. The leading argument in favor of it, on the other hand, is that the elector should not be confined to party lines in seeking the best candi-

dates for office. Some sentiment appears to exist in California for
the open primary.

The Abolition of Cross-Filing

For forty-six years, 1913 to 1959, candidates were allowed to
seek the nominations of parties other than their own in partisan
primaries. No test of party affiliation was required of an aspirant
for any party's nomination. If the cross-filer succeeded in securing both major-party nominations, his name appeared on the
November ballot with the label "Republican-Democrat" or "Dem-
ocrat-Republican." With only one candidate for the two major
parties, the final election usually became a mere formality for
the successful cross-filer.

The first direct primary law of 1909 contained a rigid party
test under which the candidate had to declare that he had supported the party at the preceding general election. The test was
dropped altogether in 1913, largely as a means of protecting incumbent officeholders who had followed Governor Hiram W.
Johnson into the Progressive party in the "Bull Moose" campaign
of 1912. Progressives were enabled to capture both their own and
the Republican nominations, and to safeguard themselves against
three-way contests in the general election.

Between 1914 and 1958 cross-filing became a dominating feature of California politics. Candidates for all partisan public
offices made use of it. Earl Warren in 1946 was the only candidate for the governorship to secure both major party nominations. Hiram W. Johnson in 1934 and 1940 and William F. Knowland in 1952 won both for the United States senatorship. In
1950 Goodwin J. Knight secured the lieutenant governorship by
successfully cross-filing in the primaries. Other state executive
offices were won by cross-filing with considerable regularity.

Nearly all serious candidates for congressional and state legislative offices attempted to win by this device. The peak in successful cross-filing was reached for the office of representative in
Congress in 1940, when 55 per cent of the seats were filled in the
primary. The top in state senate cross-filing was achieved in
1944, when 90 per cent of the districts holding elections gave

PARTISAN OFFICES

STATE	CONGRESSIONAL	COUNTY COMMITTEE
Governor Vote for One	**United States Senator** Vote for One	**Member County Central Committee**
EDMUND G. (PAT) BROWN, Democratic	WILLIAM JOLLEY, Republican	**Forty-Third Assembly District** Vote for Seven
Attorney General	Refrigeration Contractor	A. L. LAWSON
WILLIAM F. KNOWLAND, Republican	GOODWIN J. KNIGHT, Republican	Incumbent
United States Senator	Governor of California	ROBERT A. INGRAM
	ALEXANDER D. WILLIAMSON, Republican	Incumbent
	Public Accountant	LOUIS S. HAYWARD
	GEORGE CHRISTOPHER, Republican	Incumbent
Lieutenant Governor Vote for One	Mayor, San Francisco	MAY H. WHITE
HAROLD J. POWERS, Republican	CLAIR ENGLE, Democratic	Incumbent
Lieutenant Governor	Congressman	VIRGINIA C. HERZOG
GLENN M. ANDERSON, Democratic		Incumbent
Business Development		PAUL McR. JONES
		Incumbent
	Representative in Congress	KATHRYN IVERSON
	Twentieth District Vote for One	Incumbent
Secretary of State Vote for One	H. ALLEN SMITH, Republican	
FRANK M. JORDAN, Republican	Member of Congress-20th District	
Secretary of State	RAYMOND ROBERT FARRELL, Democratic	
	Attorney at Law	
Controller Vote for One	**LEGISLATIVE**	
ROBERT C. KIRKWOOD, Republican		
State Controller		
ALAN CRANSTON, Democratic	**State Senator**	
Business Administrator	**Thirty-Eighth District** Vote for One	
	RICHARD RICHARDS, Democratic	
	California State Senator	
	MARSHALL S. JOHNSON, Republican	
Treasurer Vote for One	Advertising Executive	
A. RONALD BUTTON, Republican	TILDEN W. JOHNSON, Republican	
State Treasurer	Engineer	
BERT A. BETTS, Democratic	DAVID D. PALAZZO, Republican	
Certified Public Accountant	Newspaperman	
	ERNEST A. STEWART, Democratic	
	Tax Economist	
	BRADFORD TRENHAM, Republican	
Attorney General Vote for One	Executive	
STANLEY MOSK, Democratic	ERNEST WARGO, Democratic	
Judge of the Superior Court	Real Estate Broker	
RALPH R. PLANTEEN, Republican	ALFRED A. WELLS, Republican	
Attorney at Law	Attorney at Law	
CASPAR W. WEINBERGER, Assemblyman, Republican California Legislature		
PATRICK J. HILLINGS, Republican	**Member of Assembly**	
United States Congressman	**Forty-Third District** Vote for One	
ROBERT McCARTHY, Democratic	HOWARD J. THELIN, Republican	
State Senator	Member of the Assembly- Forty-Third District	

A portion of the Republican primary ballot of June, 1958. This was the last primary before the abolition of cross-filing. Note the names of leading candidates from both parties, but each is labelled with his own party affiliation under the terms of Proposition 7 of 1952.

both party nominations to a single candidate in the primary. The maximum for state assembly also occurred in 1944, when candidates for 80 per cent of the lower house seats secured both party nominations.

By its very nature cross-filing obscured party lines. The more usual way to liberalize primaries and to reduce partisanship is to adopt the open primary, thus removing party affiliation requirements for voters. California has retained the closed primary as far as voters are concerned, but from 1913 to 1959 opened wide the gates in respect to candidates.

The first step toward repeal of cross-filing came with the adoption in 1952 of a requirement that a candidate's party affiliation be printed on the ballot. Opponents of cross-filing had placed on the ballot an initiative statute (Proposition 13) that provided outright repeal. Supporters of cross-filing succeeded in defeating it by proposing a more moderate plan (Proposition 7) which merely required the printing of party affiliation after each name on the ballot. Politicians were astounded when, in the 1954 primary, only one candidate for a statewide office successfully cross-filed. Also "settled in the primary" were 6.6 per cent of congressional contests, 27.5 per cent of assembly seats, and 55.0 per cent of state senate posts. Similar results obtained in the 1956 and 1958 primaries.

Cross-filing was abolished in 1959 by a short amendment to the elections code requiring a would-be candidate to show by his registration affiliation "with the political party the nomination of which he seeks."

The Nonpartisan Primary

The nonpartisan primary differs in several respects from the partisan one. Judicial, school, county, and municipal offices are nonpartisan. The aspirant for a nonpartisan office secures his place on the primary ballot in the same manner as one who seeks a party nomination. He pays the requisite fee and undertakes his campaign.

If a candidate for an office which is nonpartisan wins more than one-half of all votes cast for the office in the primary, he is declared elected. But if no candidate for county district attor-

NONPARTISAN OFFICES

JUDICIAL	JUDICIAL	SCHOOL
Judge of the Superior Court **Office No. One** Vote for One	**Judge of the Superior Court** **Office No. Fifteen** Vote for One	**Superintendent of** **Public Instruction** Vote for One
SAMUEL R. BLAKE Judge of the Superior Court	RICHARD FILDEW Judge of the Superior Court	ROY E. SIMPSON Incumbent
		EVERETT T. CALVERT Educator Administrator
Judge of the Superior Court **Office No. Two** Vote for One	**Judge of the Superior Court** **Office No. Sixteen** Vote for One	DAVID B. EVERETT School Superintendent
CLARENCE L. KINCAID Judge of the Superior Court	JOHN F. McCARTHY Judge of the Superior Court	HOLLAND D. ROBERTS Educator
		COUNTY
Judge of the Superior Court **Office No. Three** Vote for One	**Judge of the Superior Court** **Office No. Seventeen** Vote for One	**Sheriff** Vote for One
THOMAS L. AMBROSE Incumbent	H. EUGENE BREITENBACH Judge of the Superior Court	PETER J. PITCHESS Undersheriff, County of Los Angeles
EVELLE J. YOUNGER Judge, Los Angeles Judicial District		DAN CROWLEY Baseball Executive
IDA MAY ADAMS Judge Los Angeles Judicial District	**Judge of the Superior Court** **Office No. Eighteen** Vote for One	JOHN C. DORAN Rancher
	ALBERT E. WHEATCROFT Judge of the Superior Court	HOWARD M. KESSLER Business Man
Judge of the Superior Court **Office No. Four** Vote for One		
CLARKE E. STEPHENS Judge of the Superior Court	**Judge of the Superior Court** **Office No. Nineteen** Vote for One	**District Attorney** **(Unexpired Term)** Vote for One
	JOHN F. AISO Judge of the Superior Court	WILLIAM B. McKESSON District Attorney
Judge of the Superior Court **Office No. Five** Vote for One		
FREDERICK F. HOUSER Judge of the Superior Court	**Judge of the Superior Court** **Office No. Twenty** Vote for One	**Assessor** Vote for One
	ALFRED GITELSON Judge of the Superior Court	JOHN R. QUINN Assessor of Los Angeles County
Judge of the Superior Court **Office No. Six** Vote for One		RUSSELL L. HARDY Property Appraiser
PHILBRICK McCOY Judge of the Superior Court	**Judge of the Superior Court** **Office No. Twenty-One** Vote for One	GENE JOHNSTON Tax Economist
	MARK BRANDLER Judge of the Superior Court	ROBERT A. NUETZMAN Real Estate Appraiser
Judge of the Superior Court		

*A portion of the 1958 primary ballot covering non-partisan
offices. A candidate securing a majority of votes cast for
the office is declared elected, and need not contest the
November election.*

ney, for example, should win a majority in the June primary, a
run-off contest between the two highest aspirants takes place
at the November election. Although counties utilize the state
primaries and general elections for the election of their officers,

cities and other units of local government have separate election calendars.

The nonpartisan primary assures a majority choice. It does, however, give a considerable advantage to the incumbent of an office who is running for re-election. The challenger lacks the party label that might attract attention and votes.

Since the adoption of a constitutional amendment in 1934, state judges (Supreme Court and District Court of Appeal) have been selected by a unique procedure which is described in the chapter on the courts.

The Presidential Primary

Delegates to the national party conventions which select nominees for President and Vice-President are chosen in the various states in two different ways. A majority of the states uses state and district conventions for selecting and pledging delegates. About one-fourth of the states, including California, retain the presidential primary method, involving direct election or pledging of delegates. A determined effort to abolish the presidential primary was defeated in the 1959 session of the Legislature. Apparently it was motivated by a desire to enhance California's influence in national politics and to strengthen the hand of the state party organizations.

California's law requires that the chairmen of the party state central committees notify the secretary of state of the number of delegates to the national convention assigned to California. Nomination papers naming the slate of delegates are circulated by supporters of particular presidential aspirants. The papers must be signed by registered voters affiliated with the party equal in number to 0.5 per cent of the vote cast for the party's candidate in the last gubernatorial election. The group must secure the endorsement of the presidential aspirant himself. In practice and by law, the slate is balanced geographically, with each congressional district claiming approximately equal representation. Beginning in 1944, the presidential primary short ballot has been used. At the top of the ballot appears the heading "For Delegates to National Convention." For each presidential aspirant there is a box entitled "Candidates preferring ———

———" and a statement that an "X" in the space provided will count as a vote for all candidates preferring that presidential aspirant. No provision is made for "write-in" candidates. The names of candidates for delegate are printed on a separate slip enclosed with the sample ballot.

The presidential primary is combined with the regular primary and held the first Tuesday of June in each presidential election

---

DEMOCRATIC PARTY

16th Congressional,   38th Senatorial,   60th Assembly District

To vote for the group of candidates preferring a person whose name appears on the ballot, stamp a cross (+) in the square in the column headed by the name of the person preferred.

FOR DELEGATES TO NATIONAL CONVENTION.   VOTE FOR ONE GROUP ONLY.

Candidates Preferring **ADLAI E. STEVENSON**	Candidates Preferring **ESTES KEFAUVER**
☐	☐
A cross (+) stamped in this square shall be counted as a vote for all candidates preferring Adlai E. Stevenson.	A cross (+) stamped in this square shall be counted as a vote for all candidates preferring Estes Kefauver.

California's presidential primary has the following characteristics: delegates are elected at large; they must be pledged to a particular individual; there is no separate preference vote. Since 1944 the short ballot has been used, eliminating the names of candidates for delegate from the ballot.

year. The successful slate of delegates proceeds to the national party convention, held in July, August, or September. California law does not bind delegates to vote for the presidential candidates to whom they are pledged. It is common for the state Republican organization to pledge to a "favorite son," either the state chairman or incumbent governor, and make the best "deal" possible at the convention. The Democrats have rarely avoided an acrimonious conflict in the California presidential primary.

ELECTIONS

Election Procedure

California has long used for its general elections the day set by federal statute, the first Tuesday after the first Monday in November of each even-numbered year. On this day, the voters select the officers—federal, state and county—for which nominations have been made in the June primary, and vote on the propositions which have been proposed by the state legislature, the initiative, or the local governing body during the past two years. Regular municipal elections of the general-law cities are held on the second Tuesday of April in even-numbered years; home-rule or chartered cities and counties may have other dates, as stipulated in their charters. Special state elections on propositions or to fill vacancies in offices may be called by the governor. The governing bodies of counties and of cities possess authority to call special elections for their level of government.

Over-all supervision of election machinery is a responsibility of the secretary of state. Actual conduct of elections, however, is a local, mainly county, function. Except for San Francisco, there are no separate boards of election commissioners, but each county board of supervisors acts ex officio as such for all except municipal elections; each city council acts similarly for municipal elections. The county clerks and city clerks manage the local election machinery, but the larger counties have "registrars of voters" for the purpose.

Polling districts, or precincts, are defined by county clerks and county surveyors and approved by county boards. Precincts are established for the convenience of the voters, so that the elector will have neither too far to come nor too long to wait his turn. The size of each precinct is usually set at 200 voters estimated to cast ballots; this is a rather small number for urban places, especially where the voting machine is employed. The precinct board is composed of one inspector, one or two judges, and two or three clerks. County boards of supervisors formerly used their appointments to election boards as patronage for supporters, but the law now requires preference for those who are on civil service eligible lists for clerical positions, and for those with previous experience. The polling place is determined by the county board; it may be a home, business house, school, or other convenient site. The law specifies in detail the equipment, including voting booths and ballot boxes required for each.

The polls open at 7 A.M. and close at 7 P.M. The board is sworn in, and the ballot boxes are checked to see that no ballot has been deposited in advance. The first voter enters and states his name. His certificate of registration, bound with those of other voters in the precinct, is checked, and he is asked to sign the "roster" with name and address. If the signature is the same, a ballot is issued and the voter proceeds to the booth to mark it in privacy. When he returns, the election officials check and tear off the perforated stub on the corner ballot. The stub number must be the same as that on the ballot issued to the person; this prevents "chain voting," a corrupt procedure under which a "repeater" was given a marked ballot, which he deposited in the ballot box, and returned the clean ballot to his masters.

It is possible for watchers representing candidates or parties to challenge a person who attempts to vote on the grounds that he lacks one or more of the qualifications necessary for voting. The validity of such a challenge is determined by the board through the administering of oaths, examining of records, or giving of tests. A printed record of voters registered in the precinct is kept posted, and the board checks off the names of all who vote, in order that campaign workers may know where to go to bring out nonvoters. Under the state constitution, each voter is entitled to two hours off from his employment with pay in order to vote.

At the appointed hour, precinct officers close the polls and proceed to deface all unused ballots, which must be returned to the county clerk and destroyed by him. The valid, used ballots are then canvassed, to see that their number agrees with the number of names on the roster. The count begins with the election board members sharing the work of reading and tallying. Voters have a right to witness the count being made and to challenge any procedure which appears to depart from the law. When returns are completed, the results are posted at the polling place, and all ballots, materials, tally sheets, and equipment are returned to the county offices. The county board canvasses the vote and declares the final results. In practice the results usually are known far in advance of the final proclamation, because precinct boards release unofficial figures to the press as quickly as they become available.

California, along with nearly all the states, permits a voter who is away from home on election day to vote by "absentee ballot." The procedure is simple; either the voter goes to the county clerk and casts his ballot in advance, or five to twenty days before an election he writes for a ballot and fills it out. The ballot is sealed in a special envelope and returned by mail.

Ballot Form

In form, California's ballot would be described as (1) largely consolidated, with federal, state, and county candidates and propositions on the same ballot, a separate one being used for municipal propositions and officers voted on at state general elections;* (2) office block, grouping candidates by office rather than by party, providing no party column or emblem, and having no arrangement for straight party voting with one mark.

This state goes to unusual lengths to prevent corruption. In addition to the comparison of signatures between register and roster, and the use of perforated stubs on ballots, the state also uses a secret watermarked ballot paper, which may be obtained by the counties only from the secretary of state. The printing is done in the counties. A sample ballot, replica of the official ballot, is distributed to every voter by mail in advance of the election, and if propositions are to be voted upon, publicity pamphlets containing descriptions of the proposed measures are included.

The presidential short ballot was used for the first time in the 1940 election. Previously, the names of all candidates for presidential electors appeared on the ballot, although any considerable voting for individual electors had long since ceased. Now the presidential electors section, which formerly took several columns, is reduced in size to a few lines. At the head of the

---

* Since 1959, counties have been empowered to use a separate ballot for nonpartisan offices and local measures if the general election ballot would otherwise be too large for convenient handling.

column appears, "Vote for One Party," and the list of presidential and vice-presidential candidates follows, together with their parties. More than one-half of the states, including most of the larger ones, use the presidential short ballot. Voting machines are authorized but little used in California. San Francisco employs and likes them. Los Angeles County acquired a few but has stopped using them and has sold the equipment. Besides the usual deterrents to their adoption (expense, for example) the extremely long ballot in this state complicates the situation considerably. It takes a very large machine face to handle the multiple offices and propositions in a normal California general election. Returns were unusually late in the 1958 general election, bringing renewed interest in punch-card and other mechanical and electronic methods of voting and tabulating returns. Los Angeles County has contracted with a manufacturer to develop a vote tabulating machine.

Further Reading

Anderson, Dewey, *Voting in California*. Washington, D.C.: Public Affairs Institute, 1958.

Baker, Gordon E., and Bernard Teitelbaum, "An End to Cross-Filing," *National Civic Review*, XLVIII (June, 1959), pp. 286-291.

Burke, Robert, "Cross-Filing in California Elections, 1914-1946," Unpublished M.A. thesis, University of California, Berkeley, 1947.

California, Secretary of State, *Statement of Vote*. Issued following each primary, special, and general election.

Harris, Joseph P., and Leonard Rowe, *California Politics*, 2nd ed. Stanford: Stanford University Press, 1959.

Hazen, Evelyn, *Cross-Filing in Primary Elections*. Berkeley: Bureau of Public Administration, University of California, 1951.

Jones, Harold T., *Administration of Elections in Los Angeles City, County and the State of California*, Los Angeles: Office of the City Clerk, 1955.

League of Women Voters of California, *California Voters' Handbook*, Pasadena: The League, 1957.

McHenry, Dean E., "Invitation to the Masquerade," *National Municipal Review*, XXXIX (May, 1950), pp. 228-232.

Pit-hell, Robert J., "The Electoral System and Voting Behavior: The Case of California's Cross-Filing," *Western Political Quarterly*, XII (June, 1959), pp. 459-484.

Four

The Pattern of

Politics

THE PATTERN OF CALIFORNIA POLITICS has many unique features. Political parties play a less important role than in the nation or in most other states. Pressure groups are unusually powerful. The ballot is long, both because so many offices are elective and because of the large number of propositions (mainly constitutional amendments) put up to popular vote. The primary has an extraordinary importance in the political process, because of factionalism in the parties, and the extent of non-partisanship.

PARTY POLITICS

The Legal Status of Party

The Elections Code stipulates in great detail what a political party is, how it is organized, what it may and may not do. A party is defined in the law as an organization which is "qualified for participation in any primary election." Qualification is achieved if the conditions mentioned on page 41 of Chapter Three are met. Obviously, those criteria are inadequate for general use, and are meant mainly for primary-election purposes. But they provide the foundation of legal status and are therefore important. At the end of 1959 only two parties were officially qualified: Democratic and Republican.

Party Organization

The state convention stands at the head of the party hierarchy in California. It meets once every two years, on a stipulated Saturday of August or September, and is composed of delegates each of whom represents one of the party's nominees for the directly elected federal and state offices in the state. (There was a total body of 160 during the 1950's.) Some of the delegates are the nominees or officeholders themselves, some (where there is no party nominee) are appointed by the state or county central committee of the party. The convention has two main functions, neither of which is of great importance. First, it adopts the state platform of the party. Second, in presidential-election years, it selects the party's candidates for presidential electors.

The state central committee also meets biennially, on the day following the convention. Unlike similar bodies in other states, it is huge, being composed of all delegates to the convention, all chairmen of county central committees, and three appointees of each convention delegate. The total membership of the committee between 1952 and 1960 reached 700 on some occasions. The law prohibits a state central committee chairman from succeeding himself and requires that the chairmanship alternate between northern and southern California. Committee members may vote by proxy. The duties of the committee, as defined by law, are nominal and vague, including the responsibility to "conduct party campaigns" and to organize "as it deems suitable or desirable and for the best interests of the party." The full committee may, and in practice does, delegate its powers and duties to an executive committee. In consultation with the party's nominees for representatives in Congress, this committee may set up still another unit, a party congressional committee to manage the campaign in each congressional district.

The county central committee is the only level of party organization with popular election. The number of members varies considerably: San Francisco has five members for each of the six assembly districts in the city and county; Los Angeles has seven for each of its thirty assembly districts. In the smaller counties, election is by supervisorial districts and the members are apportioned according to the vote for the party's candidate for gov-

CALIFORNIA PARTY ORGANIZATION

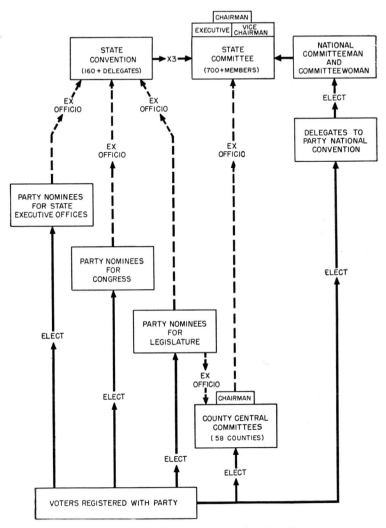

Complicated and cumbersome, formal political party organization in California rarely works effectively.

ernor. The term of office is two years in all counties. Election takes place in the June primary. In addition to the elected members, the party's nominees for state senate and state assembly are ex officio members of the county central committees. The county committee has the general responsibility of conducting a campaign within the county. Should a vacancy occur in the party's list of nominees for offices within the county (state senate or assembly), the county central committee fills it.

The Party in Practice

By statute, California has attempted to do more than provide a framework for party organization. It has tried to legislate in detail on the functions as well as the form. The result is a structure resembling a pyramid in shape, and virtually as lifeless. For various reasons, California's parties have almost been hollow shells, without true roots in the electorate. Over the years, the state parties have been riding along on the coattails of national issues, furnishing in meager fashion the crystallization of opinion and of provision of responsibility—recognized functions of political parties.

The first question is, Who are party members? Virtually all of the registered voters consider themselves members of one or another of the parties. For the 1938, 1948, and 1958 general elections, the party registration in the state stood as follows:

	1938	1948	1958
Republican	1,293,929	1,908,170	2,676,565
Democratic	2,144,360	2,892,222	3,875,630
Other parties	58,875	38,033	32,268
Decline to state	114,252	223,572	167,958
Registration totals	3,611,416	5,061,997	6,752,421

Under state law, whoever declares his party preference as Republican is a Republican, and whoever tells a registration deputy he is Democratic belongs to the Democratic party. This involves no searching test of party ties of the past and no promises about the future, but is a mere declaration of preference.

In view of the overwhelming Democratic majority in registration, how did Republicans win so many state and congressional offices? Among the many explanations offered, the following appear most plausible: (1) Many of the "Democrats" are such in name only, having long since abandoned voting for the party of their youth, family connection, section of origin, or depression-era loyalty. (2) Republicans are more apt to vote on election day than are Democrats. (3) The Democratic party has been short on attractive candidates. (4) Republicans have made skillful use

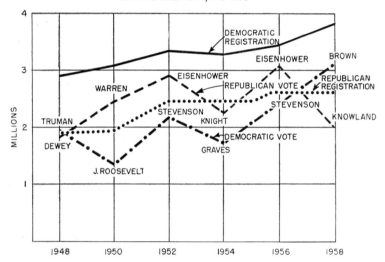

TRENDS IN STATE-WIDE
PARTY REGISTRATION AND VOTING
(FOR PRESIDENT AND GOVERNOR)
GENERAL ELECTIONS, 1948-1958

*The overwhelming Democratic registration and the re-
markable Republican electoral victories until 1958 pose
one of the most tantalizing questions in California politics.*

of their greater monetary resources and newspaper support. (5) State legislative and congressional districts in the 1940's and 1950s were gerrymandered to give Republican candidates the advantage.

What should a party do? In theory, a political party should perform, among others, the following services for democratic government: (1) It should canalize and crystallize opinion and narrow the policy alternatives before the voters by compromising the diverse views of individuals and groups. (2) It should act as broker of candidates for office by selecting and promoting them, and should narrow the candidate alternatives before the voters; (3) It should educate and interest voters in politics through publicity and leadership. (4) It should provide responsibility, the party in power being held accountable for its stewardship of office, and the minority party furnishing criticism. (5) By producing compatible groups of officeholders, a party should help to overcome the diffusion of government authority which results from the separation of powers between the legislative, executive, and judicial departments.

Has the California political party done its job? Only in part. In normal campaigns its policy declarations are so vague that the voter has a poor index to what may happen. Party discipline, until recently, was so lax that a program proposing definite reforms was not likely to be binding on officials elected under the party's label. In this respect it was a real failure, for the enforcement of discipline was virtually unheard-of in state politics. This was due to many factors—lack of party-affiliation tests for primary candidates, poor leadership, absence of patronage, neglect by the public, and other causes.

Moreover, California parties have few facilities for issuing literature or information except during campaigns, when the more blatant propaganda is used. Leadership, save for a few individuals, has been rather uninspiring. The party is most successful in its task of selecting and pushing candidates and of narrowing the candidate alternatives.

Reasons for the Failure of Party

The residue of cross-filing has been examined in the preceding chapter. The impact of the practice upon the vitality and prestige of the party was destructive, and is likely to be felt for many years to come.

The average voter does not follow closely the business of government; indeed, various surveys have shown that the level of civic information is exceedingly low. The voter, however, may develop a rough value judgment concerning the work of the parties. Until the repeal of cross-filing, accountability for a legislative program, for example, was almost impossible to establish. In the Legislature of 1959 the senate had 27 Democrats, of whom 17 were elected under the Republican label as well as their own, and 13 Republicans, of whom 6 successfully cross-filed and also secured the Democratic nomination. The situation was less confusing in the assembly, but the party lines were often blurred there too.

2) Lack of leadership is another reason for the failure of the party. One of the state buildings in Sacramento bears the inscription: "Bring Me Men to Match My Mountains," and California has produced some outstanding political leaders who have inspired interest in public affairs. But few in recent years have brought vitality to party organizations. Many have inclined to a posture of nonpartisanship, standing aloof from their own parties even in campaigning.

3) Making county central committees elective has not helped matters. Because the committees have little power and no real organizations below them, many able people decline to seek election. Some who are elected lack the initiative and energy necessary to build an organization in precinct and assembly district.

4) Active party workers frequently complain over the lack of patronage, or jobs for deserving politicians. Actually, the number of political appointments is quite small. The 1934 civil service amendment, as described in a subsequent chapter, leaves few posts which may be filled at the discretion of the governor or legislature. In the Rolph administration (1931-34) a considerable amount of patronage accrued through probationary appointments and other devices. For several years, the State Relief Administration, an exempt agency, provided jobs for the faithful. Although an organization can be built through patronage and spoils, various citizens' groups offer clear evidence that one can be built without them. Reliance upon incentives other than spoils may produce a more effective organization, if interest in governmental affairs is maintained at a high level. At any rate, the merit system is firmly established in the state, and parties may as well become reconciled to the absence of any considerable amount of state patronage.

The standing of the political party in California is further endangered by a rather widespread attitude of contempt for things political. This point of view is not confined to our state, but it is often expressed in particularly violent form here, even though justifications for it are somewhat less than in most states. Many who do not persist in the "politics is a dirty business" attitude reserve no place in their lives for civic activities and take no part or interest in public affairs; actually they participate little more in their government than does a European living under a communist or fascist dictatorship.

Informal Party Organizations

One of the consequences of the failure of official parties has been the rise of extralegal party groups. Party clubs and associations are set up to meet the need for local bodies to organize the precincts and recruit supporters among the electorate. Although these bodies are often chartered by county central committees, they are essentially private groups unregulated by the laws governing formal parties. Each party now has a predominant extralegal organization to perform some essential functions. The California Republican Assembly and the California Democratic Council are the leading informal party organizations in California.

The Republican Assembly was established in 1934 to rejuvenate the party. Younger elements in the party used this vehicle to infuse new personnel and program into the party. They soon turned to the selection and endorsement of candidates in advance of primary elections. Assembly candidates often were the only Republicans on the primary ballot for a particular office, and thereby could concentrate on securing a plurality in the Democratic primary by a vigorous appeal that eschewed partisanship and stressed "the man." With the Democrats disorganized, the Republican Assembly scored victory after victory in the late 1930's, the 1940's, and the early 1950's.

A key device of the assembly is the "candidate and fact-finding committee" set up to examine would-be candidates, examine the situation, and recommend one as the "endorsed" candidate. These committees were formed for most offices for which a contest was in prospect, whether statewide or district. Their nominations of endorsed candidates are subject to ratification by assembly state convention or district bodies. By such methods Richard M. Nixon and Goodwin J. Knight were brought into public life.

During the 1950's the Republican Assembly was unable to contain some factional fights within the party. In 1954 its endorsed candidate for lieutenant governor was defeated in the Republican primary. In 1958 it was unable to prevent a primary contest between Goodwin J. Knight and George Christopher for the United States senatorship. Despite these cracks in unity, however, the assembly remains a potent force in the Republican party, and its local sinews of strength—while weakened by the abolition of cross-filing—are likely to remain substantial.

The California Democratic Council was organized in 1953 following the Republican sweep in the election of the year before. Long denied the fruits of victory by factionalism among themselves and by superior organization among their opponents, leading Democrats sought a formula for capitalizing on their predominance in numbers of registered voters. The result is an organization that rather parallels the Republican Assembly in techniques, but may have deeper roots in the local communities. Dozens of Democratic clubs were organized during the 1952 campaign, and they have multiplied since that time. The CDC on district and statewide levels is a federation of local Democratic clubs and organizations.

In its first test of strength, the 1954 primary, the CDC endorsed in convention all Democratic candidates who subsequently won party nominations for statewide offices, but in the November election all except Attorney General Edmund G. Brown lost to Republicans. In 1956, the CDC endorsed state senator Richard Richards for the United States senatorship, and played a large part in securing the Democratic nomination for him despite a hot contest with both Samuel Yorty, its endorsee in 1954, and Thomas H. Kuchel, Republican incumbent who subsequently won in the general election. In legislative and congressional districts, however, Democrats—many with CDC endorsements—made significant gains.

The 1958 primary and general election raised the CDC to the peak of its influence up to that time. All of its endorsees for statewide offices won their party nominations, and all offices except the secretaryship of state were won in November. The landslide

62 THE PATTERN OF POLITICS

victory obscured for a while latent cleavages in Democratic ranks that may again open up under stress. The CDC and the club movement it represents was not *the* Democratic party in the sense that CRA became, for a time at least, *the* Republican organization. There are other important pockets of power: the official party organization in the state and counties, the incumbent officeholders, the large contributors, the trade unions. When there is substantial agreement among these elements, Democratic candidates are likely to have uncontested primaries and unified support in general elections. When they split, the chances of a Republican resurgence are good.

PRESSURE POLITICS

Organized Groups in the Political Process

The role of special-interest groups in politics has only recently attracted the attention it deserved, but the great American tendency to join and to organize has long been recognized. "Americans of all ages, all conditions, and all dispositions," wrote Tocqueville more than a hundred years ago, "constantly form associations."

Pressure-group politics has been known in California since the beginning of the state. The activities of lobbyists gave the first legislature, which convened at San Jose in 1850, the name "legislature of a thousand drinks." After 1869 and the completion of the transcontinental railroad, economic power became concentrated in the Central Pacific Railroad. The "Big Four"—Leland Stanford, Collis P. Huntington, Charles Crocker, and Mark Hopkins—were enthroned not only as economic but also as political masters of California. For the next forty years the railroad was the dominant force in state and local politics. The railroad machine was bipartisan, and sought to control the conventions of both parties.

The Railroad Machine

In the early nineties Stanford resigned from the presidency of the railroad, and was succeeded by Huntington. With a new name, the Southern Pacific, and a new political head, William F. Herrin, the company embarked upon a new era. Under Herrin's control, the Southern Pacific machine maintained a control over local and state politics that was relatively unbroken until the progressive "revolution" of 1910. Allied with the railroad in the political machine, and often called by reformers the "associated villainies," were other interests requiring political protection. The methods of the Herrin machine are disclosed in the memoirs of Fremont Older and in the legislative reviews of Franklin Hichborn.

The end of the Southern Pacific machine as a dominant political force occurred in 1910, when the progressive faction of the Republican party nominated and elected Hiram W. Johnson as governor and won a majority in both houses of the legislature. This progressive victory coincided with other far-reaching economic and political changes in the state: the emergence of organized labor as a powerful and independent force, the enfranchisement of women, the rise of new industries and utilities such as the electric power concerns, and the shift of religious and moral groups to political influence. Neither political nor economic power was now a monopoly of any group. Therefore the methods of pressure-group politics changed; the old lobby, with its strong-arm methods was dead; and the new one, dressed in the modern garb of persuasiveness, came into being.

Why Groups Are Powerful

The unusual importance of pressure-group politics in California may be attributed to several special conditions. This has been a one-party state during most of the last half-century. Republicans held the governorship continuously from 1898 to 1958 (except 1938-42), a majority in the assembly from 1893 to 1959 (except the sessions of 1937 and 1939), and a majority in the senate every session from 1889 until the two parties tied in 1957. Both parties were weakened by the long preponderance of one party in power. Party lines, as shown before, were confused by the practice of cross-filing in the primaries. The tradition of party discipline has been lacking. The real division in state politics for two decades after 1910 was between progressives and reactionaries in the Republican party. With parties playing less than the usual role in state politics, pressure groups have tended to operate directly in primary and general election campaigns and have crossed party lines in their lobbying activities.

Group politics has also been given impetus by the presence of the new instrumentalities of popular control—the initiative, referendum, and recall. If a party caucus in the legislature should whip its members into line, an organized group can use the referendum to defeat its affirmative actions, and the initiative to overcome its refusal to act. Even if a partisan united front were achieved, it could be broken through the recall. A direct fight before the electorate on a proposition involving a major economic interest, such as retail chain stores, petroleum companies, or electric utilities, brings the expenditure of hundreds of thousands of dollars to propagandize the electorate. Such a campaign may be run directly by the organized group or by specialists employed for the purpose.

The Groups and Their Methods

The major state organizations which engage in group politics and secure special representation may be classified by the interest served:

1. Public utilities—electric and gas companies, California Railroad Association, trucking industry

2. Farm—California Farm Bureau Federation, California State Grange, Agricultural Council of California (large cooperatives)

3. Labor—California State Federation of Labor (A.F. of L.), now merged with California C.I.O. Council; railroad brotherhoods

4. Schools—California Teachers Association, Affiliated Teacher Organizations of Los Angeles, California Congress of Parents and Teachers

5. Insurance—National Board of Fire Underwriters and individual companies

6. Employers—California Manufacturers Association, Merchants and Manufacturers Association of Los Angeles, Industrial Association of San Francisco, Associated Farmers

7. Petroleum Industry—Independent Petroleum Producers and Consumers Association, major oil companies

8. Public Employees—California State Employees Association and others

In addition to the interests and bodies mentioned, there are dozens of other important groups at work in California politics. The methods of pressure groups in politics may be classified as follows: (1) dissemination of information—preparation of legislation, furnishing of information, argument at hearings; (2) social pressure—development of contacts, currying favor through personal acquaintance; (3) issuance of publicity—spreading propaganda to influence the public and concentrating individual pressure on public officials; (4) campaign activities—endorsement of candidates, rendering of financial assistance, securing of pledges from candidates.

The informational function of special-interest groups is well known and is of considerable value. Organizations provide direct, authoritative representation for industries, fields, or memberships. Public officials need authentic information from the groups concerned in order to make proper decisions on the question at hand. If compromise is an important part of democratic government, then certainly the executive or legislator who is a craftsman of the compromise should have the fullest possible information on all sides. Bills are often drafted by group attorneys; pamphlets and letters are written for informational inducement; group spokesmen present their point of view to committee hearings and conferences.

Social pressure is a well-known lobbying technique. The clever lobbyist, engaged in either executive or legislative work, studies his quarry and makes the most discreet and telling approach possible. On the invidious side, this often begins with the picking out of an official's weaknesses—he cannot resist women, or liquor, or poker, or something else; then the lobbyist approaches and may play hard on the weakness. On the harmless side, the group representatives provide entertainment and fellowship, and seek only to reach the official ear with straightforward arguments under favorable circumstances.

Publicity or propaganda is issued by virtually all groups interested in influencing the formation of public policy. Much of it is intended to induce public reactions which can be translated into pressure on public officers. Groups with large memberships may secure an adequate number of letters and telegrams within their own organization; business concerns are forced to rely upon special organizers and widespread advertising. Campaign activities constitute a major function of most organized groups with political goals. The amount of their participation varies greatly. A mild form of intervention on the campaigning front involves the circulation of questionnaires requesting information on candidates' views, and the publication of the answers. Some groups publish factual summaries of the record, including important roll calls in the legislature, often indicating the "good" and "bad" votes of the various legislators. Still others make open endorsements of candidates and designate enemies. A few groups enter campaigns with vigor, spend large amounts of money directly and indirectly, and assign campaigning responsibilities to members.

SECTIONAL POLITICS

North versus South

Sectional cleavages in California politics fall into two classes: north versus south, and rural versus urban. The controversies between northern and southern California have on several occasions become so bitter that state division has been very seriously discussed. In late 1958, two events reminded Californians that separatism is not dead. Sponsors of a new state of "Shasta," to be formed from the eight northernmost counties, inquired about the procedure for obtaining statehood. A San Francisco newspaper reported the results of a poll in which 55.7 per cent of respondents (presumably northern) indicated that partition between north and south into two states was desirable.

The north, led most of the time by San Francisco and the bay district, was predominant in state politics from 1850 to around 1930. This leadership was secured at first from the concentration of population in the north during the gold rush, and the earlier development of agriculture and manufacturing there. After southern California began to exceed the north in population, northern political control was maintained through obstructing reapportionment of the legislative and congressional districts and similar acts.

In the legislature of 1931 the south won a victory in a violent reapportionment struggle, securing representation according to population in both the assembly and the national House of Representatives. During the last decade sectional lines have reappeared many times. Usually the southern element has shown itself in control, although its potential power is not fully realized due to cohesiveness of the northern politicians and to the diffusion which prevails in the south. Moreover, the state senate and the State Board of Equalization are apportioned in such a manner as to overrepresent the north. The reapportionment fight of 1941 ended in another victory for the south; in 1951 partisanship was probably a larger factor than sectionalism. The ten counties below the straight line formed by the northern boundaries of San Luis Obispo, Kern, and San Bernardino counties contained, in 1950, 56 per cent of the state's population; the forty-eight counties above had 44 per cent of the people.

Water has been a great bone of contention between north and south in recent sessions of the legislature. In general, northern California is a "have" area and southern California is "have not." The north is anxious to reserve for itself a sufficient supply for future development. Although both regions have grown rapidly since the war, the population of the San Francisco Bay area has been more stable, while in Los Angeles people move oftener and consequently are more difficult to organize both politically and industrially.

Urban versus Rural

The urban-versus-rural split is now of even greater importance. It occurs more frequently in American states than does the division between two great metropolitan areas. In this state earlier urban-rural conflicts were subordinated to north-south controversy, but occasionally they became intermingled. The "federal plan" of apportioning the state senate, described in the chapter on the legislature, represents a rather complete victory of rural over urban forces. The rural areas were able to establish this system in 1926 only with support from San Francisco, which was given in part to spite Los Angeles and was often regretted afterward.

He who would win votes in the California legislature must defer to rural sentiment. Party groups, urban elements, individual politicians, and pressure groups—all must bow to the supremacy of the "country" or "cow counties" in the state senate. Although vigorously challenged via an initiative constitutional amendment in 1948, rural predominance in the senate continues.

The most acute split on issues, in recent years, has been over water. "Counties of origin," largely northernmost and astride the Sierra Nevada, prefer to have population and industry come to them rather than have their water siphoned off to the thirsty and urban southern counties.

CAMPAIGNS AND FINANCE

Primary Campaigning

The conduct of a campaign in California differs considerably from that in states with strong political organizations. The primary, both partisan and nonpartisan, often has been wide open, with nominations frequently won by dark-horse or insurgent aspirants. In the past there has been a tendency on their part to stress regional and personal issues, and to minimize partisanship. Since the partisan primary can be won by a plurality, aspirants often are numerous. The position of the incumbent seeking renomination is thereby strengthened. The nonincumbent therefore may resort to spectacular antics, such as a "hillybilly" campaign, or to support of some farfetched panacea, such as a pension scheme, which will appeal to a considerable sector of the electorate.

Electioneering is amateurishly conducted, even though campaign workers often are paid. Lacking any definite machinery in the precincts, the primary aspirant rounds up friends, tries to collect a war chest, and spends available cash for the usual purposes. A part goes for printing literature, which is thrown on residential doorsteps or mailed to voters. Some is spent for radio and television time, which the candidate uses to pour forth his persuasive words. Posters and billboards are utilized to press indelibly onto the consciousness of John Q. Public that the honorable August Blowhard has consented to become a candidate for this or that office. Thorough personal canvassing, except by candidates for minor local offices, is rare.

The General-Election Contest

When the partisan nominee faces an opponent of the other major party in the general election, he adjusts his strategy according to circumstances. If his party has the minority in registration, he attempts to overcome this obstacle by winning over voters from his opponent's party, by stressing issues which will appeal to certain elements, and by attacking his opponent's weakest points. Should his party, however, be in a majority position, then he concentrates on holding his partisans together by extolling party history and virtues.

The general-election campaign is conducted with the full knowledge that California voters are an independent lot. Given respectable candidates, a majority may follow traditional party prejudices; but there exists an unusually large element of independent, insurgent voters, who may upset the best-laid plans of those who count on narrow partisanship. The middle group is progressive in inclination, but unlikely to accept candidates to whom the "radical" label is successfully attached.

Professionals in Campaigns

One relatively unique feature of campaigning in California is the large role played by public relations firms and campaign management specialists. Whether for a statewide or a district campaign, whether for a candidate or a proposition, professional campaign direction is available for hire. Some argue that it is cheaper per vote obtained to put a campaign in the hands of a specialist than to build up and maintain a permanent political organization. It allegedly has the advantage of a tractor over a horse: no need to feed it when it is not working.

Several characteristics of California have produced a climate in which professional campaign specialists could flourish. The initiative and referendum required many economic interests, usually well-financed, to have occasional access to the electorate. The state is large and diverse. Party organizations were weak. New mass media, first radio and then television, required special skills. Cross-filing tempted candidates to "go for broke" in the primary in the hopes of capturing both party nominations and thereby avoiding a contest in the general election. The pre-primary endorsement procedures evolved by the Republican assembly required intricate negotiations and preparation that often could be best supplied by a professional.

The best known of the firms engaging in campaign management is Whitaker & Baxter, a husband and wife team that has scored a remarkable string of victories for their clients. They have managed successful campaigns for Earl Warren, Goodwin J. Knight, and some of the largest corporations that operate in the state. Murray Chotiner helped win victories for Richard M. Nixon, William F. Knowland, and other leading candidates.

Although some regard the emergence of the professional campaign specialist with alarm, this phenomenon might have been expected to come from the situation that prevailed in California. It is too early to see whether the reemergence of party will reduce the dependence of candidates on public relations firms. If so, then there will still be plenty of business from the associations and corporations that must reach the public during and between campaigns.

Financing Political Activities

California has a corrupt-practices law, the "Purity of Elections Act of 1907," as amended. Candidates and campaign committees must file itemized statements of receipts and expenditures. Political parties are not required to report. Financial statements must be filed within thirty-five days after each primary or general election. Sources of contributions are little restricted; both corporations and trade unions are permitted to donate. Since 1949 there has been no total-expenditures limit set in the law, either for candidates or committees.

The list of purposes for which lawful expenditures may be made does not include such common items as parades and spectacles, refreshments or amusements. On the prohibited list are rental of premises on which liquor is served and printing that does not reveal the name and address of the person responsible.

Since 1957 political contributions of $100 or less in any primary or general election are deductible for state income tax purposes.

Maximum expenditure limits were abandoned because they were virtually unenforceable. The old limitations were based on the salary and term of office. The candidate for the governorship, for example, was permitted to spend 20 per cent of one year's salary. The allowable amounts were ridiculously low. Some conscientious candidates reported expenditures far in excess of the permitted amount, but there was no record of successful prosecution. Many avoided open violation by attributing expenditures to a committee that supported a party slate rather than a single candidate. In a state as large and complex as California, rigid limits on the amounts that can be spent in campaigns have proved ineffective. Although the law is improved by eliminating expenditure maximums, the legislature has not taken the next logical steps of fixing the responsibility for political spending firmly on the candidate, his designated representative, or committee treasurer.

In the hot gubernatorial contest of 1958, close to $950,000 was spent in the primary, and over $1.5 million in the general election were reported for the two candidates. More than $600,000 was spent in the final election campaign for the United States senatorship.

Reforming the Political Process

Nonpartisanship and Other Reforms

Political parties in California fail to perform adequately the services which justify their existence. Should parties, therefore, be abolished? Or should parties be strengthened? Over these questions a very long controversy has raged.

The case for nonpartisanship may be stated simply: it is alleged that national party lines and issues have little application to state politics; the choice of the majority is not assured by the partisan system. The reform legislature of 1911 wiped out party designations for all judicial and school offices. The 1913 session made local governmental offices nonpartisan. In 1915 a bill was enacted making all remaining state positions nonpartisan. The measure was held up in referendum and defeated in a special election in October 1915 by a light vote of 156,967 against 112,-681 in favor. Since that time, election of governor, lieutenant governor, controller, treasurer, attorney general, secretary of state, legislature, and four members of the Board of Equalization have continued on a partisan basis.

Although party designations could be removed from the ballot by statute, party groups might continue making open endorsements as they have in Minnesota's nonpartisan plan. State parties or political leagues might emerge and function much like national parties in national affairs. In 1955 the senate passed a bill making state legislative offices nonpartisan, but the measure was killed in the assembly after sharp objections were raised by the California members of Congress.

The case for retaining and strengthening partisanship relies upon the traditional arguments for parties: parties have a role in the process of crystallizing opinion; they provide a measure of corporate responsibility. The layman, as we have seen, may have an opinion upon the general conduct in office of a party, but may be unable to recognize an individual candidate's merits and demerits. As state and national governments became more interdependent, national party principles have more and more application to state issues. In 1935 an advocate of nonpartisanship asked: "What has the tariff, the League, or the World Court to do with how you believe on the Sacramento Valley Project?" Today, the federal government has the major role in the central valley project, and continued progress in a dozen fields of state activity are bound up with federal-state cooperation.

Conclusion

California politics is different from the politics of other states, more in terms of emphasis and degree than in any unusual fundamental force. Through a combination of historical factors, the nature of the population, and unique legal devices, party has been relegated to a meager and nominal role—impotent, starved, and ill organized. Into the vacuum created by the shrinking of party, the pressure groups have entered. Purposeful, well organized, and well financed, they have thrown their weight and influence around both in campaigns and in the legislature.

Denied the emblem of party, both through the adoption of nonpartisanship for all local, school, and judicial offices (and for forty-six years through the practice of cross-filing) the voter has been forced to grope through the excessively long ballot without proper aid. Since he is confronted with a task that staggers the most alert citizen, the average man must pick up his civic data on a hand-to-mouth basis. The newspapers thereby secure great leverage in political influence. So do those who have the means to hire the other principal media of information dissemination.

Although possessing many of the trappings of democracy, such as the direct primary and the initiative, California falls short of truly responsible politics. In every state and nation of any size, political parties have been found essential to the proper functioning of democratic politics in big government. Therefore, California should explore every avenue of strengthening parties. Reform properly began with the abolition of cross-filing. Party bodies should be given sufficient power to activate themselves and freedom to adopt their own organizational forms. Party committees of pre-primary conventions might well be empowered to indicate preferred candidates on the primary ballot. Consideration should be given to returning to the convention plan of nominating statewide candidates, as is done in New York.

The high cost of campaigning, accentuated by the advent of television, poses problems of extraordinary difficulty. Several possibilities are worth exploring. A small fee might be collected at the time a voter registers, and turned over to official party bodies for use during and between campaigns. Candidates might be given the privilege of furnishing literature, of limited size and affirmative appeal, to county clerks and registrars of voters for inclusion with the sample ballot which is mailed at public expense.

The existing situation is unsatisfactory and untenable. Either parties ought to be given conditions under which they can live and provide the expected services, or they ought to be eliminated.

On the other hand, in presidential-election years, California's parties receive sharp stimulus. The size of their delegations to the national conventions, the state's large electoral vote, and its pivotal role in deciding national elections combine to set the stakes of politics very high.

In 1960 as never before, California's strategic position in the presidential nominating process is felt. On the Republican side, Californian Richard Nixon led the preconvention field as a possible nominee for the presidency. Although Governor Edmund G. Brown is widely considered as a "favorite son," the shifting tides of the Democratic convention of 1960 could give him a place on the national ticket. In any case, California's large delegation is likely to be a decisive force. Perhaps vitality can be restored to California's parties through transfusion of enthusiasm from national politics.

Further Reading

Anderson, Totten J., "Bibliography on California Politics," in *Bibliography on Western Politics*, a supplement to *Western Political Quarterly*, XI (December, 1958), 23-51.

———, "The 1958 Election in California," *Western Political Quarterly*, XII, Part 2 (March, 1959), 276-300.

Burke, Robert, *Olson's New Deal for California*. Berkeley and Los Angeles: University of California Press, 1953.

Carney, Francis, *The Rise of Democratic Clubs in California*. New York: Holt, 1958.

Chinn, Ronald E., *Democratic Party Politics in California, 1920-1956*. Unpublished Ph.D. dissertation, University of California, Berkeley, 1958.

Cresap, Dean R., *Party Politics in the Golden State*. Los Angeles: Haynes Foundation, 1954.

Farrelly, David G., and Ivan H. Hinderaker, *The Politics of California: a Book of Readings*. New York: Ronald Press Co., 1951.

Harris, Joseph P., and Leonard Rowe, *California Politics*, 2nd ed. Stanford: Stanford University Press, 1959.

Lee, Eugene C., "The Politics of Non-Partisan Elections in California Cities." Unpublished Ph.D. dissertation, University of California, Berkeley, 1957.

McHenry, Dean E., "The Pattern of California Politics," *Western Political Quarterly*, I (March, 1948), 44-53.

Mowry, George E., *The California Progressives*. Berkeley and Los Angeles: University of California Press, 1951.

Pitchell, Robert J., "The Influence of Professional Campaign Management Firms in Partisan Elections in California," *Western Political Quarterly*, XI (June, 1958), 278-300.

———, "Twentieth Century California Voting Behavior." Unpublished Ph.D. dissertation, University of California, Berkeley, 1955.

Rowe, Leonard C., "Political Campaign Funds in California." Unpublished Ph.D. dissertation, University of California, Berkeley, 1957.

Thompson, Bruce A., "Campaign Contributions and Expenditures in California," *California Law Review*, XLI (Summer, 1953), 300-319.

Five

The Initiative,

Referendum

and Recall

VOTERS AT CALIFORNIA STATE elections decide upon a greater number of propositions than do the voters of any other state. It is not uncommon for twenty-five measures to appear on the ballot at a general state election. This is the result of two practices that have been current in California for more than a generation: the amending of the state constitution by relatively easy procedures, and the involvement of voters in direct legislation. Both are products of the "Progressive Revolt" of 1910 in California politics, a slogan of which, "Let the People Decide," continues to prevail in political operations.

THE PEOPLE DECIDE

Because the state constitution is long and contains many provisions that are detailed and legislative in nature, frequent amendments are proposed. Every constitutional amendment, regardless of the method by which it originates, must be approved by a majority of the voters if it is to be valid. This requirement is one of the principal causes of the long ballot in California. In Chapter 2 it was explained that amendments may be proposed either by (1) the legislature, (2) an initiative petition, or (3) a constitu-

76

tional convention. Most constitutional amendments originate in the legislature. Since 1911, when the initiative method was adopted, the legislature has submitted a total of 337 constitutional amendments to the voters, whereas initiative petitions have introduced 79, and no constitutional convention has been convened during that time.

The initiative and referendum have contributed to the length of the ballot, and, in recent years, have produced some unusual processes in California politics. Adopted as reform measures in the early 1900's to assist in breaking the hold of a state political machine upon the legislature, they have produced at mid-century two unusual phenomena of state politics: paid petition-circulators who will, for a fixed price, obtain the necessary signatures to qualify a petition, and the political public relations firm which will conduct the campaign to adopt or defeat a measure if provided with sufficient campaign funds. Popular legislation has become a process of large scale organized politics, and a small corps of specialized practitioners has sprung up to act as paid champions for clients that have sufficient money to conduct the required procedures. Direct legislation has become a significant part of group political strategy.

LEGISLATION BY PETITION

Direct legislation is based on the theory that the citizens should have the opportunity to participate in the legislative process by voting directly upon specific propositions. The initiative is the device used to bring a proposal to a vote of the people. A petition signed by registered voters equal in number to 8 per cent of the vote for governor at the last state election places a proposed statute or constitutional amendment directly on the ballot at the next state election. This is known as the direct initiative. The measure so proposed is a complete statute or constitutional amendment, and if adopted, becomes law in the form proposed.

Another type, known as the indirect initiative, requires only the equivalent of 5 per cent of the vote cast for governor, and places a proposed statute automatically before the legislature for consideration. No legislature has yet adopted a measure proposed by an indirect initiative petition, hence the initiated proposition must be submitted to the voters at the next state election. This type of initiative is illustrated by an incident in 1951. An initiative petition proposed to abolish cross-filing, but the legislature declined to act upon the proposal, and submitted to the voters a competing proposition which required that the party affiliation of each candidate be printed after his name on the ballot. The voters adopted the legislature's alternative proposal and defeated the initiative proposition.

Billboard advertising and use of catchy slogans in regular use by campaigners on initiative and referendum measures. It is an expensive means of campaigning. Courtesy of Manchester and Crocker, Pacific Outdoors.

Statutes submitted to the voters by initiative petition become law if approved by a majority of the voters participating in the election. A special protection is given statutes proposed and adopted by this method: although the legislature may propose to amend or repeal those statutes, such changes are effective only if approved by the voters.

The *referendum* is a device used to suspend a statute that has passed the legislature and been signed by the governor, and to bring it to a vote of the people at the next state election. If a majority of the voters reject a referred statute, it is void. If the majority vote is favorable, the statute goes into effect immediately thereafter. Most bills do not take effect as laws until ninety days after the governor has attached his signature; during that period of time a referendum petition may be circulated for signatures. The constitution exempts several classes of bills from the referendum. For example, bills calling elections, providing levies of taxes, or appropriating money may not go to a referendum. If bills on such subjects could be held up until the next general election, the normal operation of the state's government might be seriously upset. Also some legislation cannot wait for ninety days or longer; it is needed as soon as the legislature can draft and vote upon it. Therefore, the constitution directs that urgency measures dealing with the public peace and safety shall be exempt from referendum action, and that if two-thirds of the members of both houses of the legislature agree that a certain situation requires emergency action and pass a bill to meet the need, the act shall become law immediately after the governor signs it. Such emergency measures must, however, contain a clause that sets forth the reasons why the legislators believe an emergency exists. Almost every legislative session since 1933 has passed a small number of bills with emergency provisions. Occasionally a taxpayer or other interested party has gone to court and charged that an "emergency" bill was not in fact dealing with an emergency but was pushed through the legislature with an emergency clause to escape being submitted to the voters by a referendum petition. In such cases the California courts have shown a tendency to inquire into the reasons given by the legislature, although none has been invalidated to permit a referendum to qualify.

The Petition

Circulation of a petition is the first formal step in either the initiative or the referendum. Virtually the entire procedure for conducting petitions is set forth in the constitution and remains practically unchanged from the method adopted in 1911. Petition circulators must observe numerous legal details if they wish to produce a valid petition that will get a place on the next election's ballots. The most significant requirement is the quota of valid signatures that must be obtained. Some states set this quota in terms of a flat number or a percentage of the qualified electorate. California uses a formula based upon a percentage of the votes cast at the last election for governor.

Direct initiative petitions, requiring 8 per cent, will need 420,462 signatures to qualify between 1960 and 1962, and an

---

INSTRUCTIONS FOR CIRCULATING INITIATIVE PETITIONS

Caution: Under the law, you cannot circulate this petition unless you are now a registered elector in the county.

1—Do not circulate this petition or obtain signatures outside of the county in which you are now a registered elector.

2—Any voter of the county, male or female, who is now a registered elector in the county and whose registration has not been cancelled, can sign this petition. Others cannot.

3—IT IS A FELONY FOR ANY PERSON TO WRITE ANY NAME IN THIS PETITION EXCEPT HIS OR HER OWN.

4—THE PETITION MUST BE SIGNED JUST AS THE SIGNER HAS REGISTERED AS A VOTER. (The law requires that in registering, a voter shall give his full Christian name. In other words, Mr. Jones should sign—John K. Jones—and not merely J. K. Jones.)

A married woman must sign her own given name—NOT her husband's. For example: May Jones must sign her name—May Jones—and not Mrs. John Jones. THE PETITION MUST BE SIGNED JUST AS THE SIGNER HAS REGISTERED AS A VOTER.

Proponents of an initiative measure try to obtain signatures in excess of the minimum needed to allow for invalidations resulting from violation of these requirements.

indirect initiative will require 262,789. A referendum petition also requires the equivalent of 5 per cent of the vote for governor, and therefore will require 262,789 signatures.

Numerous attempts have been made to control the form of the petition to ensure the honesty of its use. Few people are likely to read the complete text of a proposed statute, therefore it is important to have a concise and accurate summary available.

INITIATIVE MEASURE TO BE SUBMITTED DIRECTLY TO ELECTORS

LEGISLATIVE REAPPORTIONMENT. Initiative Constitutional Amendment. Amends Article IV, section 6, of Constitution. Requires legislative districts be reapportioned every ten years according to population shown by Federal census, commencing 1950. Substitutes State Controller for Surveyor General on Reapportionment Commission. In forming senatorial districts eliminates provisions preventing division of counties or cities and counties or uniting parts thereof with others; permits county or city and county to contain more than one senatorial district; removes limitation on grouping of counties of small population. Until such reapportionment is made designates the senatorial districts and what counties or portions thereof included therein.

NAME	RESIDENCE Street and Number	City or Town	Date of Signing 1942	Precinct
23.				
24.				
25.				
26.				
27.				
28.				

An initiative petition has a brief digest of the contents which must appear at the top of each sheet. Many separate petitions may be circulated.

Certainly some impartial person must be given the assignment of preparing such a summary in order to avoid suspicion or trickery. Fewer ambiguous phrases are likely to be produced by an impartial person to confuse those who will be asked to sign a petition. Therefore, sponsors of a petition are required to apply to the attorney general for a title and summary containing not more than a hundred words to be placed at the head of each sheet on which signatures will be obtained. It is also required that signatures and summary appear on the same sheets of paper, lest unscrupulous petition circulators add signatures fraudulently.

If a single petition were to contain 420,462 signatures it would require a gigantic roll of paper. Therefore, the law permits petitions to be circulated in sections for convenience, yet the sections that have been circulated in any one county must be brought together finally and filed with the county clerk or registrar of voters. This official has the signatures of all registered voters in the county in his files, and can determine from those records if the persons who have signed the petitions are legally registered voters.

Who Signs It

Obviously it is more attractive to petition-circulators to present petitions in the large, populous counties such as Los Angeles, San Francisco, and Alameda, because more signatures can be obtained with less effort than can be done in counties such as Trinity and Alpine. However, most petitions are circulated in at least ten counties in order to make people in various parts of the state familiar with the proposal before it reaches the ballot, and to avoid the charge that the proposal is being made entirely by city people.

What is meant by "valid" signatures to a petition? A citizen must be a registered voter at the time he or she signs the petition. There are also certain other requirements regarding the manner in which the signer indicates his name and address, aimed primarily at assisting the county clerk in identifying a signer. One common situation arises from married women's signatures. A married woman might sign as "Fern Smith" on some occasions, and as "Mrs. John C. Smith" on others. Yet, are they the same for legal identification purposes? Again: are "J. C. Smith" and "J. Calhoun Smith" the same person, even though the address is the same for both? The law requires the county clerk to be certain that the signer is a registered voter.

Time to Circulate

Persons circulating initiative petitions are forced to work within time limits. Probably anyone with a plausible idea and a sum of money could secure enough signatures to a petition over a long period of time. But, would the result guarantee any serious support for the proposition? When an initiative petition is circulated, it must be completed and submitted to the county clerk in the counties where circulated within ninety days after the official summary is received from the attorney general. The clerk must complete his check within twenty days and certify his findings to the secretary of state. Petition sponsors may then have an additional forty days to secure more signatures, and the county clerks have ten more days to check this batch and certify results. If fewer than the specified number of signatures have been secured, the petition fails. If, however, the secretary of state finds that the petition contains the required number of valid signatures, he must assign the measure proposed by it a place on the next state election ballot.

Referendum petitions have but ninety days in which to qualify. The constitution specifies that the bill signed by the governor becomes law within ninety days, and within that period a referendum may qualify. Therefore, even more than in the case of initiatives, a referendum petition requires organized effort to obtain the signatures within the time limit.

Petition Pushers and Drum Beaters

In California—with its big population that continues to grow with the arrival of thousands from other states, with its many cities, and with its diverse sectional and group interests—petitions to propose legislation can scarcely materialize spontaneously. Considering the time limits set by law, a group that wishes to circulate a petition successfully must either have an organization of its own prepared and ready to function on signal, or hire an organization that is prepared to do the necessary work. Even such groups as labor unions, fraternal organizations, churches, and pension organizations are not geared for quick activity in a political campaign. Therefore, professional petition circulators have found a rich field in which to work. One man, Joseph Robinson of San Francisco, has made a business for many years of obtaining signatures for direct legislation petitions. It is reported that he guarantees clients that he will qualify a petition or accept no compensation. Fees for petition circulating are in the neighborhood of fifty cents per name—approximately $200,000 for an initiative petition. Robinson and other circulators employ a corps of part-time workers who go door-to-door or work in crowded downtown areas collecting signatures to petitions. These workers are paid so much per name for valid signatures.

Each of the three initiatives on the state ballot in 1958 were placed there by petition circulating firms working for the sponsoring groups. Robinson qualified two: the sales and income tax measure, and the private school tax proposal. Los Angeles firms —Benton, Keaton, and others—promoted the "right to work" initiative.

Once a petition has qualified and a place on the ballot is assured, proponents of an initiative or referendum are faced with the same political difficulties as before in reaching the millions of California voters with persuasive arguments. Here again the professional is available for hire. Several public relations firms are equally experienced in handling direct legislation campaigns as they are in publicizing candidates for public office. The San Francisco firm of Whitaker and Baxter began in 1933 with the Central Valley Project bond referendum and has managed numerous campaigns since, including the 1956 oil control proposal and the 1948 freight train crew measure. Harry Lerner, also of San Francisco, managed the campaign to defeat the 1956 oil control proposal and the 1958 private school tax proposal. In the 1958 fight over "right to work," two professional publicity firms staged the battle: Steve Wells of Los Angeles for the proponents, and Gross and Roberts of San Francisco for the winning opponents.

Under the direction of skilled technicians in crowd appeal, billboards, car stickers, posters, full-page newspaper ads, mailed pamphlets and letters flow out to catch the eye with slogans, arguments, and catchy phrases. Spot announcements on radio and frequent TV appearances hammer away at the listener about oil conservation, the "oil hog," "labor bosses," "preserve the American Way," etc. The final three weeks before a November general election becomes a confusing time with all known media of advertising being brought to bear to condition the voter to react in the desired manner when he goes into the election booth with his ballot.

All this skill in campaigning costs big money. Just how expensive it is is never fully known, although for many years state law has required groups campaigning on ballot propositions to file a statement of expenses with the secretary of state. Final statements are filed considerably later than the election and detail the "official" expenses of the sponsoring groups. They do not contain listing of the various supporting expenditures made by groups or individuals who were not a part of the sponsoring group. Proponents of the right-to-work measure in 1958 reported over $900,000 spent, and the opponents reported $2,491,597. Proponents of the private school tax at the same election reported $470,000 and the opponents admitted spending approximately $1,340,000. Big expenditures in direct legislation campaigns are not entirely recent developments, however. The sum of $661,595 was spent in 1922 on the State Water Power Act, and in 1936 the proponents and opponents of the chain store tax spent a total of $1,207,764. The record indicates that, almost without exception, the group that spends the most money wins!

PRODUCTS OF THE INITIATIVE

The Constitutional Initiative

Of the twenty-two constitutional amendments proposed by initiative petition and adopted since 1911, several are of prime importance in state government. The state-budget amendment adopted in 1922 is a leading example. This amendment centered the responsibility and authority for preparing a comprehensive state budget upon the governor. A comprehensive state civil service system was established by initiative amendment in 1934, replacing a weak legislative-established system that had been patched and amended many times. Another amendment extended the powers of the attorney general to make that officer the head of state law enforcement and prosecution. Two others sought to speed up trial of criminal cases in state courts and yet protect the rights of defendants. One amendment permitted persons accused of a felony to plead guilty before a magistrate at a preliminary hearing, and the other permitted trial court judges to comment to the jury upon the failure of a defendant to testify.

State financial support of the public school system is largely based upon constitutional sections proposed by initiative petitions which were sponsored by school organizations. Amendments proposed in 1920, 1944, 1946, and 1952 determine the amount of state aid that will be provided the public schools and the basic conditions under which it will be administered.

Apportionment of seats in the two houses of the legislature is determined by constitutional provisions proposed by the California Farm Bureau Federation by initiative petition in 1926. This is the so called "federal plan" of apportionment. Another significant amendment is the one giving the state power to regulate distribution and sale of intoxicating liquor. This was adopted in 1932 after the voters approved repeal of the state prohibition act, a law which also had originated in the initiative process. In an earlier era, California abolished its poll tax, using an initiative constitutional amendment proposed by the State Federation of Labor to do so.

Initiative constitutional amendments adopted during the first twenty years after the adoption of the procedure were mostly concerned with improving the structure and operation of the state government. The depression years of the 1930's brought into California politics many new issues and personalities. Several groups were preoccupied with old-age pensions and with various economic panaceas. Although the legislature and some governors were inclined to revise and liberalize the welfare laws and to adopt measures to deal with the state's economic problems, groups that wanted more drastic action were apt to turn to such procedures as the initiative. The "Ham and Eggs" pension plans of 1938 and 1939, both defeated by the voters after noisy campaigns, are among the more famous examples of this new element. Various versions of this plan continued to circulate every election year. Perhaps the most outrageous scheme proposed by the "Ham and Eggs" promoters was the one put forth in 1948 under the title "California Bill of Rights"—a plan pertaining to pensions, taxes, Indians, ministers, gambling, state senate reapportionment, and a large number of other subjects. The proposed amendment contained twelve sections and more than 21,000 words. The state supreme court sustained an action to prevent the secretary of state from putting the proposition on the ballot because it amounted substantially to a revision of the constitution in the guise of a single amendment.[1]

Two other major pension groups succeeded in getting one or more initiative amendments on the ballot. In 1944, a modified version of the plan proposed by Dr. Townsend of Long Beach, called "$60 at 60," was defeated by the voters by a decisive majority. The group headed by George McLain of Los Angeles had greater success than any other, although its success proved short-lived. The famous Proposition Four of the 1948 election was the product of the McLain group. Groups that normally oppose such schemes as this appear to have concentrated their fire on other measures in this election, with the result that Number Four won by a small majority. This amendment ousted the director of social welfare who had been appointed by the governor, made the position elective, and named the secretary of the group that promoted the measure as director until the next election. It increased old-age pensions and aid to the blind, and made all such charges a prior lien on state income. It called for the transfer of administration of old-age aid and blind aid from the counties to the state. Reaction to this scheme was vigorous, with the result that in 1950 the voters approved the repeal by a large majority.

Another panacea proposal that has appeared on the state ballot several times is the single-tax plan to finance government by a tax upon the increase in land values. The single tax was defeated in 1916, 1918, 1920, and again in 1938. Because some

---

[1] *McFadden v. Jordan*, 32 Cal. (2d) 330, 196 Pac. (2d) 787 (1948).

schemes like the single tax and certain pension proposals have reappeared a number of times in more or less the same basic outline, some political leaders have proposed from time to time that once an initiative proposition has been defeated it should be prohibited from appearing on the ballot again for a specified time, such as five years. A limitation of this type has not gained support, however. It would be exceedingly difficult to determine what constitutes the "same" or "substantially the same" measure. Furthermore, such a plan might well invite "hijacking," whereby a group deliberately proposes a crudely drawn plan in the expectation that the voters will reject it and thereby block out a more responsible group from proposing anything on the subject for several years.

Conservatism has characterized the voters' attitude towards most initiative constitutional amendments. Of seventy-nine proposed since the inauguration of the initiative method in 1911, only twenty-two have been adopted. Most of those adopted have remained in effect for long periods, the 1948 pension measure having the shortest life of any. Although numerous efforts have been made to alter the legislative apportionment plan, it continues in effect.

Initiated Statutes

Of the fifty-six statutes that have been proposed by petition, only fifteen have been adopted, and several of those have since been partially amended or wholly repealed. For a short time after the adoption of the initiative there was a tendency to make considerable use of the device. For example, the largest number of initiatives proposed at any one election, nine, was presented in 1914. Of these nine, only three were adopted. Seldom in recent years have more than three initiatives appeared on the ballot; frequently there has been none.

What has the initiative contributed to California government? One contribution that can scarcely be called the product of special interest group politics is the permanent registration law. Details of this law were drafted by experienced election officials with the objective of improving the law regarding registration of voters. Opposition to various proposals made on the subject in the legislature had prevented adoption by customary procedures, but no organized opposition was made against the initiated proposal. The law has been praised as being sound in scope.

Regulation and licensing of osteopaths separate from that of the medical practitioners was established by initiative statute. In similar fashion the law governing regulation of chiropractors has been passed and added to from time to time. Separate licensing boards have been created for each group.

California adopted daylight saving time by the initiative process after rural groups had successfully blocked similar proposals in the legislature on several occasions. The basic legislation defining usury (charging exorbitant rates of interest for loans) was adopted by initiative in 1918. Legalization of professional boxing and wrestling was similarly approved in 1924 but later repealed and replaced by legislature-written regulations. The initiative has also been used to repeal the state prohibition law and the "full train crew law" which regulated the number of crew members required to operate freight trains. The latter law had long been dear to the Railway Brotherhoods, but anti-labor forces' efforts prevailed in the 1948 election.

Measures proposed by the initiative represent a wide variety of interests. Many of the earlier ones sought to regulate morals. A 1914 initiative prohibited prize fights. Prohibition of production and sale of liquor was the subject of several early initiative proposals. In 1930 a proposition sought unsuccessfully to close barber shops on Sundays. Proposals to permit various forms of gambling and to prohibit them have come to a vote from time to time.

Since 1935 proposed initiative statutes have dealt almost entirely with economic matters, with labor-management struggles, or with interests of a particular business or profession. Naturally enough, perhaps, large campaign funds and organized campaign efforts have resulted from this shift in the focus of the initiative process. Measures are the product of group politics and are usually related to skirmishes that have been fought or are about to be fought within the legislature between strongly organized groups. In the 1958 gubernatorial election two initiatives were deeply involved in the strategy of competing election groups. Republican candidate William Knowland strongly supported a "right to work" initiative which was fought successfully by organized labor. Earlier in the campaign, labor leaders had fostered an initiative to repeal the state sales tax, an object long advocated by organized labor. Strategy changed during the course of the campaign, however, and the tax repeal law was given reduced support, with the result that it lost also.

The Indirect Initiative

The indirect initiative has received relatively little use. The first was in 1937 when a quarrel developed between the fish canners and those fishing interests that served fertilizer reduction plants. The canners sought to oust the fertilizer plants and, being unsuccessful in the legislature, they turned to circulating initiative petitions. They sought and obtained the necessary 5 per cent of signatures to submit to the legislature. The senate considered the matter and rejected it; the assembly declined to act at all. The secretary of state thereupon placed the matter on the November 1938 ballot, and it passed. In 1940, a group that had sought unsuccessfully to have the law regarding building and loan associations rewritten made use of this method. In this instance, both houses of the legislature declined to act and the matter went to the ballot in 1942 and was defeated. The 1951 session of the legislature received two 5 per cent initiative petitions. One, sponsored by the League of Women Voters and others, proposed to repeal the cross-filing system of nominating state officers. The other was an old age pension plan proposed by the McLain group. The legislature declined to act on either measure; however, it submitted a proposal to require candidates to disclose their party affiliations on the state ballots and submitted it to the voters in the 1952 election in competition with the initiative anti-cross-filing measure. The voters accepted the legislature's proposal and rejected the initiative. The McLain pension initiative was defeated also.

Two features of the 5 per cent initiative tend to discourage its use. The length of time that must elapse between circulation of a petition and final presentation to the electorate destroys the momentum of public interest. Publicity built up during the circulation of the petition is lost, inasmuch as the proposal cannot go on the ballot until almost a year later. Also, if the legislature is inclined to submit a competing measure, the latter can be drawn in a manner to take advantage of the strong features of the initiative proposal and it can enjoy the prestige derived from adoption by both houses of the legislature and approval by the governor.

Petition Referendum Results

Thirty-five statutes have been referred to the voters of California since 1912, and in only thirteen instances has the legislature been upheld. The comparatively small number of acts referred, of the total emanating from the legislature, would seem to indicate that the voters are reasonably satisfied with the normal legislative process. There was a tendency to make more use of the referendum shortly after its adoption in 1911 than there has been in recent years. Every election between 1912 and 1922 saw from one to five referendum measures on the ballot. From 1942 to 1952 the procedure was not used at all. In 1951 a bill to exempt schools maintained by religious and charitable organizations from property taxes met much opposition. After the governor signed it a referendum petition qualified, and the campaign that followed was vigorously conducted by both sides. The bill was upheld by the voters in 1952, but its opponents later carried the matter to the courts on constitutional issues. In 1958, an attempt was made to repeal this measure, in effect, by an initiative constitutional amendment. This move was likewise unsuccessful.

Evaluation of the Referendum

In California, referendum measures have excited great interest in the voters; usually more voters express themselves on a petition referendum than on the constitutional amendments that appear on the same ballot. Among the measures that have been attacked by referendum petitions but have been approved by the voters include the "red light abatement act," the "blue-sky law," and the public water control act, all of 1914. Others included a liquor enforcement act, the "federal plan" of legislative reapportionment, an act to prevent leasing of beaches for oil drilling, and the Central Valley Project Act of 1933. Measures defeated in referendum votes include one in 1915 that would have made nomination of state officers nonpartisan, a tideland oil drilling bill, two bills to tax oleomargarine, and the chain store license tax act.

One may well ask: Why don't those who are opposed to a bill spend their energies opposing it while it is going through the legislature rather than springing to action after the bill has passed? Often when the full story of a referendum campaign is made clear it becomes evident that the group which circulated the referendum petition and directed the publicity campaign for the ensuing election had lobbied, albeit unsuccessfully, at every stage of the legislative process and also had sought to persuade the governor to veto the bill. The usual processes of legislative pressure having failed to produce the desired results, the group had then sought to persuade the voters that their group interests were identical with the "public interest." Referendum campaigns are apt to be expensive; therefore groups interested in defeating legislation usually regard them as a last resort. One of the more expensive campaigns took place in 1936, when the chain store license tax act was defeated. The California Retail Stores Association filed affadavits that it had spent $1,142,033.29 to defeat the bill, whereas the Anti-Monopoly League acknowledged that it had spent $65,731.56 in the unsuccessful effort to persuade the voters to support it.

LOCAL DIRECT LEGISLATION

The Initiative and Referendum in Cities

Voters of every city and county in California are guaranteed the initiative and referendum for local affairs by the state constitution. Those cities or counties that have a municipal or county charter may set any special provision regarding number of signatures required or other features. Other cities and counties are governed in these matters by the general state laws. In general, local direct-legislation petitions require signatures equal to 10 per cent of the vote at the last local general election for initiative petitions and 5 per cent for referendums. In other respects the rules for local direct legislation are similar to those for the state at large.

Several subjects that are important in local government are exempt from the initiative and referendum because they are administrative in nature. These include street improvements, purchase of supplies, location of public buildings such as city halls and police stations. Tax rates and appropriations are also exempt by law and left exclusively to the elected officials and the administrators working under their direction.

The first exercise of the local initiative in California was made in Los Angeles in 1906 when the voters of that city adopted an ordinance prohibiting slaughterhouses within the municipal limits. Several cites have adopted civil service for their employees by approving an initiative proposed by the employees and their friends. A number of cities have also established pension systems for police and fire employees in the same manner.

Somewhat more frequent use has been made of the referendum by cities. Both Los Angeles and San Francisco have had referendums against public utility franchises granted by the city councils. Several smaller cities have had referendum fights over ordinances licensing games and pleasure establishments. One of the most publicized municipal referendums in recent years was the Los Angeles vote in 1958 concerning an agreement between the city and the Dodgers' baseball club for the establishment of a stadium in Chavez Ravine. The campaign waged in this city controversy followed most of the methods employed in state elections. Both sides spent considerable money in billboard advertising, radio time, and publicity blurbs. Professional campaign managers were employed. The council was upheld.

Local governments have made less use of direct legislation than the state. One explanation for this is that city councils meet frequently, usually weekly or twice per month, and hold their sessions at the city hall—in the midst of the electorate. Although attendance by the public at council sessions may not be large, the council seldom takes action without previous discussion and contact with political elements in the community. Popular reaction to a council action sometimes leads to reversal of the decision. In a few instances, when a group has circulated an initiative petition, the council has taken part of the proposal and adopted it as an ordinance, thus putting an end to the petition. Although many disputes are to be found in local affairs, seldom is there sufficient provocation to spend the money needed to promote a referendum or initiative petition.

Direct Legislation: Evaluation

Originally adopted as a reform tool, direct legislation now appears to be firmly rooted in California politics. It has been modified, both by legislation and practice, but it has found a place in the strategy of politics. It is no longer a safety valve for spontaneous popular movements; it requires large resources and astute management. It is clearly expensive. Other objections that have been made to direct legislation are: initiative measures are often poorly drawn, initiative measures that have been defeated often reappear in slightly different form, groups interested in stable government through representative institutions must be on the alert and prepared to finance a campaign to defeat a measure, the referendum invites group political warfare. In spite of vigorous criticisms of the initiative and referendum, most groups that are active in state-wide affairs have either used the initiative and referendum at some time or have seriously considered doing so. Criticism of abusive use of direct legislation has led to modifications in the laws governing the procedures.

RECALL OF PUBLIC OFFICERS

A Theory of Responsibility

The recall is based upon the theory that an elected official should be held accountable to the electorate even before expiration of his normal term of office if a demand is made by means of a petition. Filing of a valid petition demanding recall of a public officer forces the calling of a special election to determine if that officer shall be removed or shall be permitted to complete his term.

Petitions for the recall of an officer are similar in most respects to those for the initiative and the referendum. Those proposing to recall a state officer must be signed by registered voters equal to 12 per cent of the vote cast for all candidates for the office at the last election. In the case of members of the legislature, 20 per cent is required. Petitions to recall a governor or other state-wide officer must be circulated in at least 5 counties and be signed by at least 1 per cent of the voters in the county. Although the recall is a political device, rather than a judicial one, a brief statement of the grounds upon which the recall demand is made must be placed at the top of the petition. In practice these statements are worded very broadly and leave the issues obscure.

An election to recall a state officer calls for a double action by the voter. First he is requested to vote "yes" or "no" on whether Mr. So-and-so (the officeholder) should be recalled. Second, he is asked to vote for a candidate to fill out the unexpired term, should the incumbent be recalled. Candidates to replace the officer have their names placed on the ballot by presenting a nominating petition signed by qualified voters equal to 1 per cent of the vote cast at the last election for the office. This petition must be presented twenty-five days before the recall election. The incumbent whose recall is being voted upon cannot be a candidate to succeed himself. Likewise a voter must express a choice on both parts of the ballot; he must both vote for a candidate and on the question of the recall.

The constitution does not permit the recall of a state officer during the first six months of office, the theory being that a recall should permit the removal of an officer whose performance has been unsatisfactory and should not be merely the extension of a closely fought election campaign. If a recall effort fails, the officer may not be subject to a similar effort for another six months, and the state will reimburse him for his recall-election expenses.

Development in California

The recall is a procedure that originated in California and was first adopted for the city government of Los Angeles in 1903. It was later adopted widely throughout the United States by those cities that utilized the commission plan of municipal government. It was advocated as an instrument to defeat political

SPECIAL RECALL ELECTIONS

NO VOTE SHALL BE COUNTED FOR ANY CANDIDATE TO SUCCEED AN OFFICER SOUGHT TO BE RECALLED FROM OFFICE UNLESS THE VOTER ALSO VOTES ON THE QUESTION OF THE RECALL OF THE PERSON SOUGHT TO BE RECALLED FROM OFFICE.

| Shall JOHN L. FLEMING be recalled from the office of Judge of the Superior Court of Los Angeles County? | YES |
| | NO |

| Shall DAILEY S. STAFFORD be recalled from the office of Judge of the Superior Court of Los Angeles County? | YES |
| | NO |

Candidates to succeed JOHN L. FLEMING in case he be removed from the office of Judge of the Superior Court of Los Angeles County:

Candidates to succeed DAILEY S. STAFFORD in case he be removed from the office of Judge of the Superior Court of Los Angeles County:

Judge of the Superior Court　　Vote for One

Judge of the Superior Court　　Vote for One

IDA MAY ADAMS Judge Municipal Court Los Angeles	
WILLIAM J. PALMER Judge of the Municipal Court	

ARTHUR E. BRIGGS Lawyer and Dean of Law School	
MAY D. LAHEY Judge of the Municipal Court	
WILLIAM S. BAIRD Judge of the Municipal Court	

THE GROUNDS ON WHICH SUCH REMOVAL IS SOUGHT ARE:

(1) That the actions of said JOHN L. FLEMING as Judge of said Superior Court, in connection with receivership matters pending in said Court, constitute a violation of long and well-established principles governing judicial conduct, and directly involve the interests of the public which looks to the Court for the unprejudiced determination of the rights of litigants.

(2) That said JOHN L. FLEMING has conducted himself in his judicial office in a manner prejudicial to the proper administration of justice, and that his practices have, of necessity, interfered with the proper performance of his duties as Judge, and that his conduct has cast reflection upon the integrity of the judiciary at large and engendered the belief that the rights of the people do not receive fearless and impartial consideration in the courts of justice.

(3) That by his conduct said JOHN L. FLEMING has so impaired the confidence of the public in his fitness for the high office of Judge of the Superior Court, and has so seriously affected the good repute of the entire Court that, in the interest of fair, impartial and disinterested administration of justice, he should be removed and his successor elected.

REASONS GIVEN BY JUDGE JOHN L. FLEMING OF THE LOS ANGELES COUNTY SUPERIOR COURT WHY HE SHOULD NOT BE RECALLED.

Voters of Los Angeles County:

You elected me as your Judge eight years ago by 235,000 votes. You re-elected me two years ago in the primary by a vote of over 100,000 more than my opponent.

I have served you faithfully for nine years. My decisions have been almost universally upheld by the Supreme and Appellate Courts.

In the course of my duties I have incurred the ill-will of some lawyers because I have administered justice according to the dictates of my own conscience uninfluenced by whether the attorneys who appeared before me were "big" or "little".

MY OFFICIAL CONDUCT HAS BEEN FULLY INVESTIGATED BY THE LOS ANGELES COUNTY GRAND JURY, THE UNITED STATES GRAND JURY AND BY SUPERIOR JUDGE WARNE, ASSIGNED HERE BY THE JUDICIAL COUNCIL OF THE STATE, AND NONE OF THEM FOUND CAUSE OF COMPLAINT AGAINST ME; I HAVE NEVER BEEN CHARGED WITH ANY WILFUL MISCONDUCT. IF YOU RECALL ME, YOU CONDEMN ME WITHOUT A HEARING!

Please bear in mind that this recall was started by ten attorneys, through the Judiciary Committee of the Bar Association—whereas more than 500 lawyers have written me that they are opposed to my recall.

A Judge charged with misconduct can be removed by impeachment without cost to the public, whereas THIS RECALL ELECTION WILL COST YOU NOT LESS THAN $50,000!

If you encourage this recall, you will destroy the independence of your Judiciary, because every Judge will be continually confronted with the threat of recall every time he decides a case against any powerful political group or special interest.

IF YOU BELIEVE IN JUSTICE AND FAIR DEALING—

IF YOU BELIEVE IN AN INDEPENDENT JUDICIARY—

IF YOU BELIEVE IN SAVING THE TAXPAYERS' MONEY—

IF YOU BELIEVE IN YOUR RIGHT TO ELECT YOUR OWN JUDGE—

VOTE NO ON THE RECALL!

Faithfully yours,

JOHN L. FLEMING.

THE GROUNDS ON WHICH SAID REMOVAL IS SOUGHT ARE:

(1) That the actions of said DAILEY S. STAFFORD as Judge of said Superior Court, in connection with receivership matters pending in said Court, constitute a violation of long and well-established principles governing judicial conduct, and directly involve the interests of the public which looks to the Court for the unprejudiced determination of the rights of litigants.

(2) That said DAILEY S. STAFFORD has conducted himself in his judicial office in a manner prejudicial to the proper administration of justice, and that his practices have, of necessity, interfered with the proper performance of his duties as Judge, and that his conduct has cast reflection upon the integrity of the judiciary at large and engendered the belief that the rights of the people do not receive fearless and impartial consideration in the courts of justice.

(3) That by his conduct said DAILEY S. STAFFORD has so impaired the confidence of the public in his fitness for the high office of Judge of the Superior Court, and has so seriously affected the good repute of the entire Court that, in the interest of fair, impartial and disinterested administration of justice, he should be removed and his successor elected.

REASONS GIVEN BY JUDGE DAILEY S. STAFFORD TO JUSTIFY HIS COURSE IN OFFICE

I DENY ALL OF THE ABOVE CHARGES.

A group, of long-standing political enemies, is responsible for the recall proceedings against me. This same small group, of lawyer-politicians, was against me when I was overwhelmingly elected by the people two years ago, and they are against me now.

These politicians, acting willfully, selfishly, and UNABLE TO INFLUENCE ME AT ANY TIME in my judicial actions, are making this attempt to recall me BECAUSE THE PEOPLE REPUDIATED THEM. The petty, vague and technical accusation of an alleged violation of judicial ethics, set forth as their reason for my recall, is NOT the real reason.

I AM NOT ACCUSED OF ANY WRONG-DOING. THERE IS NO CHARGE AGAINST ME THAT WOULD HAVE ANY STANDING IN ANY COURT. I NEVER HAVE VIOLATED MY OATH OF OFFICE. NO ACTION OF MINE EVER HAS REFLECTED ADVERSELY UPON ANY MEMBER OF THE BENCH. NO CITIZEN EVER HAS SUFFERED AN INJURY AT MY HANDS.

Investigation of my conduct was made by the Grand Jury; by an impartial outside Judge and, at my suggestion, by the District Attorney of Los Angeles County. ALL THREE FOUND THAT NO WRONG HAD BEEN COMMITTED BY ME. During twenty years as a public officer, interrupted only by my war service, MY PERSONAL AND JUDICIAL INTEGRITY NEVER HAS BEEN QUESTIONED. The common man and woman, without regard to race, creed or color, has ever received a fair deal in my court. Powerful, privileged groups HAVE NOT BEEN ABLE TO CONTROL ME. THE PEOPLE HAVE STAMPED THEIR APPROVAL OF ME AS A JUDGE IN THREE ELECTIONS.

To keep me on the bench Vote "NO" on this recall.

DAILEY S. STAFFORD,
Judge of the Superior Court.

Recall election ballot. State recall elections combine a vote on recall of the incumbent with the election of a successor.

96

bossism; it was based upon the thought that an elected official owes an accounting to his constituents at all times, not merely at fixed intervals. Twelve states have adopted it, but Oregon was the first to put it to state-wide use. North Dakota, in recalling a governor, has perhaps made the most spectacular use of it.

Several types of recall were advocated in the early 1900's, but the recall of elected officials has become the one generally identified with the term. Another type, the recall of appointed officials, has very nearly disappeared from modern practice. San Jose places the name of the manager on the municipal ballot every two years for decision by the voters as to whether the manager shall be retained. The preponderance of present-day thinking insists that administrative officers should be responsible either to the legislative body or to an elected chief executive and should be spared from election politics. When Arizona applied for admission to the Union in 1911, its state constitution provided for recall of judges. President Taft, himself a former federal judge, opposed this feature and declined to endorse the Arizona constitution until that provision was removed. California includes the recall of judges along with the general provisions for the recall of any elected officer.

State Use of the Recall

The recall has been used very sparingly against state officers. Soon after the 1911 constitutional amendment was adopted, three state senators were brought to recall elections and two lost their seats. Petitions requesting the recall of Governor Olson were circulated for a considerable time in 1940, but the movement collapsed.

Recall attempts against officials of counties and units other than cities have not been numerous. Kern and Fresno counties have had some experiences. Several bitter election quarrels took place in irrigation-district affairs in Imperial Valley. Los Angeles County voters recalled three superior court judges in 1932.

Municipal Recall

Recall elections have occurred somewhat frequently in California cities, especially in the smaller ones. The "Big stick behind" the door," as Theodore Roosevelt described the recall, remains well dusted. In a few communities the recall has been overused, and as a result feuding factions have kept the voters in a constant turmoil of elections. In numerous instances, however, the recall has been the result of a long-developing political explosion; the period following it has often been one of municipal peace and quiet.

Procedure for the recall of local officers has been outlined in general state legislation and in local charters. A local petition must be signed by the equivalent of 25 per cent of the vote cast for the office at the last general election. Some of the procedure is more elaborate than that required for state recalls. A statement of reasons for the recall, together with a notice of intention to circulate, must be served upon the officer concerned and must also be published in a newspaper of general circulation. Petitions may not be circulated until twenty-one days later, and the petitions must contain both the statement of reasons for the recall and the officeholder's reply. Signatures must be obtained within sixty days.

In municipal recall elections, except in the few cities whose charters require a different procedure, the voter is requested to answer two questions: (1) Shall the incumbent be recalled? and (2) In the event a majority of votes favor the recall, shall the city council fill the vacancy by appointment or shall it call a second special election for the purpose? If the council is directed to fill the vacancy, it must do so within a specified time (between thirty-five and forty days after the recall). More than one member of a city council may be forced to face a recall election at the same time. Although such plural recalls are few in practice, they are not entirely unknown. In 1932 Pasadena recalled its entire city council; Long Beach did the same in 1934. In 1951 San Fernando recalled three of its five-member council. In instances where a majority of the council are recalled at the same time, the city clerk must call a special election to fill the positions and the recalled members must remain in office until their successors take the oath of office. The city's government must go on!

Recall of municipal officers is often attempted because of alleged corruption or because some city council members have voted for an unpopular project. Most often such movements are the direct outgrowth of factional politics. In a number of instances they have arisen out of long-standing struggles that directly involve the police department and its methods of keeping the peace within the municipality.

Recall in Large Cities

Recalls in Los Angeles and San Francisco have followed a somewhat different pattern from those in the smaller cities. This is partly because of the difference in size of the cities, and also because of differences in governmental structure. A mayor elected on a city-wide vote, as in the two major cities, is as likely to be the target of a recall petition as is a city council member elected from a district.

San Francisco has had relatively few recalls; most of them occurred in the early years. It was the first city in this state to recall a member of the judiciary; in 1913 a police judge who had used his power to reduce bail in an arbitrary and suspicious manner was removed from office. In 1921 two police judges involved in corrupt connections with bail-bond brokers and vice interests were driven out. Unsuccessful attempts to recall the city attorney and the district attorney were made in 1915 and 1917 respectively. In 1946 Mayor Roger Lapham defeated a recall attempt that grew out of a dispute over municipal advertising. The election attracted nationwide attention, and Mayor Lapham signed the recall petition himself in a challenge to his opponents to fight the issue openly.

Los Angeles has made vigorous use of the recall. Mayors Harper and Shaw were removed from office; Mayors Porter and Bowron were forced into recall elections but defeated their opposition. Five councilmen have stood recall elections, and three of them were removed. One of the most dramatic recall elections took place on September 16, 1938, when the Los Angeles voters removed Mayor Frank Shaw from office. He had served one full term and had been re-elected. Rumors of corruption and machine control were often heard; many persons alleged that the city was "wide open." A private investigator gathering evidence in a suit against a political leader was bombed, and the head of the police "intelligence" squad, which worked as a political espionage group for the ruling clique, was convicted of directing the bombing. Recall petitions against the mayor quickly qualified, in spite of numerous obstructive tactics employed by his supporters. Superior Court Judge Fletcher Bowron, who had been in charge of the "crusading" 1934 county grand jury, was prevailed upon to submit his name as a candidate for mayor if the incumbent were recalled. Three other candidates filed, but popular attention centered on the contest between Shaw and Bowron. Shaw was recalled by a vote of 236,526 to 129,245, and Bowron was elected to succeed him. Upon taking office Mayor Bowron reorganized the police, fire, civil service, and public works boards of commissioners, and for some time thereafter was given full support in the council for his reorganization of the city's government.

Evaluation

The recall more nearly serves its originally-intended purpose in the cities. In a limited number of instances, long mounting political pressures for reform in a city have come to an explosion at a recall election. More often, unfortunately, recall campaigns have been merely the continuation of factional feuds or have been stratagems of harassment conducted by the "outs" against the "ins." Most frequent use of the municipal recall has been in small, newly organized cities. By and large the older, more mature communities have been satisfied to determine control at the regular elections.

Other means for removing elected officials who have violated their legal responsibilities are found in impeachment of state officers and in removal of local officers by court decision following an accusation by the county grand jury. Both these methods involve judicial procedures in which specific charges must be filed and determined by formal means, instead of by political elective methods.

One of the most serious problems in recall elections is the provision of adequate information for the voters concerning the issues of the campaign. Finally, a recall is disruptive and often leaves considerable factionalism in its wake.

Further Reading

Best, Wallace H., "Initiative and Referendum Politics in California, 1912-1952." Unpublished Ph.D. dissertation, University of Southern California, 1955.

Bird, Frederick L., and Frances M. Ryan, *The Recall of Public Officers*. New York: The Macmillan Company, 1930.

Bond, Floyd A., and others, *Our Needy Aged—A California Study of a National Problem*. New York: Henry Holt and Co., 1954.

California State Chamber of Commerce, Research Department, *Initiative Legislation in California*. San Francisco, 1939.

Commonwealth Club of California, "Direct Legislation," *Transactions*. . . . XXV (March, 1931), 409-590.

Crouch, Winston W., *The Initiative and Referendum in California*. Los Angeles: Haynes Foundation, 1950.

Jonas, Frank A., Ed., *Bibliography on Western Politics*, XI *The Western Political Quarterly* (Supplement), Dec. 1958, 23-51.

Ketcham, Ronald, *Voting on Charter Amendments in Los Angeles*, Bureau of Governmental Research, Studies in Local Government No. 3, Los Angeles: University of California at Los Angeles, 1940.

Key, V. O., and Winston W. Crouch, *The Initiative and Referendum in California*, Berkeley: University of California Press, 1939.

Worden, William L., "Tales of the Kingmakers," *Saturday Evening Post*, May 23, 1959, pp. 28ff.

Zeitlin, Josephine Ver Brugge, *Initiative and Referendum: A Bibliography*. Los Angeles: Haynes Foundation, 1939.

———, *Recall, A Bibliography*. Los Angeles: Haynes Foundation, 1941.

Six

The Legislature

"THE REAL BLEMISHES in the system of state government," wrote James Bryce nearly seventy-five years ago, "are all found in the composition and conduct of the legislatures." California was twice visited by the eminent Englishman in the 1880's, and some of the criticisms he directed against legislative bodies unquestionably applied to that of the Golden State. When the citizen of today compares the legislatures described in *The American Commonwealth* with the present California legislature, he may justifiably glow with pride over the achievements of less than eight decades.

THE LEGISLATIVE STRUCTURE

One House or Two?

When California was framing its first constitution, there was little time for experiment. The bicameral structure employed by all existing states and by the federal government was accepted without serious question. Indeed, the legislative forms used in other states, especially by New York and Iowa, were adopted rather uncritically. The whole legislative body was designated "legislature"; the upper house was called by the usual name of "senate"; the lower house was given the more usual title of "assembly," now used only in New York, Wisconsin, and Nevada. A

102

proposal to change the name of the lower house from "assembly" to "house of representatives" was defeated by the voters in November 1956.

The number of assemblymen and senators was left flexible in the first Constitution. Both houses were apportioned according to population. The 1850 Legislature finally seated sixteen senators and thirty-six assemblymen.

Plans for a one-house legislature have been discussed frequently in California and other states during the last thirty years. A wave of agitation for unicameralism in the 1910's and 1920's led to no adoptions in any state. A second campaign in the thirties culminated in success in Nebraska, which adopted the reform in 1934. Since that year, from time to time, there has been some interest in, and support for the unicameral principle in California. Initiative petitions were circulated during 1940 for a constitutional amendment which would establish a single-house legislature of eighty members elected mainly on the basis of population, and meeting for annual sessions. Insufficient signatures were obtained to place the proposition on the ballot, and there has been no subsequent initiative attempt.

The double-chambered legislature is well established. It is often argued that the second house constitutes a check on ill-considered legislation. But this is only one of several checks, which include committee action, gubernatorial veto, popular referendum, and judicial review; its presence does not guarantee proper deliberation. The committee of the first house does the greatest quantitative culling of bills.

There is a case, however, for employing more than one basis of representation in a legislature. California is a diverse state, and the use of a single basis might make important elements feel unrepresented. If the state should again consider unicameralism, a valid argument could be made for the utilization of two bases of representation, one of population and the other of area, meeting together in a single house.

Sentiment for a single house legislature has diminished in recent years. Senators, although elected mainly from rural counties, increasingly are concerned with state-wide problems and tend to resemble assemblymen in outlook and background.

REPRESENTATION

People or Places?

Legislative bodies in various parts of the world use various bases of representation: population, units of government, vocations, economic groups, hereditary elements, and others. California utilizes two—population and units of government. Originally only population was considered in apportioning the senate and assembly, but in 1926 the electorate adopted an initiative constitutional amendment embodying the so-called *federal plan.* This scheme, still in force, leaves the assembly apportioned according to population, and bases the senate apportionment primarily upon counties. It provides that no county may have more than one senator, and that no more than three counties may be grouped to form a senatorial district. As a result, Los Angeles, San Diego, and Alameda, with more than one-half of the state's population, have only three senators out of forty.

During the 1950's, twenty-one senators, a clear majority, represented 11.9 per cent of the state's 1950 population; nineteen senators represented over 88 per cent. This is probably the most drastic departure in the American states from the principle of popular representation. In the words of Professor Thomas S. Barclay, it "has perpetuated an unwarranted rotten borough system." The ablest defense of the "federal plan" is that advanced by Joseph A. Beek, veteran secretary of the senate. He argues logically that if the two houses are to have identical bases of representation, it would be sensible to have unicameralism. While conceding that "theoretically" the plan may deny majority rule and be inconsistent with the usages of democracy, he justifies rural control of the senate in terms of preserving rights of minorities against "mob rule" and saving the state from domination by urban interests.

Both senate and assembly districts are single-member districts. The assembly districts were not reapportioned on the basis of the 1920 census; the senate constituencies were recast in 1927 following the adoption of the "federal plan." The legislature's failure to act in regard to assembly districts meant that the apportionment was very disproportionate by 1930. The 1931 legislature finally enacted a reapportionment measure which formed assembly districts of substantially equal population. The action was repeated in the 1941 legislature.

The 1951 reapportionment posed more difficult problems, however, because of the impossibility of fitting eighty equal assembly districts into thirty equal congressional districts. The considerable disparity in size that resulted can be blamed in large part on the constitutional provision that an assembly district may not be divided in forming a congressional district. A remedy for this knotty problem was first offered in the 1955 legislature: alter the number of members of the lower house each decade to equal three per congressional district.

Assembly representation continues, then, on the basis of population. Senate representation depends mainly upon counties. The assembly remains a body primarily urban in character; the senate has become overwhelmingly rural.

The whole question of senate apportionment was before the electorate in 1948 in the form of an initiative constitutional amendment. It would have returned to a population basis, modified only by the proviso that no county could have more than ten senators. The proposition was defeated by a two-to-one vote.

Reapportionment Procedure

The constitution imposes several restrictions upon the legislature in the construction of senate and assembly districts. In both cases districts must be composed of contiguous territory. Assembly districts shall be "as nearly equal in population as may be," and counties may not be divided unless they contain enough population for more than one assembly district. The constitution makes decennial reapportionment mandatory, but since the courts cannot force a legislature to act, it was possible to omit reapportionment on the basis of the 1920 census, both in the state legislature and in Congress. To guard against the recurrence of such a deadlock, California provided in the 1926 constitutional amendment for a reapportionment commission, which was given full power to reapportion should the legislature fail to act in its first regular session after the federal census had been taken. The commission is now composed of lieutenant governor (chairman), attorney general, state controller, secretary of state, and superintendent of public instruction.

The crucial importance of the outcome of the 1931 reapportionment fight has been seen already. A long battle over assembly and congressional districts ensued. The spoils were great: nine new seats in Congress were ready for distribution, and eighty assembly districts were to be recast. San Francisco, with some northern rural support, fought every step of the way, but eventually was defeated by a combination of central valley and southern California forces.

The 1941 contest over reapportionment was mild by comparison. Three new congressional seats were to be allocated, and the usual assembly redistricting problem was at hand. The assembly reapportionment committee played the major role; it was composed of the chairman and one assemblyman from each congressional district in the state. Ten of the members were Republicans and eleven Democrats. The question was approached from both sectional and partisan fronts.

In 1951, reapportionment took a still different pattern. The state was now entitled to thirty representatives in Congress. Great interest was directed toward the allocation of the seven new seats. In the redrawing of assembly district lines, San Francisco lost two, San Joaquin one, and Los Angeles one. The four seats were distributed among the counties that grew more rapidly—San Diego, Contra Costa, San Mateo, and Kern. In combining assembly districts to form congressional districts, acute controversy arose. Some northern interests sought a fifteen-fifteen division of representatives between north and south. Southern forces held firm for a fourteen-sixteen split, which was closer to population distribution, and the bill was passed on the latter basis.

Democratic party leaders considered the possibility of testing the reapportionment in a referendum, but finally decided not to undertake it. An unsuccessful attack on the redistricting was made in the courts. The two major complaints were that congressional districts were quite unequal in population and that municipalities and natural communities were arbitrarily cut into

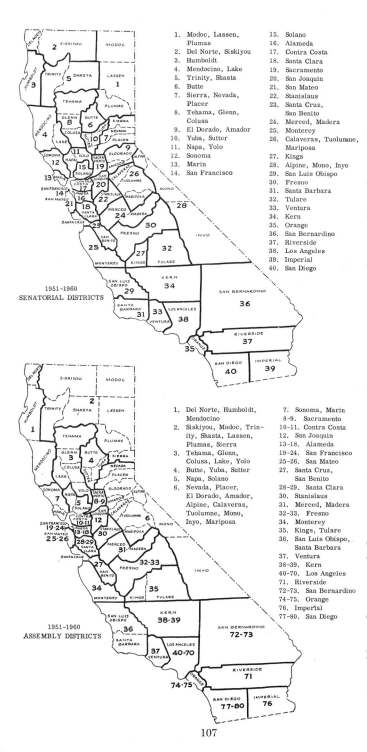

1951-1960 SENATORIAL DISTRICTS

1. Modoc, Lassen, Plumas
2. Del Norte, Siskiyou
3. Humboldt
4. Mendocino, Lake
5. Trinity, Shasta
6. Butte
7. Sierra, Nevada, Placer
8. Tehama, Glenn, Colusa
9. El Dorado, Amador
10. Yuba, Sutter
11. Napa, Yolo
12. Sonoma
13. Marin
14. San Francisco
15. Solano
16. Alameda
17. Contra Costa
18. Santa Clara
19. Sacramento
20. San Joaquin
21. San Mateo
22. Stanislaus
23. Santa Cruz, San Benito
24. Merced, Madera
25. Monterey
26. Calaveras, Tuolumne, Mariposa
27. Kings
28. Alpine, Mono, Inyo
29. San Luis Obispo
30. Fresno
31. Santa Barbara
32. Tulare
33. Ventura
34. Kern
35. Orange
36. San Bernardino
37. Riverside
38. Los Angeles
39. Imperial
40. San Diego

1951-1960 ASSEMBLY DISTRICTS

1. Del Norte, Humboldt, Mendocino
2. Siskiyou, Modoc, Trinity, Shasta, Lassen, Plumas, Sierra
3. Tehama, Glenn, Colusa, Lake, Yolo
4. Butte, Yuba, Sutter
5. Napa, Solano
6. Nevada, Placer, El Dorado, Amador, Alpine, Calaveras, Tuolumne, Mono, Inyo, Mariposa
7. Sonoma, Marin
8-9. Sacramento
10-11. Contra Costa
12. San Joaquin
13-18. Alameda
19-24. San Francisco
25-26. San Mateo
27. Santa Cruz, San Benito
28-29. Santa Clara
30. Stanislaus
31. Merced, Madera
32-33. Fresno
34. Monterey
35. Kings, Tulare
36. San Luis Obispo, Santa Barbara
37. Ventura
38-39. Kern
40-70. Los Angeles
71. Riverside
72-73. San Bernardino
74-75. Orange
76. Imperial
77-80. San Diego

Assembly and senatorial districts, 1951-1960. Note the pattern of regional strength in the two houses. If the northern boundary of San Luis Obispo, Kern, and San Bernardino counties is considered the line between northern and southern California, the distribution is: Assembly—35 north, 45 south; Senate—30 north, 10 south.

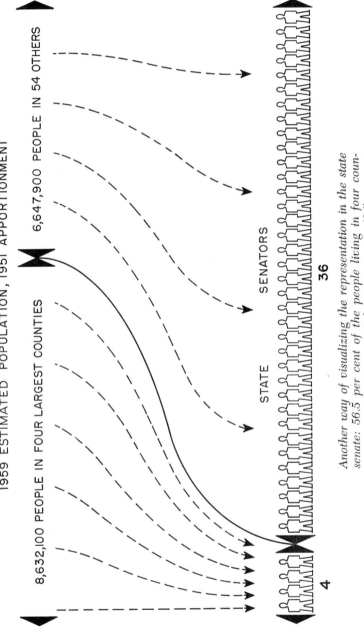

REPRESENTATION IN CALIFORNIA SENATE
1959 ESTIMATED POPULATION, 1951 APPORTIONMENT

8,632,100 PEOPLE IN FOUR LARGEST COUNTIES

6,647,900 PEOPLE IN 54 OTHERS

STATE   SENATORS

4

36

Another way of visualizing the representation in the state senate: 56.5 per cent of the people living in four counties receive 10 per cent of the senate seats; 43.5 per cent in other counties get 90 per cent.

pieces. Defenders of the 1951 act replied that the constitutional prohibition against dividing an assembly district to make a congressional district prevented uniformity among the latter. On balance, it appears that the 1951 reapportionment involved less blatant gerrymandering than sometimes takes place in other states. But there is much evidence of the arrangement of districts for personal and partisan advantage.

Will partisan majorities weight future reapportionments in their favor? Much will depend on the rules in force and on the size of the majority. The most promising reform measure was proposed in the form of a constitutional amendment by Senator Richards of Los Angeles county. It would vary the number of assembly districts with the number of members of the United States House of Representatives allocated to California by Federal law. Each congressional district would be composed of three assembly districts. If the 1961 census brings California's congressional representation up to thirty-seven seats, the "three for one" plan would require 111 members of the Assembly. Equality in district size is assured, under the "three for one" plan, by provisions that assembly districts may not vary more than 15 per cent in population, and congressional districts must be within 10 per cent. The plan failed of passage in the senate in 1955, 1957, and 1959; unless it or something like it is adopted, legislative majorities will continue to have wide latitude in arranging assembly and senatorial districts to suit themselves.

SESSIONS

Annual or Biennial?

In the Constitutional Convention of 1849 considerable discussion arose over the question of annual versus biennial legislative sessions. Annual-session proponents won out with the argument that the first years of the new state would require much new legislation. Amendments adopted in 1862 changed the basis for regular sessions from annual to biennial, and this arrangement has remained.

Sentiment for annual sessions returned, however, and the

Plans	A Constitution Art. IV, Sec. 6 Until 1926	B Constitution Art. IV, Sec. 6 From 1926	C Collins Proposal Initiative 1946	D Sliding Scale Idea 1956	E "Equitable Representation" Plan 1960
Basis	Population	Counties, except none over one senator and not over 3 small counties grouped.	Population, except no county may have more than 10 of 40 senators. Prop. No. 13 of 1948.	One senator for first 100,000; second for next 200,000, third for next 300,000, etc.	Sectional balance; 20 senators to north and 20 to south; counties and population are factors.
Number of senators large counties.*	(1911-1926) LA —8 SF —7 Ala —4 SD —1	(1927 to date) LA —1 SF —1 Ala —1 SD —1	(Est. on 1940) LA —10 SF —4 or 5 Ala —3 or 4 SD —2	(Est. on 1950) LA —8 or 9 SF —3 Ala —3 SD —2 or 3	(Est. on 1960) LA —7 SF —2 Ala —2 SC —2 Orange —2 SD —2

Grouping of smallest counties.	Third district had 5 counties. Twelfth district had 8 counties.	Several districts have 3 counties each.	Probably one district of 10 or 11 counties, another of 7 or 8.	Probably one district of 5 or 6 counties.	Probably some districts of 6 or 7 counties.
Comments	In use 75 years.	The "federal plan."	Defeated 1948 election, 2 to 1.	Never seriously considered.	Petitions circulated in 1960.

FORMER, EXISTING, AND PROPOSED
BASES OF REPRESENTATION
IN THE CALIFORNIA SENATE

* LA, Los Angeles; SF, San Francisco; Ala, Alameda; SD, San Diego; SC, Santa Clara.

1939, 1941, 1943, and 1945 legislatures submitted constitutional amendments providing for regular sessions each year. The voters rejected the first three of these proposals, in 1940, 1942, and 1944, probably because a salary increase for legislators was included. In 1946 the annual-sessions proposition was carried by a two-to-one vote. Thus the present provision in the constitution is that the legislature shall meet annually. In odd-numbered years the session is called the "general session," and any matter within the competence of the legislature may be taken up. In even years a "budget session" is held, at which only the budget bill, revenue measures, constitutional amendments, urgency measures requiring a two-thirds vote, acts calling elections, and acts providing for expenses of the session may be considered.

The necessity for annual sessions grew out of the great increase in the amount of legislative business. For more than a decade, special sessions called by the governor in even-numbered years had come to mean that the legislature was actually meeting annually. The regular annual session makes possible annual budgets and more rigid legislative control over finances. It helps the legislature to function as a continuous critic of the administration. It enables the legislature to keep abreast of the changing conditions in the state.

The length of legislative sessions is limited under the terms of the constitution. The general session convenes in early January of the odd years and continues until its work is done, but not to exceed 120 days, exclusive of Saturdays and Sundays. Budget sessions commence in February of even years, and may not exceed thirty calendar days, but may recess up to thirty days after the introduction of the budget bill. Special sessions may be called by the governor, who must specify the subject matter with which they are to deal.

Unified or Split?

After nearly fifty years, the legislature in 1959 returned to the unified session plan. Since 1911 the constitution had required a unique split or bifurcated general session. In practice this meant that the legislature convened in early January of odd-numbered years, largely for the introduction of bills; took February for a "constitutional recess"; and returned for March, April, and May to take action on bills. The theory was that the recess gave legislators and constituents an opportunity to discuss pending bills. In practice the volume of bills grew so large that the legislative counsel could not draft them in the pre-recess period, and the state printer could barely get them printed during the recess. To avoid the strict rule against introduction of bills after the recess, legislators often introduced "skeleton bills" on various subjects, but with no or meager provisions. If no such "spot" were available, another bill on the subject might be "hijacked" or taken over for a purpose other than the one originally intended by its introducer.

The voters rejected propositions that would have abolished the split session at the elections of 1940, 1942, and 1944. In 1958 a constitutional amendment providing for abolition was adopted by a narrow margin. Its provisions forbid committee hearings or passage of bills for 30 days after their introduction, unless waived by a three-fourths vote. Some such deadline is deemed necessary to prevent a "sneak play" in the closing days or hours of a session. The 1958 amendment excluded Saturdays and Sundays from the 120 day limit on the length of general sessions. Joint rules have been adopted which ban, except in emergencies, introduction of bills and constitutional amendments after the first 120 calendar days of a general session. Departmental bills (excluding those of the governor) cannot be introduced after the forty-fifth calendar day of a general session.

LEGISLATORS AND PERQUISITES

Terms and Pay

Since 1862 the terms of senators have been four years, and those of assemblymen have been two. All state legislators are nominated in the partisan direct primary in June and elected in the November general election. The forty senators have overlapping terms, with one-half of the seats up for election every two years. All eighty members of the assembly are elected at each biennial general election.

Members of the lower house would like to have longer terms.

The two-year assembly term reduces the attractiveness of service in that body and intensifies the problem of turnover. A proposition to amend the constitution to provide for four-year assembly terms and six-year senate terms, and to limit the governor to two four-year terms, was rejected by the voters in 1954. The legislature in 1959 voted to submit to the electorate a constitutional amendment that would raise the assembly term to four years, one-half elected each two years, but leave the senate term at four.

California legislators receive salaries of $6,000 a year, plus allowances of $14 a day during sessions, and $15 a day plus mileage while on interim committee business. The legislative salary was only a nominal $1,200 a year until 1949, when the voters approved a constitutional amendment raising it to $3,600. The increase to $500 a month was ratified by the electorate in 1954. The per diem allowance during sessions was sought for some time before it was approved in 1944. The electorate in 1958 rejected a proposed constitutional amendment to permit the fixing of legislative salaries by statute, subject to certain limitations. Even though, in 1959, California appeared to have one of the best-compensated state legislatures in the nation, salaries were not high considering the responsibilities. Legislative work now takes nearly full time, and the public has belatedly recognized that more adequate pay is required. Since 1947 legislators have been eligible to participate in a contributory retirement plan. The 1959 legislature submitted to the voters an amendment that would provide a salary of $9,000.

Legislative Personnel

To be eligible for membership in the assembly or senate, one must have been a citizen and inhabitant of the state for three years, and of his district for one year. Each house judges the qualifications of its own members.

A high proportion, more than two-thirds, of California legislators are college-trained. Almost all senators and assemblymen have attended the public schools. The University of California, in all its campuses, leads as an alma mater for legislators, followed—in equal numbers—by Stanford University and the University of Southern California. Many of those who attended college took a professional course, usually law.

Occupationally, lawyers and businessmen lead in both senate and assembly. Farming, real estate and insurance, teaching, and publishing are frequently represented among the private endeavors of California legislators.

From 50 to 90 per cent of the legislators in any given session have had previous legislative experience. They have been engaged mostly in municipal and county affairs, although state service is common; but rarely ever does federal experience precede state legislative work. The assembly turnover is greater than the senate's, having reached forty out of eighty in 1933, whereas the senate in one session (1929) had only three new members out of forty.

Many factors operate to condition the personnel of the California legislature. Free public education from kindergarten through university is provided, and other educational opportunities are available. Some occupations combine with legislative work much better than others. For example, an attorney or real estate man may leave business with an associate or partner, while a physician or other person might find legislative work too intermittent to combine with his profession.

LEGISLATIVE PROCEDURE

A Bill Is Born

The idea for a bill may originate in any one of many sources, including individual constituents, organized groups, state and local public agencies, and legislators themselves.

A bill may be drafted in final form by private attorneys, but with increasing frequency proposed legislation is submitted for at least the finishing touches to the legislature's own bill-drafting agency, the legislative counsel. This office has a staff of attorneys who specialize in drafting bills and amendments. Its service is provided for legislators, legislative committees, and other state officers.

Each bill must carry an enacting clause, "The people of Cali-

ASSEMBLY BILL No. 118

Introduced by Messrs. Munnell, Crown, Ralph M. Brown, Thelin, Don
A. Allen, Bane, Bee, Biddick, Britschgi, George E. Brown, Burton,
Cameron, Crawford, Mrs. Davis, Messrs. DeLotto, Dills, Miss Dona-
hoe, Messrs. Elliott, Gaffney, Garrigus, Samuel R. Geddes, Hanna,
Hawkins, House, Lowrey, Luckel, Lunardi, Masterson, McMillan,
Miller, Nisbet, O'Connell, Pattee, Petris, Porter, Rumford, Thomas,
Unruh, Waldie, Williamson, Charles H. Wilson, Winton, and Z'berg
(At the request of the Governor)

January 8, 1959

REFERRED TO COMMITTEE ON ELECTIONS AND REAPPORTIONMENT

*An act to add Section 2501 to, to amend Sections 2793, 2893,
2894, 2896 and 2899 of, and to repeal Sections 2674, 2742,
2794 and 2795 of, the Elections Code, relating to partisan
candidates.*

The people of the State of California do enact as follows:

1 SECTION 1. Section 2501 is added to the Elections Code, to
2 read:
3 2501. No declaration of candidacy for a partisan office,
4 either by the candidate himself or by sponsors on his behalf,
5 shall be filed unless at the time of presentation of the declara-
6 tion and continuously for not less than three months immedi-
7 ately prior thereto, the candidate is shown by his affidavit of
8 registration to be affiliated with the political party the nomi-
9 nation of which he seeks.

SENATE BILL No. 968

Introduced by Senators Robert I. McCarthy and Cobey

January 21, 1957

REFERRED TO COMMITTEE ON REVENUE AND TAXATION

*An act to add Section 17210 to the Revenue and Taxation
Code, relating to deduction for political contributions.*

The people of the State of California do enact as follows:

1 SECTION 1. Section 17210 is added to the Revenue and
2 Taxation Code, to read:
3 17210. In computing taxable income there shall be allowed
4 as a deduction political contributions by any person, except
5 a corporation, not in excess of one hundred dollars ($100), in
6 any primary election.

fornia do enact as follows: . . ." The title must convey an accurate idea of the contents of the bill. Beginning with the 1959 session, the joint rules required that each bill be accompanied by a digest prepared by the legislative counsel. The bill banning cross-filing carried the following digest at the bottom of its first page:

LEGISLATIVE COUNSEL'S DIGEST

A. B. 118 as introduced, Munnell (Elec. & Reap.). Elections, crossfiling.

Adds, amends, and repeals various sections, Elec. C. Eliminates crossfiling for partisan offices.

No limit has been placed on the number of bills that can be introduced by a senator or assemblyman. The member or members of either house who wish to introduce a bill merely sign their names across the typewritten manuscript and send it to the clerk's desk. The clerk takes the bill in order, reads the title rapidly, and assigns it a number. Ordinary bills are designated "AB" for assembly bills and "SB" for senate bills. Constitutional amendments are indicated by "ACA" and "SCA." Joint resolutions, used exclusively for matters connected with the federal government, are assigned the symbols "AJR" and "SJR." Simple one-house resolutions are known as house resolutions and senate resolutions.

The clerk's reading of the title constitutes the first reading within the meaning of the constitution. In the assembly the bill is then passed back to the presiding officer, the speaker, who refers it to the appropriate standing committee. The senate committee on rules has the responsibility for referral of bills to a committee in the upper house. Sometimes the bill is of such a

---

The form of assembly and senate bills. AB 118 is the cross-filing abolition measure of 1959. The 43 co-authors, a clear majority, virtually assured passage in the assembly; gubernatorial sponsorship guaranteed approval by the chief executive. SB 968 is the 1957 measure through which political contributions were made deductible for state income tax purposes.

nature that it might go to any one of several committees. Therefore, legislators and lobbyists often attempt to influence the choice of committee.

The Bill in Committee

After first reading and reference to committee, the bill is printed and distributed to legislators and to others who request it from the legislative bill room. In addition, it is listed in the *Daily History* and *Weekly History* of the house in which it was

A legislative committee hearing. This is an assembly committee, meeting in the state building, Los Angeles. Photo courtesy California State Employees Association.

introduced. It is indexed in the *Legislative Index*, and its provisions are described briefly in the next issue of the *Legislative Digest*. It is now in the committee stage of the first house, the most crucial test and the point of the greatest quantitative culling.

The standing committee to which a bill is referred has full power over it and, in investigating and studying it, may subpoena witnesses and documents. The more important bills are set for public hearing and the hearing dates publicized. Occasionally the committee fails to get a quorum on the appointed day, and citizens who have trekked to Sacramento for a hearing find it necessary to return later. Persons who wish to testify on a bill may find that the committee's time is so limited that they are cut off after a very short period. When discussions and hearing are over, the committee members vote on the question of recommending the bill.

If a majority approves, the recommendation "do pass" is given. If the majority disapproves, the bill is tabled, eventually to be reported out at adjournment sine die "from committee without further action," and the bill is killed. Occasionally a rather evenly divided committee will report out a controversial bill without recommendation; in this case the House might or might not pass it. In extraordinary cases, a majority on the floor of the house concerned may recall or withdraw a bill from a standing committee; in the senate this may be done "at any time" with twenty-one votes; the assembly requires forty-one votes and two days' advance notice.

Consideration on the Floor

The constitution provides that each bill must be read three times. The first reading occurs when a bill is introduced; in practice even the titles are not read in full if they are long. The bill reported out of committee is placed on the *Daily File* of the house concerned. The senate *File* and the assembly *File* are printed each day, and list bills on second reading, bills on third reading, special orders, and unfinished business. Committee hearings may be announced through the *File*. Bills are listed on "second reading" file in the order received from committee. Amendments may be offered on second reading; if amendments are adopted, the bill is sent out for reprint.

Since 1959, uncontested bills can be handled on the floor of the two houses through "consent calendar" procedure. To qualify for such special handling, a bill must have unanimous support in committee, no opposition expressed to it by any person present during committee consideration, and a request by the author for consent calendar listing prior to final action by the committee. After second reading, bills certified by chairmen as uncontested may be placed on the consent calendar unless some member objects. Bills on consent calendar are taken up on the second day of their listing as the last order of business. Debate on them is not permitted, but questions may be answered.

Other bills take their place at the bottom of the third reading file, in the order in which they passed second reading. On third reading the author may take up the bill for final passage, or put it on file and wait for a more advantageous situation. When he chooses to take it up, it may be amended and sent out for reprint. The author usually claims the privilege of opening and closing the debate. California legislators generally speak from their desks, and in both houses public-address equipment is available. Closure in debate is obtained through moving the previous question; if it is carried, the author gives the closing argument and the roll is called. Final passage requires an affirmative vote of a majority of the members elected to each house, twenty-one in the senate and forty-one in the assembly.

A constitutional provision requires that the ayes and nays must be recorded in the journal of proceedings if three members request it, and on final passage all bills must be read at length and the vote recorded. Reading at length is impossible under modern conditions, and the two houses continue to call a clerk's muttering of the title "reading at length." The requirement of a recorded roll call on final passage intensified the difficulties of the assembly during the closing rush. Each roll call took several minutes, and a great deal of legislative time was wasted. A treacherous device known as "substitute roll call" was developed to save time; it involved a simple motion to pass bill "A" with the same vote by which bill "B" was enacted. Hundreds of bills passed the assembly by this device, and legislators were recorded as voting for measures to which they were opposed.

Fortunately, the assembly in 1933 adopted an electric roll-call system which is both speedy and accurate. It saves great amounts of time. Each member has a push button marked "yes" and one marked "no." Opposite his name on score boards (at the speaker's right and left) a light flashes on, green for "yes" and red for "no." The speaker calls for all to vote, then orders the board closed. An electrical machine punches the roll call on printed sheets, which may be distributed to the press representatives, and which goes into the permanent records of the house. The senate continues to use oral voting.

Second House and Executive Action

The process described in connection with the first house is duplicated in the second. The bill is transmitted to the second house, where it is referred to an appropriate committee. Hearings are held in a like manner, and the bill is reported out or pigeon-holed. The second and third readings take place, and it is up for final passage. If adopted in the form in which it was passed by the first house, the bill is sent to the governor, who then has ten days in which to sign it or return it to the house of origin without approval. If the governor takes no action, the bill becomes law in ten days without his signature. If he vetoes it, his action may be overridden by a vote of two-thirds of the elected members of each house. However, if the legislature adjourns before the ten-day period has elapsed, the governor then has thirty days in which to sign. Unsigned bills are dead after thirty days; this is called "pocket veto." The governor has power to veto or to reduce any item in an appropriation bill.

Should the second house pass the bill of the first house in amended form, it is sent to the first house with the request that the amendments be concurred in. If the first house declines to accept such amendments, and the second house refuses to recede from them, a conference committee of three members of each house is set up. A compromise version of the bill is worked out, and the conferees take their suggestions back to each house. If these are acceptable to both houses, the bill goes to the governor. If not, another conference committee may be appointed to try again.

LEADERSHIP

Mr. Speaker & Co.

The speaker of the assembly is a powerful political officer, often ranked second to the governor in influence. In addition to the usual responsibilities connected with presiding, the speaker appoints all committees, is often the real leader of the lower house, and serves ex officio as a regent of the University of California.

The selection of a speaker often sets the pattern of policies and atmosphere in the assembly for the biennium. Except in the late thirties and late fifties, the contest for the speakership usually has been between Republicans who are supported by rival factions composed of economic and other interest groups. After the 1958 election placed the Democrats in the majority, members-elect caucused to consider the speakership and other matters. The caucus selected Ralph M. Brown of Modesto over Augustus F. Hawkins, and the election of Brown by the Assembly came at the outset of the 1959 session. He received both Democratic and Republican votes. Continuing the bipartisan tradition, Speaker Brown appointed as chairmen of standing committees nine Republicans and nineteen Democrats.

The rules committee of the assembly plays a leading part in the management of the business of the house. Its chairman is appointed by the speaker, but the remaining six members are ratified by the assembly after proposal, three each, by majority- and minority-party caucuses.

Recognized in the rules, and of importance in an understanding of the legislative process, is the assembly majority floor leader. He is now a partisan officer, appointed by the speaker "after consultation with the members of his supporting majority" and serves as the speaker's "personal representative on the floor."

This is in contrast to the situation which prevailed from 1940 to 1958 when the floor leader led a bipartisan coalition.

The duty of the speaker pro tempore is to preside in the absence of the speaker. The chief clerk is in charge of records, personnel, and routine. The sergeant at arms enforces the will of the house with respect to keeping order and provides for the convenience and comfort of members. Many attaches—clerks, stenographers, assistant sergeants at arms, page boys—are employed by the senate, and provide a few possibilities for jobs for relatives, supporters, and friends of the members. Since 1957 "legislative interns" sponsored by the graduate schools of California universities have served the assembly; they receive practical experience and a modest stipend, which is furnished equally by the assembly and one of the foundations.

Senate Officers

The lieutenant governor presides over the senate as its president. He votes only in case of tie, and has the general duty of keeping order.

In recent years, the president pro tempore has emerged as the most powerful officer in the senate. Not only does he substitute for the lieutenant governor when absent, but he fills the role of majority floor leader and heads the important rules committee. As floor leader the president pro tempore provides direction for the whole body, as the rules state, "to secure the prompt and businesslike disposition of bills and other business before the Senate." As chairman of the committee on rules, the president pro tempore bears the major responsibility for that body's selection of committees, general management of the functioning of the senate, and recommendations for senate confirmation or rejection of the governor's appointments. The president pro tempore is elected by the senate, usually on the basis of personal popularity and rural, as opposed to urban, support. Under the terms of a constitutional amendment adopted in 1948, the president pro tempore succeeds to the lieutenant governorship when that office falls vacant; Harold J. Powers in 1953 became lieutenant governor when Goodwin J. Knight succeeded to the governorship.

Other senate officers include the secretary of the senate and the sergeant at arms, both of whom are elected by the upper chamber.

Committee System

Committees of the assembly are traditionally appointed by the speaker. Normally the speaker is elected by a bipartisan combination, and he rewards his supporters in the speakership fight with the best chairmanships and committee posts. Members of the assembly make written and oral requests for committee assignments, and, of course, similar appeals are made by representatives of pressure groups.

The senate formerly allowed its president, the lieutenant governor, to appoint its standing committees. However, beginning in 1939 this function was assigned to its committee on rules, which consists of the president pro tempore and four other senators, who are elected by the senate. The pattern of assignments to senate committees, then, is determined mainly by the outcome of the contest for president pro tempore and the four rules committee posts.

California legislative standing committees in the past have been both numerous and ill-coordinated. In 1939, for example, the assembly had fifty-eight standing committees and the senate had forty-two. The average assemblyman served on eight committees and the average senator on six. Some of the committees were of great importance and had large numbers of bills before them for consideration; others had no bills at all. On the assembly side, a member occasionally had two or three of his committees in session simultaneously.

The senate reworked its committee system in 1941. There were twenty-one committees in the 1959 session, ranging in size from five to fifteen. The average committee had ten members, and the typical senator had five committee assignments.

The assembly reformed its committees in the 1943 session. In the 1959 session there were twenty-seven standing committees in the assembly, ranging in size from two to twenty-two. Assembly rules state that no member should serve on more than three standing committees, but waivers are granted and most members served on four committees in 1959.

Interim Committees

The power to investigate is considered an auxiliary of the power to legislate. The California legislature exercised this power freely until 1938. Early in 1938 a judge of the Los Angeles Superior Court declared that an assembly interim committee had no lawful existence, holding that a one-house resolution could not create a committee authorized to function after adjournment. This decision was sustained in the state supreme court.

Shortly afterward a second case arose over a senate committee; the senate is not a continuing body; a two-house resolution could not create a committee with power to sit after adjournment.

For a year and a half the legislature was shorn of its investigative power. In the 1940 general election, the people approved a constitutional amendment giving the legislature or either house full power to investigate under single-house or concurrent resolution. Subsequent legislatures have utilized extensively the rewon power. From such comparative data as are available, California makes fuller use of interim committees than does any other state. In 1957-59 there were twenty-five assembly, forty-four senate, and eighteen joint interim committees.

SERVICES TO THE LEGISLATURE

Legislative Aids

Bill-drafting services are provided by the legislative counsel, an officer selected by the legislature. He maintains a staff of attorneys who will draft bills and amendments for legislators, the governor, or judges. The agency also serves legislative committees, both standing and interim. An esprit de corps of high order makes it possible for a small staff to perform a huge amount of work in a very brief period.

A relative newcomer in the legislative establishment is the

auditor general. For many years independent surveys and legislative committees had recommended that the state needed an auditing agency outside of the executive branch. In 1955 the auditor generalship was created, and placed under the direction of the joint legislative audit committee. The post was filled in 1956, and the office was staffed gradually with personnel capable of carrying out its assigned tasks of examining the financial statements of the state and reporting on them. The work of the auditor general does not displace the current and internal auditing of the department of finance and of operating agencies; some have called it the counterpart of the independent audit made by an accounting firm for the board of directors of a corporation.

To secure outside counsel and lay support the legislature in 1957 established the citizens legislative advisory commission. The large membership of this body was broadly representative of the diverse groups and interests that lead in the formulation of public policy in the state. Legislative leaders simply asked the commission to help solve the problems of organization and procedure that harassed the legislative branch. The commission set up six subcommittees, the names of which indicate the areas of greatest interest: legislative sessions, terms of office, compensation and conflicts of interest, personal assistance for legislators, legislative committees, and legislative aids and services. The adoption of a constitutional amendment (Proposition #9 of 1958) abolishing the split session often is credited to the commission. Substantial studies,* made for the commission, have added considerably to the literature on the legislative process.

The legislature's own research staff is found mainly in the office of the legislative analyst. Since 1941 the legislative budget committee, a joint body composed of five members of each house, has existed to ascertain facts and make recommendations concerning the budget, revenues, expenditures, organization, and functions. The committee appoints a legislative analyst, who in turn has recruited an able staff of research analysts. Under the joint rules of the two houses, the staff may render services to investigating committees on a contractual basis.

Informational services are offered by other public agencies.

---

* Such as those of Doubleday on committees and of Mangore Corporation on compensation. See reading list at chapter end.

The state library provides a legislative reference service by securing information and giving assistance on laws, court decisions, and procedures in other states. Unfortunately, few legislators have time and inclination to consult the excellent resources of the library.

The bureau of public administration of the University of California, Berkeley, also has a legislative service. Since 1934, the bureau has issued a series of monographs on legislative problems for each session, and has prepared special reports at the request of legislators and committees. The bureau has a capable research staff—as has its parallel, the bureau of governmental research on the Los Angeles campus—and can tap the even wider resources of the university.

Add to these the assistance given by the groups and individuals on each side of public questions, and you have the more usual aids to legislators. Bill drafting is handled adequately. Informational services are less satisfactory. Without minimizing the value of the work done by the state library and the university, the full confidence of legislators in research results may best be gained when the agency is their own.

Toward a Legislative Council?

State legislative work is becoming greater in volume and complexity, and most state legislatures have need for special machinery to share continuously in the making of public policy and to study and plan a legislative program. The major proposal for helping the legislature to keep abreast of its work is the legislative council idea. It can be described as a master interim committee empowered to gather facts, prepare a program, and recommend legislative action. In its "pure" form the council is composed of legislators only. The best of the existing councils have adequate research agencies.

More than one-half of the states have set up some form of legislative council. The nearest thing in California is the joint legislative budget committee, but it is preoccupied with an approach limited mainly to reducing the cost of government and securing greater economy and efficiency.

Some opposition to creating a legislative council in California comes from legislators who fear that the legislative power will be concentrated unduly in the hands of the small group in the council. Another objection, raised by nonlegislators, is that the lawmakers may be tempted to use such continuous machinery to meddle in administrative affairs. The extensive use of interim investigating committees, however, probably involves more ir responsible intervention in the executive branch than would prevail if inquiries were conducted under the leadership and on the authority of a legislative council.

California may have moved past the point of requiring a master interim committee. A great deal of interim work is already done by *ad hoc* committees of the legislature. The joint legislative budget committee has powers so great that some already regard it as a legislative council. There remains, however, the task of coordinating the interim work being done, and of forging an instrument that will provide the leadership to make the legislative equal to the executive branch in energy and purposefulness. Joint action during interims might lead to joint standing committees during sessions. This would mean the merger of similar assembly and senate committees, or a single set of committees for the two houses. The plan has been used successfully in Massachusetts and Maine. The joint rules of the California legislature provide that joint meetings may be arranged if the chairmen of like committees deem it proper. In practice, few such meetings are held, although they could contribute greatly to the convenience of interested citizens.

LEGISLATIVE PROBLEMS

Parties in Legislation

The political party, as seen in an earlier chapter, has been restricted in its activities in California, but not yet ruled out of the legislative field. Candidates for assembly and senate are nominated through the partisan direct primary. California was a one-party state for a whole generation, from 1900 to 1932, and developed in 1910 a fairly satisfactory substitute for national parties, in the form of factional groups within the Republican party.

The progressive faction, which was led by Hiram W. Johnson (1911-1917) as governor and then by William D. Stephens (1917-1923), and which finally expired under C. C. Young (1927-1931), had some discipline and responsibility. The conservative faction, which held the governorship through Friend W. Richardson (1923-1927), was well financed and influential even in the days of progressive supremacy. This progressive versus conservative factional cleavage worked well, and the people had a clearer choice of alternatives than would have been possible between the two major national parties during this era.

After the progressive faction expired during the Young administration, a transitional period followed, 1931-1938, in which the Democratic party emerged as a major force in state politics and in the legislature. Although the state went strongly Democratic in national elections, the nomination of Upton Sinclair as candidate for the governorship in 1934 frightened the majority of the electorate sufficiently to re-elect Republican Governor Frank F. Merriam. Democratic strength in the legislature mounted steadily, however. In 1933 five senators and twenty-six assemblymen called themselves Democrats. During the 1935 session, ten senators and thirty-eight assemblymen bore the Democratic label. The 1937 legislature had the strongest Democratic representation in several decades, with sixteen senators and forty-seven assemblymen. The Democrats proceeded to organize the lower house on a nominally partisan basis, with a Democratic speaker and an occasional party caucus. The 1938 election brought a Democrat to the governorship for the first time since Governor Budd left office in 1899; the majority in the assembly was retained.

But the legislative seas were rough, and the Democratic honeymoon proved short-lived. Democratic caucuses allegedly were held in the governor's office on the governor's call. The governor handled his Democratic legislators abruptly, and some of the more conservative among them "took a walk." In the special session of 1940 a group of Democrats went over to the Republicans to elect a conservative Democrat as speaker and helped to form an "economy bloc" which was united mainly by common devotion to conservatism. In the 1941 and 1943 sessions, this bloc continued in control of the assembly, and the official Democratic

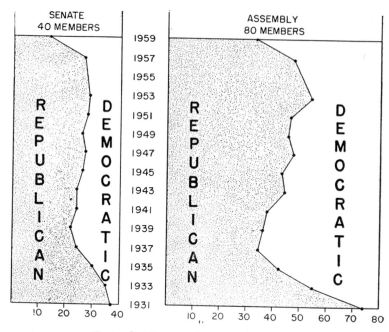

Party divisions in the state legislature.

group, now numbering about twenty-five, caucused occasionally with the chairman of the party state central committee as presiding officer. The economy bloc also met from time to time to manage the affairs of the majority. From 1945 on the normal bipartisan pattern was substantially resumed.

The senate's drift toward Democratic complexion resumed in the 1950's, but the continuous Republican control of the second chamber extending from 1889 did not end until 1957, when the two parties tied; in 1959 the Democrats took control with a two to one margin. Members of both houses go on using the labels of parties, but until recently the labels have implied no limitation on the freedom of action of a legislator. Party has now assumed a major role in the legislature, following the Democratic gubernatorial victory of 1958. Yet it is too early to forecast whether party government is here to stay or whether party influence will again become a peripheral thing, weaker than considerations of pressure group, section, and administration.

Lobbying and Pressure Groups

The task of the lobbyist is to bring the case of his special-interest group to the attention of the public official. This has been done from the beginning of government in California; the first legislature was probably dubbed "the legislature of a thousand drinks" because of the lobbying activities of favor seekers.

Techniques of the lobbyist vary with the type of organization represented, public popularity of his cause, and other factors. If his group has a large membership and impressive popular support (as farm and labor organizations) then he may rely mainly upon broad publicity and public pressure as his leading sanctions. If he represents a corporation which is in public disfavor, however, he may find it necessary to spend large amounts for advertising and propaganda, to entertain lavishly, and to bring pressure to bear from high places. Nearly all of the major lobbyists prepare legislation, furnish information, testify at committee hearings, and do some entertaining. Some special interests finance campaigns, or in some other way make payments to deserving legislators.

For many years the only official registers of information on groups and lobbyists before the legislature were those established under senate and assembly rules. The senate advocate register was commenced in 1925. The assembly began in 1937 to register "business representatives and legislative representatives."

Neither the senate nor the assembly rule on registration of lobbyists was drastic. The representative of a group, organization, or corporation simply was required to state his connections publicly. There were no penalties for violations, except the implication that an offender might be denied the privilege of appearing before committees.

Then came the explosion of 1949, which followed the publication of Lester Velie's two articles "The Secret Boss of California," in *Collier's*.* The articles told the story of Arthur H. Samish, lobbyist extraordinary. The public was shocked by the power attributed to him, by boastful quotations from him, and espe-

---

* August 13, 1949, pp. 11-13, 71-73; and August 20, 1949, pp. 12-13, 60, 62-63.

cially by the picture of the big man holding a puppet ("Mr. Legislature") on his knee.

The legislature, in special session during December 1949, enacted and the governor signed a strict bill patterned after the federal lobbying act. A more permanent act was adopted in 1950. Legislative representation committees were created in each house and given the duty of studying and analyzing lobbying. Both houses designate the legislative analyst as the officer with whom lobbying reports should be filed, then published in the Assembly *Journal*.

Criticisms of the law swamped the legislature, particularly during the 1953 session. A senate committee reported that the statute was too vague and ambiguous, and recommended that nonprofessional lobbyists should not be subjected to the reporting requirement. Others complained that the lobby reports required too much detail and were so lengthy that the proper purposes of the law were not served. In 1959 the legislative counsel ruled that a person who merely appeared before a committee when a bill was heard need not register.

The constitution also makes "lobbying" a felony, but clearly such improper influence as bribery and intimidation is meant. No record of prosecution in a court of law is known. The main features of existing California statutes governing lobbying call for registration, financial reports, prohibition of contingent fees, and penalties for violation. Left untouched, however, are the problems of getting the campaign contributions of interest groups on record and of recording data on the relationship of lawyer-legislators to interests with legislative goals.

The Executive in Legislation

The governor has several direct constitutional powers over legislation. He has authority to veto, to call special sessions, to submit the budget, and to reduce or eliminate items from appropriation bills. Indirectly he influences the course of legislation through his power over appointments and by his ability to appeal to public opinion. His veto power includes the "pocket veto" after adjournment and the "item veto" of appropriation bills. In calling an extraordinary session of the legislature, the governor specifies precisely what questions may be dealt with, and the legislature has no power to enact laws on other subjects.

Recent governors have developed some staff to cope with the large volume of legislation. Governor Olson appointed a former legislator as his "contact man"; Governor Warren added a "legislative secretary" to his official family, and his successors have followed suit. In addition, several departments and agencies of the state government maintain regular lobbyists before the legislature. Agency and department heads are asked to file advance written authorization for their spokesmen with committees before which they intended to appear. Indeed, the time may be at hand when a formal system of clearance of legislative measures by the executive will be advisable. Joint rules require that departmental bills be introduced in the first forty-five days of a general session, but the governor is exempt from this deadline.

Quantity of Legislation

The California legislature for many years ranked first among the American states in the volume of legislation introduced and enacted. This doubtful distinction may have been shed, however, with the abolition of the split session. An impression of the quantitative aspects of the legislative mill may be gained from an examination of the records of recent general sessions of the legislature, before and after the change in sessions:

COMPARISON OF ACTION ON BILLS, SESSIONS OF 1957 AND 1959

Assembly		Senate
	Total introduced	
4,118	1957	2,680
2,912	1959	1,489
	Passed first house	
1,875	1957	1,212
1,738	1959	978
	Passed both houses	
1,580	1957	1,098
1,489	1959	874
	Became law with or without governor's signature	
1,449	1957	975
1,402	1959	794

The large volume of legislation has caused apprehension in some quarters. The great quantity is attributable in part to the diversity of the state and the mental fertility of legislators, pressure groups, and constituents. But another reason for this flood of legislation is the tendency for the California legislature to deal with detailed and petty matters. They are far from the important questions of public policy that ought to claim the legislative attention. Some examples of minor matters that claimed the attention of a recent legislature will serve to illustrate this point:

SB 626 defines jumping frog contests.
AB 336 makes unlawful the selling or distribution of hydraulic brake fluid without a license and sets standards for fluids.
AB 1970 establishes and describes dimensions of standard container for nectarines.

These are questions not of high public policy but of detail, and they can be settled more competently by administrative bodies than by legislators. The legislature might well reserve the power to review rule making by executive agencies, but no good reason exists for expecting 120 legislators to waste time and money wrangling over whether or not black-tailed jack rabbits are predatory animals.

Delegation of decisions on minor matters to administrative agencies would require extensive changes in existing procedures and codes of law, but it could be done after thorough review of the statutes by the legislative counsel or by the Law Revision Commission personnel. Most proposals made for reducing the quantity of legislation have centered on setting a maximum limit on the number of bills a single legislator could introduce. No doubt there is a great deal of duplication among bills and much introduction in order to accommodate a single constituent or group. Quantitative limitation would appear to restrict unjustifiably the freedom of the legislator and to miss getting at the basic cause of the problem—namely, the mass of detailed provisions in the existing law.

Law Revision

The law revision commission has been, since its creation in 1953, the state's principal agency engaged in continuous study

and improvement of the law. It consists of one senator, one assemblyman, and seven appointees of the governor. Its task is to
examine the law and judicial decisions, to locate defects, and to
recommend changes needed. Proposals by public officials, by the
bar, by learned bodies, and by other groups are considered. Recommendations for bringing the law into harmony with modern
conditions may be made by the commission.

A forerunner, now expired, was the code commission, which in
two decades completed the monumental task of codifying the
statutes of the state. It began in 1929 with four codes and about
21,000 laws. When its work was finished in the early 1950's the
statutes had been combed, obsolete laws sifted out, and unconstitutional and inoperative acts eliminated. The statute law of the
state was grouped and systematized into twenty-four "codes."

The Legislature and the Public

What can the conscientious citizen do about keeping informed
on state legislative matters? The first essential is to find out who
his representatives are. Then as he obtains information on issues,
he can check the record of the senator and assemblyman upon
whose stewardship of office he will pass next election day. His
most obvious source of data is the newspaper, but few even of
the metropolitan papers report Sacramento news thoroughly. He
may belong to a special interest group which publishes a journal
or newsletter carrying legislative news in season.

But if Mr. Citizen wishes to follow legislation in detail, it will
be necessary to learn to use some of the official documents. They
are available in good public libraries, and most may be obtained
from one's assemblyman or senator. First, he will need a *Handbook, California Legislature* for the current session. There he
can find the bills of interest to him by checking the *Legislative
Index;* he can see a brief summary of each bill in *Legislative
Digest.* To find the status of a bill, he can look at the histories,
Senate Weekly History or *Assembly Weekly History,* and after
the session is over, the *Final Calendar of Legislative Business.*
They contain the titles and individual history of each bill, summaries on committees and authors, and other useful information.

Should Mr. Citizen then wish to see the text of a certain bill, he can either ask to see it in his public library, or write to the Legislative Bill Room, State Capitol, Sacramento, for it. He should remember, however, neither *Digest* nor public library copies of bills include amendments. If he wishes to check on how a particular legislator voted, he must look in *Senate Journal* or *Assembly Journal* under the date given in the history as passing the house concerned. The journals do not carry debates, but only motions, roll calls, and the like. After a session is over, the *Summary Digest of Statutes Enacted* offers the most convenient review of the bills passed.

Mr. Citizen's task of looking up how his legislator voted may be made easier by using some of the interest-group reports on legislative sessions, especially those of the State Federation of Labor, the California State Chamber of Commerce, and the League of Women Voters.

Further Reading

Barclay, Thomas S., "The Reapportionment Struggle in California in 1948," *Western Political Quarterly,* IV (June 1951), 313-324.

Bemis, George W., "Sectionalism and Representation in the California State Legislature, 1911-1931." Unpublished Ph.D. dissertation, University of California, 1934.

Beek, Joseph A., *The California Legislature.* Sacramento: State Printing Office, 1957.

California, Legislative Analyst, *California Interim Legislative Committees and Reports.* Sacramento: State Printing Office, biennial.

California State Government: Its Tasks and Organization. Background papers prepared for the California Conference on State Government, held at Stanford University, Sept. 13-16, 1956, in cooperation with The American Assembly. See particularly papers by Leary and Hinderaker.

Collings, Rex A., "California's New Lobby Control Act," *California Law Review,* XXXVIII (August, 1950), 478-497.

Commonwealth Club of California, "How Should Legislative Investigating Committees Operate?" *Transactions . . . ,* XLV (July, 1951), 154-178.

Doubleday, Jay, *Standing and Interim Committees of the California Legislature* (Citizen's Legislature Advisory Commission). Sacramento: State Printing Office (May, 1959).

————, "Legislative Review of the Budget in California." Unpublished Ph.D. dissertation, University of California, Berkeley, 1958.

Hardy, Leroy, "The California Reapportionment of 1951," Unpublished Ph.D. dissertation, University of California, Los Angeles, 1955.

Hinderaker, Ivan H., and Laughlin E. Waters, "A Case Study in Reapportionment—California in 1951," *Law and Contemporary Problems*, 17 (Spring, 1952), 440-469.

Larsen, Christian L., *The Use of Special Committees and Commissions by the California Legislature.* Berkeley: University of California, Bureau of Public Administration, 1937.

Lee, Eugene C., *The Presiding Officer and Rules Committee in Legislatures of the United States.* Berkeley: University of California, Bureau of Public Administration, 1953.

McHenry, Dean E., *A New Legislature for Modern California.* Los Angeles: Haynes Foundation, 1940.

Mangore Corporation, *The California Legislator.* A study made for the Committee on Compensation and Conflicts of Interest, Citizens Legislative Advisory Commission. Los Angeles: Mangore, 1958.

Staniford, Edward F., *Legislative Assistance.* Berkeley: University of California, Bureau of Public Administration, 1957.

Streamlining State Legislatures. Report of a Conference held at the University of California, Berkeley, Oct. 27-29, 1955.

Young, C. C. (ed.), *The Legislature of California—Its Membership, Procedure, and Work.* San Francisco: Commonwealth Club, 1943.

Seven

The Executive

Branch ··

CALIFORNIA HAS BEEN slowly modernizing its executive branch. Law and political processes have combined to make the position of governor a very important and powerful one. This is the result of fifty years of steady development. There yet remains much to do, however, if the governor is to be a chief executive in the style of the President of the United States or the executive head of a large business corporation. The constitution continues to provide for popular election of five other executive officers—secretary of state, controller, treasurer, attorney general, state superintendent of instruction—together with a lieutenant governor and an independent board of equalization. Each executive officer performs such functions as are designated by the constitution and statutes without much coordination with the others. The political parties do not provide the unofficial coordination that is needed, and in recent years at least one officer has belonged to a different party from the others.

Salaries and other perquisites have been improved recently, recognizing in part the enhanced status of the executive. In 1944 and 1946 salary figures of the state's executives were removed from the constitution and the legislature was directed to set salaries at figures not less than $10,000 a year for governor and $5,000 for other officers. The governor's salary is now $40,000.*

---

* The Attorney General receives $26,000, the Lieutenant Governor, Superintendent of Public Instruction, and Controller receive $20,000; the Treasurer and Secretary of State receive $19,500; and each member of the Board of Equalization receives $16,000 per year.

138

In addition he has an official mansion provided, although the present building is so old that it has been proposed that the governor be furnished a modern house rather than a museum.

THE GOVERNOR

What the Governor Does

Formal responsibilities of a governor include preparing the state's budget, preparing a program of legislation to guide the legislature, signing or vetoing bills adopted by the legislature, appointing numerous top state officers, maintaining general supervision over law enforcement, calling special sessions of the legislature if the needs of the state require such action, exercising clemency in appeals of persons convicted of a felony. He is broadly responsible to see that law is enforced and the welfare of the state and its citizens is protected.

Informally, the governor is a political leader and activities of this role take a large part of every governor's time. There are dinners to be attended, speeches to be made, bridges and buildings to be dedicated, conferences to be attended, and thousands of individuals and groups to be met and listened to. In his role as political leader the governor presents his policies to the voters, receives advice that shapes much of his policies, and seeks to project his own personality to the voters and to political leaders. The formal and the informal responsibilities are never distinctly separated. One role supports and determines the other. Both types of duties begin as soon as the governor is elected, even before he is sworn formally into office, and continue until his term ends.

When the successful candidate finds himself governor-elect of California, he is immediately faced with many responsible tasks. Elected on the first Tuesday in November, he must be prepared to face the legislature, elected at the same time, when it meets on the first Monday in the following January. Before the legislature organizes he must have his own program in shape to be presented by the executive's "spokesmen" in the legislature. Messages to the legislature must be prepared. Furthermore, governors have often exercised a behind-the-scenes influence in the selection of legislative officers. The incoming governor's most important duty is the preparation of the state's budget for the fiscal year beginning the next July 1. By law, the governor-elect is permitted access to the financial records of the state, and the civil servants in the finance department assist his finance director-designate to formulate the budget before he formally takes the oath of office as governor.

Executive Budget

The governor is required to submit a budget to the legislature each year. Under the legislative session plan adopted in 1946, meetings in even-numbered years are devoted chiefly to the budget, whereas meetings in odd-numbered years deal with the budget in addition to all other legislation.

The budget division of the Department of Finance, staffed by permanent civil service finance specialists, does the enormous job of developing the details of the annual budget, subject to policy directions from the governor. Each administrative department of the state government prepares an estimate of the money that it will need to pay salaries, purchase equipment, and meet the various expenses involved in carrying out the work assigned to it by existing laws. The Department of Finance receives the estimates from the departments, organizes them as a tentative budget, and conducts studies to determine how the departments may improve their administration and get along with less money than requested. The governor's budget basically comprises the estimates compiled by the Department of Finance from departmental proposals, although each governor has certain programs that he emphasizes and supports more strongly than others in his budget proposals. Estimates of the revenues from existing state taxes also have an important effect on the size of the state budget. If estimated revenues are likely to prove insufficient or the expenditures proposed by the governor are likely to exceed the estimated revenues under existing law, the governor is responsible for recommending changes in the revenue laws. If, as occurred between 1946 and 1952, there is a surplus of income over expenditures, the governor proposes a fiscal policy appropriate to that condition. In 1959, Governor Brown found it essential to recommend new taxes as well as to trim many departmental estimates in order to prepare an adequate budget.

The constitution directs the governor to submit to the legislature an appropriation bill to carry out the features of the state budget, together with an explanatory message. The bill is introduced into both houses by the respective chairmen of committees dealing with appropriations. The governor may send over supplements or amendments to his original bill at any time during the session. Until the governor's budget bill has been adopted, however, the legislature may not pass any other appropriation bills, except those for salaries, mileage (cost of legislators' travel to Sacramento), and expenses of the two houses, nor may it attach an appropriation clause or rider onto another bill.

Before the executive budget plan was adopted appropriations for the expenses of state government were made in a series of bills that originated with legislative committee chairmen. No one in the state government was responsible for comparing appropriations with an estimate of revenues. Also the only scrutiny of departmental requests for money was the political one made by committees of the legislature while the particular bill was before them. The entire process of appropriations was haphazard and uncoordinated. The struggle to develop a systematic budget system with the governor as the responsible head was begun about 1904 and culminated in the 1922 constitutional amendment. Governors and the Department of Finance have been engaged since then in improving the administrative processes of budgeting.

The Governor and Legislation

The constitution of 1879 specified very few of the governor's executive powers, but the most important directed him to recommend measures for the good of the state. Governors in recent years have made extensive use of this prerogative to urge the passage of certain bills, to protest others, or to pass on to the legislators information on a variety of matters concerning the state and its business. (See Chapter Six for further discussion of this.)

The governor may call the legislature into extraordinary session and may outline the subjects that may be legislated upon at the session. The constitution prohibits the consideration in extraordinary session of any legislation other than that contained in the governor's call, except to provide for the legislators' own expenses. During the period of economic distress in the 1930's and during the war period, the governors found an increased number of occasions to call special sessions. These ranged in length from two or three days to several weeks. Now that the legislature meets annually, there are fewer occasions to call special sessions, although some have been called simultaneously with budget sessions.

Whenever a bill has passed both houses of the legislature it must be laid before the governor. The constitution permits him ten days in which to consider the bill if the legislature is in session. If he signs it, it becomes law. If he does not sign it within the ten-day period, he may return it to the house in which it originated, together with a message outlining his objections, or he may retain the bill beyond the ten days and allow it automatically to pass into law. Most governors have followed the formal veto procedure, although a few have permitted some bills to pass without their signature. In the 1939 session, for example, Governor Olson permitted forty-five bills to go without his signature. Governors Richardson, Rolph, and Olson had difficulties with the 1923, 1933 and 1939 legislative sessions respectively. Richardson rejected more bills or parts of bills than has any other governor. Governor Rolph had more vetoes overridden by legislative majorities than any other governor. Governor Olson had a few vetoes over-ruled in each session. In 1959, Governor Brown had close relations with the legislature, hence the veto problem was at a minimum.

Before signing or vetoing most bills the governor receives a great deal of advice from his personal advisers, administrative departments, legislators, and persons interested in the defeat or passage of the measures. Political pressure upon him to influence his decision upon a controversial bill often becomes intense indeed. Telegrams and letters pour into the executive offices, and interested persons attempt to telephone or see the governor personally. Governors have a personal staff to shield them from some of this direct pressure upon their time and attention and to help channel the contacts with the public.

In the normal course of legislative action many bills are presented to the governor in the closing days of the session. In order that the governor may give intelligent attention to these bills, the constitution allows him, not ten days, but thirty days after the close of the legislative session in which to study the bills and sign or reject them. The refusal of the governor to sign one of these bills is known as a pocket veto. Most governors, even those who maintained a harmonious record with the legislature in session, have not hesitated to use the pocket veto liberally. Most pocket-vetoed measures are those of minor or local interest that do not have strong backing and are allowed to lie untouched while the governor devotes his time to the more urgent ones in the stack. The governor's veto power does not apply to constitutional amendments or to initiative statutes.

The Item Veto

California was one of the first states to permit the governor to veto individual items in an *appropriation* bill. In all states allowing the item veto (now four-fifths of the Union) the governor may eliminate one or more items altogether. California goes further, and permits him to reduce items below the figures voted by the legislature, according to his discretion. He has no authority to increase an appropriation. When the governor reduces or rejects an item, he is required to state his objections, and the rejected part becomes law only if the legislature overrides his veto. In going over the budget bill (the major appropriation bill of any legislative session) after the legislature has acted, for example, the governor may approve most of the items, completely reject some that the legislature may have added, and scale down items that the legislature has raised above the figure recommended in the governor's budget proposals. Consequently the item veto has given the governor the opportunity to take a strong lead in determining the state's fiscal policies. Two instances of the exercise of this veto by Governor Merriam throw light on the extent to which this power may be used. In the first, the legislature increased the appropriation for the Department of Industrial

Relations beyond that proposed in the governor's budget and earmarked a portion for certain activities. The governor eliminated the earmarked item and reduced the total appropriation. In the second, the governor vetoed the earmarking or limitation placed upon a part of the $48,000,000 relief bill, but directed that the total should stand undiminished. These uses of the veto power were upheld by the supreme court in contested cases.

The item veto has been used sparingly. As might be guessed, it has been used most when the governor's political strategy has been to make a record for economy and the legislature has been under pressure to spend. Most governors have sought to expand the state's programs and hence have had little reason to reduce the legislature's appropriations.

The Governor's Appointing Power

The courts have wisely said that the power to appoint subordinate officers was one of the most important executive powers. Most of the appointing power of California's governor is derived from statutes rather than from the constitution directly. For example, the constitution directs that there shall be a state board of education, but leaves the mode of selection to be determined by statute. The constitution authorizes the governor to appoint five members of the Public Utilities Commission, the sixteen members of the Regents of the University of California, the five members of the Fish and Game Commission. The governor also appoints the judges of the state Supreme Court and the district courts of appeal. Other executive and administrative offices are created by statute and the legislature determines whether the governor is to be allowed the patronage.

Among the important and high-salaried positions that the governor may fill are department heads such as directors of finance, agriculture, corrections, mental hygiene, veterans affairs, motor vehicles, natural resources, professional and vocational standards, public works, social welfare, alcoholic beverage control, and industrial relations. Among the officers with the title of division head, or the equivalent, serving at the pleasure of the governor are the state librarian and the building and loan commissioner. To a very considerable extent, the quality of a governor's record as a chief executive of the state is determined by the quality of appointments he makes to high administrative posts, and it is well that he have a relatively free hand in making selections.

Establishment of the state civil service for the administrative employees has removed from the governor the responsibility of selecting the thousands of technically trained persons who carry out the state's day to day work. He does, however, have the power to select the top policy-making and policy-implementing administrators.

The governor's appointing power is qualified in some instances by the requirement that the appointee must also receive approval of the state senate. Examples of such appointments are the insurance commissioner, seven members of the state Board of Health, and the ten members of the state Board of Education. The governor may not dismiss an officer appointed with the confirmation of the state senate without the approval of that body.

The governor's patronage has steadily grown with the creation of numerous boards and commissions to which he may appoint members. Some, like the veterans board and state racing commission, have extensive responsibilities set forth in legislation. Some, like the welfare commission, make rules and give advice. Many, typified by the numerous boards in the department of vocational standards, are licensing and regulating bodies. Still others, like Governor Brown's metropolitan study commission and the conference on mental health, are study groups created largely to advise upon a broad area of public policy.

Vacancies in superior and municipal court judgeships are filled by governor's appointment, as are vacancies on county boards of supervisors. Membership on district agricultural boards in numerous counties is determined by gubernatorial selection also.

The Governor and Law Enforcement

The governor is often referred to as the chief law-enforcement officer of the state. This position derives from the exercise of authority given him by numerous statutes. For example, he may require the attorney general or the district attorney in any county to inquire into the affairs of any private corporation. He may direct the attorney general to assist a district attorney in law enforcement. As the chief executive, the governor plays a prominent role in the extradition of persons in California charged with the commission of crimes in another state. After he has signed the papers allowing a person to be extradited, he may request the attorney general and the district attorney of the county in which the person is located to assist in carrying out the action. The governor is also the key officer in arranging for extradition from another state of persons charged with having violated California law and having escaped. California law-enforcement officers must apply to him to make the request to the governor of the other state for extradition.

In other fields of law enforcement the governor moves less directly, because law enforcement is traditionally a responsibility of local government. The governor has no state police force at his command (the state highway patrol is limited to law enforcement on the highways). The prestige of his office is such, however, that if he calls upon a law-enforcement officer to undertake certain responsibilities considerable attention is given to the request. If local law enforcement breaks down, the governor may call into action such state forces as the militia to enforce law and keep the peace.

Acts of Executive Clemency

One of the traditional powers of the governor is to exercise executive clemency toward persons convicted of a felony. Although he may not interfere with a court trial, he may grant a reprieve, commute a sentence, or pardon a convicted person if convinced that justice and mercy call for such an action. A full pardon by the governor restores all rights and privileges of which the person was deprived by conviction of a felony. When the governor grants executive clemency of any sort he must report the action to the next session of the legislature. Although the number of pardons, reprieves, or commutations of sentence is not large in any one year, the nature of this authority places a grave responsibility upon the governor. He must be guided not only by the laws that determine his authority, but also by the advice of judges, prison administrators, and high officers in correction administration.

The National Guard

The governor is commander in chief of the state militia and may call it to active duty in cases of emergency. He may consider that an emergency exists if local law-enforcement officials cannot cope with a riot or other civil disturbance, or if a flood, earthquake, or other catastrophe disrupts the normal activities of protecting persons and property. He may call out the militia at his own discretion or at the request of local mayors or sheriffs, or at the request of the President of the United States. In California the governor has seldom resorted to calling out the militia. One of the more recent occasions was in March, 1933, when Long Beach and the surrounding area were struck by a severe earthquake.

The traditional state militia has been reorganized and integrated with the National Guard, which has both state and federal connections. A National Guard Reserve has been organized to perform some of the traditional militia duties when the National Guard may be in national service. Many of the governor's military responsibilities are carried out by the adjutant general, an appointee of the governor.

Civil Defense

A modern responsibility of great importance that has been assigned to the governor is the headship of the civil defense organization of the state. This duty involves him in cooperation with the federal program and brings him into close relations with civil defense staffs and law-enforcement officers of the local governments within the state. A state civil defense organization has been set up within the governor's executive offices to plan and prepare for alerting and protecting the civil population in case of enemy military attack. The governor has authority to establish rules governing the declaration of an emergency in which the defense organization will be called into action and determining what warnings will be given. He also has the power to authorize local defense organizations to plan and stage practice alerts and drills.

Who Gets Elected?

There are few constitutional limitations upon the people's choice of a governor. He must be a citizen, at least twenty-five years of age, and must have resided in the state for at least five years. Not many of the governors have been native sons, but most have been seasoned veterans of California politics. Although the numerous and arduous administrative duties that fall to the governor today make the selection of younger men desirable, recent governors have been well beyond the constitutional age minimum. Governors have come to their duties equipped with a variety of experience. Hiram Johnson was the exception: the governorship was his first major office; his reputation had been won as a special prosecutor in the San Francisco graft trials. William D. Stephens, Johnson's successor, had been in Congress for six years before his appointment to the lieutenant governorship in 1916. He became governor when Johnson resigned to go to the United States Senate. Friend W. Richardson had had a considerable career in state politics, first as state printer and then as state treasurer. C. C. Young (1927-1931) and Frank F. Merriam (1934-1939) had somewhat similar careers of officeholding. Both began their state careers as assemblymen—Young from Berkeley, Merriam from Long Beach. Each became speaker. The final preparation for each was the lieutenant governorship. Both men were thoroughly skilled in legislative affairs and knew the capitol well before assuming the chief executive's duties. James Rolph, Jr., had been mayor of San Francisco for nineteen years previous to his election in 1930. Culbert L. Olson, the first Democrat to hold the office since James Budd's administration (1895-1899) served a term in the state senate prior to winning the governorship. Both Olson and Merriam had held elective office in other states before coming to California, the former in Utah, the latter in Iowa. Earl Warren was elected to the governor's office in 1942, after a long and successful period as district attorney in Alameda County and one term (1939-1943) as attorney general. Goodwin Knight served as judge of the superior court in Los Angeles County and as lieutenant governor for two terms. He became governor when Warren resigned to accept the position of Chief Justice of the United States Supreme Court, and was re-elected for a full term in 1954. Edmund G. Brown became governor in 1958 after serving two terms as attorney general and several as district attorney of San Francisco.

Few California governors have been re-elected. Johnson and Warren have been the only ones to be returned for additional four-year terms, and Warren was the only one re-elected twice. In 1946 he was re-elected at the primary election by securing the nomination of both major parties. A proposal to limit governors to two terms was defeated by the voters in 1954 in connection with a proposal to lengthen legislators' terms.

OTHER EXECUTIVE OFFICES

Succession to the Governorship

In this era when chief officials are expected to travel widely by every modern vehicle in performance of public duties, and the destruction of cities by nuclear attack is a topic of discussion in an uneasy world, many people have given sober thought to determining how an orderly succession in the headship of the state government could be determined. The position of lieutenant governor was created originally to ensure that an elected official would be available to act if the governor were incapacitated. When the governor of Oregon and a group of high state officials perished in a single airplane crash, it was recognized that more detailed provision for succession was required. California adopted two constitutional amendments in 1946 and 1948 which spelled out the order of succession to the governorship in case of great emergency. If the offices of governor and lieutenant both became vacant, the president pro tempore of the state senate, the speaker of the assembly, the secretary of state, the attorney general, the treasurer, and the controller succeed in that order to the chief position. In 1959, the legislature authorized the governor to designate seven citizens who succeed, in turns, if the constitutional officers were unavailable in time of great emergency.

Lieutenant Governor

The reason for creating the office of lieutenant governor originally was to have a state-wide elected officer who could act if the elected governor was unable to perform the duties of his office. Such inability might arise from death or resignation, or from absence from the state. Two California governors have died in office and five have resigned.

On a number of occasions the governor leaves the state for a short time—to attend a meeting of the Governor's Conference, transact state business in Washington, D.C., attend a presidential nominating convention, or make political speeches for his party. When he leaves, the lieutenant governor becomes the acting chief executive until he returns. Usually an informal understanding between the two men determines what official activities the lieutenant governor shall undertake and how he will perform them as acting governor. Normally the activities are limited: he may sign an application for extradition, and keep routine engagements. A somewhat unusual proceeding was Lieutenant Governor Knight's signing of legislative bills with Governor Warren's approval during the absence of the latter in 1952.

A second function that the lieutenant governor has had since 1850 is that of presiding over the state senate when that body is in session. That activity is not connected with the executive work of the state government, but it does give the lieutenant governor a reason for being at the state capitol periodically, and it keeps him prominently active in politics. Such influence as the lieutenant governor exerts upon legislation in the senate depends largely upon his personal popularity and party standing. In a formal sense he has little to do with the legislative process other than to rule upon points of parliamentary law and to vote in case there is a tie in the senate voting. Several lieutenant governors have come to their office after several years service in the legislature; and in such instances they have wielded considerable influence informally. Lieutenant Governor Glenn M. Anderson served several terms in the assembly.

In recent years there has been a tendency to place the lieutenant governor on numerous state boards and commissions, thus bringing him more into some of the administrative activities. He is an ex officio member of the Regents of the University of California, and, at present, holds membership in the California toll-bridge authority and the state lands commission. An important function of the latter body is to determine oil-drilling leases on state-owned tidelands. The 1926 constitutional amendment which established the procedure for apportioning seats in the legislature made the lieutenant governor chairman of the commission that is to undertake reapportionment if the legislature should fail to do so.

Few lieutenant governors have had the opportunity to rise to the governorship. Stephens followed Johnson when the latter was elected United States Senator, Merriam was elevated upon the death of James Rolph, Jr., and Goodwin Knight moved up when Earl Warren was appointed Chief Justice of the United States Supreme Court. C. C. Young stepped from the lower office to the higher by election. The usual practice has been for a lieutenant governor to serve one term and then give way to someone else.

Although governors and their lieutenant governors have usually been of the same party in this state, they have not always been close personally, nor have they usually worked in close cooperation. Occasionally there has been real political rivalry. The notable example of close cooperation, however, was that of Hiram Johnson and John M. Eshleman (1910-1914).

Attorney General

Second only to the governor in public prominence is the attorney general. A 1934 constitutional amendment which was proposed by district attorneys and law-enforcement officers throughout the state added to the traditional duties and prerogatives of the attorney general to make the office really the head of the law-enforcement system of the state, in both civil and criminal matters. As the director of the Department of Justice he heads a criminal law enforcement program which includes the division of criminal identification and investigation and the division of narcotic enforcement. Under the 1934 amendment he is required to assist and to supervise the work of the district attorneys. If either the district attorney or the sheriff of a county is away or unable to cope with a situation, the attorney general may appoint someone to take over the officer's duties during the crisis. It was not intended that the attorney general should interfere with the locally elected officers, but that he should be given authority to aid them and to strengthen the statewide system of law enforcement. The new powers have very seldom been employed; the attorney general has worked in close cooperation with the local enforcement officials.

One civil duty that requires a large amount of work is that of advising executive officers, the legislature, administrative departments and boards, and district attorneys of the various counties regarding their legal authority and liabilities. The attorney general passes upon the legality of proceedings for all state bond issues and upon state contracts. His deputies appear in courts ranging from a justice court to a United States Supreme Court to represent the state or its officials when they are parties to suits involving them in their official capacities. Hearings before such state agencies as the medical board and the personnel board also require the services of the attorney general's staff. Many of the cases in courts involve the state's interest in public lands and in the collection of contested taxes. The attorney general is expected to be constantly alert to protect the interests of the state. In discharging his duty he must occasionally decide to start a suit against large and powerful interests which will fight back in both the courts and in political campaigns.

Stanley Mosk was elected in 1958. Previously he had been superior court judge in Los Angeles. At one time he was secretary to Governor Olson.

State Controller

The controller has one of the largest responsibilities in the state government, yet this office seldom figures in the limelight of publicity. Part of this responsibility arises from the basic nature of the office, part from the fact that the controller serves as a member of the Board of Control and the Board of Equalization. This officer stands at the gate of the state treasury, so to speak. Checks for salaries and supplies and for services rendered the state can be issued only if the controller draws warrants authorizing the payments. He must be satisfied that money has been appropriated by the legislature for these things and that the proposed payments are in line with the requirements laid down by the legislature. Sometimes the exercise of this responsibility brings him into conflict with departments of the state government, and on such occasions the disagreement is taken to the courts for a decision. Only the courts may overrule the controller; or the legislature may alter his instructions.

Central control accounts for all state funds and agencies are maintained in the controller's office. The detailed accounts are maintained in the agencies concerned, but the controller keeps records in order to be certain that authorizations for payments are in order and should be allowed. He also prepares and publishes figures on county, city, and special-district financial transactions for the information of the public. The controller is also responsible for enforcing tax collections for the state government. He supervises collection of the inheritance and gift taxes, and enforces collection of the motor fuel and motor vehicle transportation taxes, and the state tax on insurance companies and on petroleum and gas assessments.

Alan Cranston, who was elected controller in 1958, had not previously held state office although he had been active in state politics for a number of years prior to being a candidate.

Treasurer

The state treasurer receives the money collected by the controller, the franchise tax commissioner, the Board of Equalization, and others; he keeps custody of the funds, and pays out the money when authorized to do so by warrants from the controller. Also when the state has a bond issue the treasurer arranges for the sale of the bonds and administers the payment of interest and the final redemption. Most of the treasurer's work is accomplished through banks; the state keeps accounts in numerous banks throughout the state. He is required to keep an account of all money received and paid out, and to keep separate accounts of the many funds that have been established by law. Although this is a responsible office, many people question whether it should really be an elective one. Policies controlling the activities of this office are fixed in considerable detail by the legislature to ensure honesty in the handling of state money.

Bert A. Betts, who was elected treasurer in 1958, had not previously held office. He won the position in the first two-party contest held in several years.

Secretary of State

In California the office of secretary of state is a clerical and custodial one, although at least two of its activities are of great interest to certain groups. One of these is the processing of the official papers required for a business to incorporate as a company under the laws of California. Whenever a corporation is formed, changed, or dissolved, a proper certificate must be filed with this office. Efficient handling of these papers is important to the business community. The department collects several hundred thousand dollars per year in fees for these services.

A second important activity of the secretary of state is that of the state's chief election administrator. All petitions for statewide initiative, referendum, and recall proposals must be filed with him. He also prepares the ballot for each state election, determining the place assigned to each constitutional amendment and each initiative and referendum proposition. Because of this exercise of discretion, the secretary of state may be subject to considerable persuasion by groups that desire to have a measure in which they are interested given Number 1, 2, 7, or some other favored number. Many do not wish to draw Number 13! Purchasing the official ballot paper and supplying it to county election officers is another responsible job. After the election, the secretary of state canvasses the returns and officially declares the result. When there is a close contest the actual result may not be known until this canvass is completed.

Among the more routine tasks of the secretary of state is included the custody of all legislation passed by the legislature, the official version of the state constitution, oaths of office of state officials, certificates showing incorporation of cities and annexation of territories to them, and city and county charters and their amendments. He also has charge of the Great Seal of the state, which must be affixed to all official documents.

Secretary of State Frank M. Jordan was elected to the office first in 1942 and has served continuously since. For many years he was chief deputy to his father, Frank C. Jordan, who was secretary of state from 1906 until his death in 1940.

AN ELECTED BOARD

Board of Equalization

The state Board of Equalization is one of the few multiheaded agencies created by the state constitution. Basically this is a tax board, although between 1933 and 1954 it also administered the liquor-regulation work of the state—a function which plunged it into the hottest glare of publicity. Its original function was to prepare rules for assessment of property for taxation, and to equalize the valuation of taxable property so that there would be some semblance of uniformity throughout the state. Most evaluation work, however, is done at the county level by elected county tax assessors. The board also was designed to assess certain businesses, such as insurance companies, that are subject to state taxes, and others, such as railroads, whose operations are statewide and whose property is subject to taxes in several counties.

The board also has tax-collection duties in connection with the motor vehicle fuel tax and motor transportation tax. This requires a staff of field investigators and auditors and a system of records. When the state adopted a retail sales tax in 1933 the legislature assigned the collection and enforcement work to the board of equalization. Administration of the sales and use taxes likewise requires a field investigation and auditing staff to check with the thousands of retail merchants in the state who collect the tax with their sales and pay over the collection to the state. The board determines the rules that control the enforcement of the tax—that is, who pays and under what conditions. The board also administers a uniform sales tax for counties and cities when a county and the cities within it agree to a common plan.

Four members of the board are elected from districts, the boundaries of which are determined by the legislature. Their term is four years. The state controller serves ex officio as the fifth member. Included in the board's permanent civil servant staff at Sacramento are outstanding specialists in taxation and property evaluation. Numerous proposals have been made in recent years to revamp the board and to reassign its functions, particularly those involving tax collection, to other departments.

Further Reading

Bell, James R., "The Executive Office of California Governor under Earl Warren, 1943-1953." Unpublished Ph.D. dissertation, University of California, 1956.

Book of the States. Chicago: Council of State Governments. Published biennially with supplements. See appropriate sections relative to each elected state officer.

California. Senate Interim Committee on Governmental Organization, Organization of the Executive Branch of State Government. Sacramento, 1958.

Isom, Warren R., "The Office of Lieutenant Governor in the States," American Political Science Review, 32 (October 1938), 921-926.

Lipson, Leslie, The American Governor: From Figurehead to Leader. Chicago: University of Chicago Press, 1939.

————, "The Executive Branch in the New State Constitutions," Public Administration Review, 9 (Winter 1949), 11-21.

Eight | State Administrative Departments and Activities

STATE SERVICES and activities are numerous and varied, and reach into every part of the state. The state not only carries out its work through state employees of various administrative departments but also through local districts and county departments that are partly financed from state funds and controlled by state law. This chapter will be concerned chiefly with the work of state administrative departments.

At present the departments that provide service functions employ the largest number of state workers and spend the largest share of the state's annual budget. They touch the interests of every person within the state, directly or indirectly. The Department of Mental Hygiene and Department of Employment are examples of organizations that provide some type of service directly to individuals. Examples of agencies that provide services less directly but to all persons in the state are the division of highways in the Department of Public Works which designs, constructs, and maintains our highways; the division of beaches and parks in the Department of Natural Resources that protects our major recreational spots; and the division of forestry that protects our timber resources. The Department of Education carries out a host of activities to assist the public schools which are administered by the school districts at the local level.

A considerable number of other administrative activities involve enforcing laws and standards; hence they are known as *regulatory* functions. These include the investigating and court-trial work of the attorney general and his staff, the licensing and permit-issuing duties of the various boards of examiners in the Department of Vocational and Professional Standards, and the activities of inspectors in the Department of Agriculture and the Department of Public Health. This group of functions also includes the work of the utilities commission, the insurance commissioner and the commissioner of banks, and many others.

A third group of activities may be classified as *staff and housekeeping* functions. They contribute to the servicing, control, and management of the state government. Examples include: the State Personnel Board, the Controller, Department of Finance, and the treasurer's office.

SELECTED ACTIVITIES

Administrative activities of the state of California are so extensive and varied that only brief discussion of selected ones can be undertaken. Many are of recent origin. All affect the people of the state.

Roads and Highways

The Department of Public Works is the largest in the state administrative organization. The 1959-60 executive budget authorized it to employ more than 5,300 employees to assist in designing and supervising construction of state buildings, to purchase land for construction projects that totaled a quarter of a billion dollars, and to design and construct highway and bridge projects costing slightly more than 297 million dollars. This department has three main divisions that perform specialized tasks. The division of architecture supervises the design and construction of state buildings. The division of highways, which is much the largest of the three divisions, designs and constructs highways and bridges; a special unit within it obtains the land necessary for rights-of-way over which highways are routed. This unit operates much as a very large real estate agency for the state government. The third division is that of San Francisco Bay Toll

Crossings which is assigned the study of additional crossings of that waterway.

California's vast highway system is generally rated to be one of the best in the nation, but the whole activity has been developed during the lifetime of persons now living. The first state road in California, built in 1865, was one leading to Yosemite, but the state highway system dates only from 1902. Development of the automobile and settlement of the state by large numbers of people who have arrived in succeeding waves of migration since 1910 have combined to make necessary the construction of a highway system that reaches into all parts of the state. Agreement that the system should be statewide in extent produced the decision that the main task of locating, designing, constructing, and maintaining the major routes should be given to the state rather than to counties or any other local government. The resulting system produced important consequences for the economy of the state. Farmers in remote areas have been able to get their produce to the main rail and water transportation centers, mountain and beach scenic spots have been made accessible to tourists and residents, and our metropolitan areas have yet another important transportation link between them. It is also now concerned with caring for the needs of the vast automobile and truck traffic of the metropolitan areas of San Francisco Bay, Los Angeles, and San Diego.

Since 1946 the state has become increasingly concerned with constructing freeways to handle the volume of traffic in the metropolitan areas and their adjacent regions. The cost of such projects is usually beyond the ability of local governments to finance; also the problem of metropolitan traffic has come to be more than a local problem.

At one time travelers on state roads had to pay tolls to private bridge and ferryboat companies in order to cross certain rivers or bays. As the state highway system developed, it was decided that the best policy in the public interest would be for the state to take over the construction and operation of bridges. Most bridges on the state highway system are free of charge, but a few extremely expensive ones like the ones crossing San Francisco Bay are operated as publicly owned toll bridges. The money

California Highway Patrol enforces traffic laws. The highway patrol operates throughout the state to enforce state motor vehicle laws. It is not a general police force. Courtesy, California Highway Patrol.

collected is used to repay that borrowed for the construction and to pay maintenance costs.

Motor-Vehicle Regulation

Almost as soon as automobiles appeared on the roads in California, a policy was worked out to determine the division of responsibilities between state and local governments for their regulation. It was agreed that the state should license drivers and machines and that licenses should be a prerequisite for operating a vehicle legally upon any street, road, or highway. Local police were to aid in enforcing this requirement as well as to enforce state and local traffic laws. Licenses are issued by state inspectors in accordance with standards set by the state. This part of automobile regulation is carried on by the Department of Motor Vehicles.

Several years after licensing was established the state undertook to enforce traffic safety laws on the highways. City police perform traffic regulation in addition to their traditional law-enforcement duties. However, much traffic is truly statewide. Early attempts at traffic regulation by local governments demonstrated that there was a lack of uniformity in enforcing the laws. All of this caused motorists' organizations and the public to look for some other form of traffic-law enforcement. For a time the idea of a general state police force was discussed, but it was dropped. Local law-enforcement departments were opposed to having such a force, and many powerful groups were afraid that the development of a state police organization would result in shifting the real control of general law enforcement away from the local governments, where it had been close to the people. Interest in automobile regulation produced the state highway patrol which is limited to enforcing the motor-vehicle laws and to keeping the peace along the state highways. It operates chiefly in the country areas, although it does patrol to a limited extent along state highways or freeways within cities. The highway patrol, which has a force of approximately 3,400, is organized as a separate department of the state government.

Policing and Detection

A few specialized law enforcement activities are performed by the state although general law enforcement is a function of cities and counties. A special narcotics division of the Department of Justice investigates the transportation and sale of narcotics and assists federal and local officers in making arrests. Food and drug inspectors of the Department of Health investigate the processing of food and drugs to prevent the manufacture and sale of impure commodities. Much of the work involves laboratory testing. Again, the work is in most cases conducted cooperatively with federal and local officers.

The crime laboratory, fingerprint files, and police records maintained by the State Department of Justice, supplement and strengthen local general law enforcement programs. Fingerprints and other records in the state's collection are contributed by local police and sheriffs' departments and are made available to any local department upon request. The state also maintains a police teletype system which connects several of the main population centers of the state. Over this communications system emergency messages and information regarding wanted criminals are dispatched regularly. These facilities were organized at the request of local law-enforcement officers and responsibility to determine the operating policies of the state organization is vested in a board of governors selected by police departments and sheriffs. The program is a cooperative effort to improve law enforcement throughout the state.

Prisons and Correctional Institutions

Traditionally the state government provides prisons to hold those who have been convicted of serious violations of law and who have been sentenced to long terms of servitude. The jails maintained by cities and counties are for the retention of prisoners awaiting court trial and of persons convicted of less serious breaches of law, whose terms are less than a year. For many years the two prisons at San Quentin, near San Francisco, and Folsom, near Sacramento, were California's penitentiaries. Growth of the state's population and development of new centers of population in southern California and elsewhere have made it necessary for the state to develop a number of penal and correctional institutions in various parts of the state as well as new ideas of penal administration. The two original prisons are now for the custody of hardened criminals. Included among the new penal institutions is a women's prison at Chino, in San Bernardino County. New ideas of penal administration are being demonstrated in new types of institutions. One near Chino is for men prisoners whose conduct indicates that high stone walls, cells, and armed guards will not be necessary. This "minimum security" institution has only wire fences surrounding dormitories and work fields. At Soledad and at Tracy are "medium-security" prisons where prisoners are given opportunities to work, under guard, and to rehabilitate themselves to rejoin society. Another special institution is the California Men's Colony near San Luis Obispo, where old men who are not dangerous prisoners are kept. A new medical facility near Vacaville cares for inmates who are mentally ill, are sex offenders, or have some serious disease. All

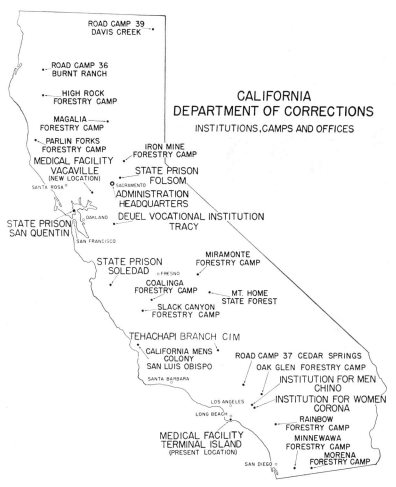

California state correctional institutions and camps. The state's correctional institutions range from maximum-security prisons to forest camps where prisoners work with a minimum of guarding. Courtesy, State Department of Corrections.

of these institutions for adult offenders are under the administration of the Department of Corrections.

Many who have been convicted of offenses may not be sentenced by the court to serve a prison term, or they may receive a relatively short assignment to a correctional institution and then be placed on parole. Adult men who have been placed in one of the state's penal institutions come under the supervision of the Adult Authority. This body may fix the term of imprisonment and

Visiting day at Chino Institution for Men. At this correctional institution many of the traditional features of a prison are absent, thus facilitating the return of the individual to normal society. Courtesy, State Department of Corrections.

set the punishment for male prisoners. The emphasis is upon studying the individual case and shaping penalties according to the offense and the individual's record. The Adult Authority may determine that a prisoner is eligible for a parole or it may revoke the privilege if, after parole is given, his conduct is bad. Every effort is made by the authority to rehabilitate those who will demonstrate by their conduct that they can benefit by careful, personal treatment.

The Youth Authority has the responsibility for classifying and assigning youthful offenders to correctional programs, conducting rehabilitation work, and administering the paroles of this group. It also advises the judges, county probation officers, and local law-enforcement officers on juvenile work. A considerable portion of the Youth Authority's work is to operate a number of institutions of various types. Reception and assignment of boys and girls is done at two regional centers: the northern one near Sacramento, the southern one at Norwalk in the Los Angeles

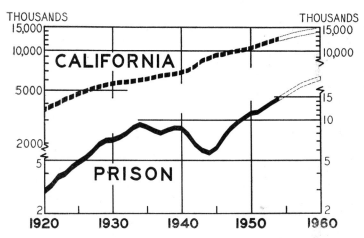

Comparison of state and prison population since 1920. As the state's population has risen, the number of persons in correctional institutions has risen, except during World War II. Courtesy, State Department of Corrections.

area. Three forestry camps are operated for boys between 17 and 21, where they may do useful work building fire breaks, trails and roads, while under the jurisdiction of the authority. A correctional school for young boys is maintained in the mountains of Calaveras County; and one for boys of an older age group is located at Whittier. A third boys' school is at Paso Robles. The Preston School of Industry, in Amador County, is for boys 16 to 21 years old. Correctional schools for girls are located near Santa Rosa and Ventura.

Care of the Sick

Public hospital policy makes distinction between state and county responsibilities for hospitals that is similar to the division discussed previously in prison and correctional work. General medical care (for those who cannot afford to finance their own care) is the responsibility of county governments; the state undertakes only more specialized types of hospital service.

At the present time the state of California concentrates attention upon caring for the mentally ill and mentally defective. The department of mental hygiene operates eight hospitals, located in various parts of the state, to care for mentally ill persons who have been assigned to a hospital by courts that are responsible for making such decisions. It also maintains three separate hospitals for mentally defective persons, and two additional institutions that accept both types of persons. The average population of these hospitals was about 46,000 patients in 1947-48 and it was estimated that in a short time the total patient load would be nearly 50,000. The Department of Mental Hygiene and its hospitals employ 13,516 persons, including psychiatrists, nurses, kitchen workers, and others to administer the program, which costs approximately $65 million a year. In addition to the hospitals, the department supports a number of mental hygiene outpatient clinics to provide treatment for persons who do not need hospital care and who may be prevented from becoming hospital cases.

To encourage local governments to provide general hospital services the state helps finance construction of hospitals that will be administered by local governments, including hospital districts. It may provide one-third of the construction cost, another third is provided by the federal government, and the remaining third is financed by the local government. State funds have been limited for this program, however. For many years California has also assisted counties to construct tuberculosis hospitals separate from general public hospitals and conforming to state standards for the care of persons afflicted with that disease.

Recreation

The state, as well as local governments, is extensively involved in providing facilities for public recreation. However, some effort has been made to draw a distinction between types of recreation facilities that will be provided by the state and those provided by local government. Cities operate various types of parks, golf courses, swimming pools, and playgrounds. Counties generally maintain rural parks and picnic sites; some large counties also provide beaches, golf courses, and other facilities. The state has devoted its funds to three types of projects. One type consists of state parks in the mountains and at the beaches, where people may camp and enjoy a short holiday. Several state parks have also been set up to preserve such natural beauty spots as redwood groves. A second type of project has been the purchase of beaches in order to preserve these natural recreation areas for public use. Many of these beach areas have not yet been developed; a few are leased to local governments which provide life guards and other services. A third type of state project is to purchase and preserve houses and landmarks that are associated with state and local history. Examples of this include Sutter's Fort in Sacramento and Sutter's Mill at Colma, where gold was first discovered. Many of these places are visited by thousands of vacationers every year.

Education

The state has been the keystone in the arch of public education in California since 1850. Conduct of education at the elementary and high-school level is the responsibility of local school districts governed by locally elected school boards. A large portion of the money that finances these schools is provided by state taxation, however, and large sums of state money have been loaned and granted to districts for school construction. School building construction must conform to state standards of safety. Teachers and school administrators must possess state credentials which are granted only after applicants have satisfied state standards of education and professional training. Local school districts select the teachers, determine what shall be taught, and provide the books and equipment used in the schools.

The State Department of Education, headed by the elected state superintendent of public instruction, stands at the top of the public-school organization in California. It apportions state school money as directed by state law, grants credentials to teachers, reviews and approves textbooks, advises the local school administration, and stands as the principal adviser to the governor and the legislature on matters requiring legislation. The state superintendent is assisted in a number of policy-determining matters by the state Board of Education, which is appointed by the governor. In addition, the board exercises a number of important duties given it by law, one of which is to act as the governing body for the eleven state colleges and the California Polytechnic School.

The state colleges, situated at San Diego, Long Beach, Los Angeles (two), Fullerton, Fresno, San Jose, San Francisco, Hayward, Sacramento, Chico, and Arcata, were originally established for the education of teachers. In recent years their programs have been expanded to provide a variety of subjects and these schools have become regional colleges. The California Polytechnic School at San Luis Obispo with branches at Pomona and San Dimas, offers agricultural and technical training at the college level. The state colleges are financed almost entirely from the state budget.

University education comes under the Board of Regents of the University of California. For many years, the university has not only provided a distinguished center of learning but it has made an impact upon every section of the state. Starting with one campus, at Berkeley, the university has expanded since 1868 to comprise seven campuses: Berkeley, Los Angeles, Davis, San Francisco (medical), La Jolla-San Diego, Santa Barbara and Riverside. Two new ones are planned. University extension conducts adult education activities throughout the state. Agriculture extension and the agriculture experiment station have worked in every part of the state. Under contracts with the Atomic Energy Commission, the university has administered physical science research programs at Berkeley, Los Angeles and Livermore, and at the huge Los Alamos station in New Mexico.

In support of education generally is the state library at Sacramento. The library represents one of the important collections of books, documents, newspapers, and similar materials in the state. It serves state departments and members of the legislature in Sacramento, and maintains a loan service to county libraries throughout the state. This loan service has long been an important element in strengthening the educational resources of the smaller and more rural counties.

Regulation of Utilities and Occupations

Certain types of business activities which offer essential services under near-monopoly conditions, although owned by private stockholders and companies, are of special importance to the public interest. Not every enterpriser who might wish to do so can be allowed to go into these businesses. Also their nature is such that direct competition in the market is reduced and hence the traditional determinants of prices do not operate upon them. It has been found desirable to set the rates which these businesses may charge and to regulate their activities. These are generally referred to as *public utilities,* a group that includes railroad, electric-power, gas, water-supply, and telephone companies. Regulation of public utility businesses within the state of California has been given to the state Public Utilities Commission, composed of five commissioners appointed by the governor. The commission employs a staff of rate experts and other specialists to assist in determining rates and regulations.

Licensing of corporations and individuals that engage in businesses other than utilities is a form of government regulation that also has come to be widely adopted in the United States. No one may undertake an activity that is so regulated unless he obtains a license. In order to get a license the individual or company must meet certain tests or conditions which relate to ability to conduct the type of activity. Licensing, as discussed here, does not extend to setting prices or rates. After a license has been granted, it may be revoked if the person or company violates the regulations attached to it. Attempting to operate without a license becomes a punishable offense in itself.

California has adopted the licensing method to control the practice of several occupations and trades, including those of doctors, dentists, chiropractors, osteopaths, morticians, building contractors, real estate brokers, and beauty operators. Attorneys come under a comparable regulation. To obtain a license for one of these occupations, a person must apply to a state licensing board and must show that he has achieved the required education and training and that he has a knowledge of the state law and regulations that apply to his particular work. The regulations seek to establish standards of proper conduct so that the public who come to a licensed person can be assured that they are being served by a person who is qualified by knowledge and ethics to serve them properly. A medical practitioner, for example, may have his license revoked by the state medical board if he prescribes drugs improperly, splits fees with persons who refer patients to him, commits immoral acts, or becomes incompetent and neglectful in the practice of his work. Most licensed professions and occupations have sought state regulation in order to eliminate unqualified or unscrupulous persons who have endeavored to pass themselves off on a trusting public.

Agriculture

Agriculture has supplied a major portion of this state's wealth since the beginning of statehood. Agricultural production has been extremely diversified. In the central valleys one finds wheat, barley, and oat crops, wine grapes and table grapes, fruit, and vegetables. Cotton production in the San Joaquin Valley places California ahead of many states of the Deep South in this crop. Large-scale dairy farming is found in many sections of the state. The oranges and lemons of southern California have been known throughout the world, and the early melons and vegetables of the Imperial Valley go to markets throughout the country. In the coastal areas are beans, sugar beets, and walnuts. Apples are produced at higher elevations and in coastal areas. The vineyards and fruit orchards in the Sonoma valley and adjacent areas have long been prominent in the agricultural economy of the state. With such a diversified and highly productive agricultural activity, California has been understandably interested in supporting agricultural research, market analysis, standardization of weights and measures, eradication of plant diseases and pests, and improvement of farming methods and marketing activities. The state's Department of Agriculture employs more than 1,900 people and spends a budget of more than $15 million per year. The activities of the department are organized into three major divisions: plant industry, animal husbandry, and marketing. Eradication of plant diseases and pests that threaten the state's crops is a continuing major concern of the state Department of Agriculture. One of these activities is known to every motorist who has driven into the state. At the state border, fruit and vegetable inspectors from the Bureau of Plant Quarantine inspect any agricultural produce that a motorist may be bringing into California. This is to prevent the spread of plant diseases and pests that might attack crops.

Milk produced within the state for human consumption must be processed in accordance with state agricultural standards regarding sanitation and quality before it may be sold. State milk regulation has been established to ensure a high standard throughout the state and to reduce the necessity of numerous and uneven local regulations. In addition to establishing sanitation standards, the state establishes prices that may be charged for milk. This is to prevent "price wars," which may result in the reduction of quality. State milk inspectors check dairies and milk-handling and -processing establishments. In some cases the state has authorized city and county inspectors in place of state inspectors to enforce the state standards.

Meat prepared for sale within the state comes under regulation and inspection by state inspectors in the Department of Agriculture. A statewide enforcement organization has replaced local inspection. Cities may, however, regulate the sanitary conditions in stores selling meat and milk in order to give added protection to the health of their citizens.

An important protection both to the honest farmer and produce merchant as well as to the consumer is the enforcement of standards of weights and measures. Packages and containers for measuring and selling fruits and vegetables must have standard dimensions; otherwise it is extremely difficult for the merchant or the purchaser to determine whether he is getting his money's worth in a purchase. Unless recognizable standards are maintained, it is difficult to determine adequate prices for boxes of oranges or crates of berries, or even to determine what are first-grade apples or peaches.

Administration of many programs of interest to agriculture involves cooperation between three levels of government and the farmer. Much of the work of the California Department of Agriculture is done in cooperation with the federal agriculture program, although the federal work figures most prominently in research activities. At the county-government level is the county agent or agricultural commissioner. This officer is paid partly from local funds and partly from state and federal funds. He is engaged directly in helping the farmers of his county to obtain information and advice regarding every variety of farming problem. He is responsible for advising farmers about improved methods of farming, of improvements in seed, animal-husbandry methods, and a great variety of other matters. This is literally grass-roots administration.

ADMINISTRATIVE ORGANIZATION

The Field Services

Although Sacramento is the capital of the state, only the headquarters part of the state's administration is conducted there. The governor and other elected executive officers and most appointive administration heads have their principal offices at Sacramento, although facilities are also provided in San Francisco and Los Angeles. The main job of supervising and directing the state's work is performed in Sacramento, but most administrative departments have found it essential to set up many district and regional offices. Thus the activities of the state are brought closer to the people. Some cities of the state, such as San Francisco, Los Angeles, Fresno, and San Diego, have become almost branch capitals for state administration. State office buildings have been erected in each of those cities to house state activities. Many departments have their own field offices arranged in other buildings to suit the convenience of conducting their departmental work. Many such buildings are owned by the state, although much office space is rented in privately owned buildings.

To make sure that these *field offices*, as they are called, will not become "outposts" out of touch with the policies and directions of the department's headquarters in Sacramento, many kinds of communications systems have been set up. Mail, frequent telephone calls, and a teletype system connecting state office centers in most of the major cities with headquarters in Sacramento provide formal means for communication. Top administrators find it necessary to visit field offices frequently and to bring field office key people to Sacramento for conferences. It has become necessary also to appoint high caliber administrators to head field offices and to give those administrators authority to decide many problems without referring every detail to headquarters in Sacramento. State business today is big business!

Departments

Most of the administrative activities of the state government and the employees who perform them are grouped into departments. From the discussion in previous pages, it will be noted that one basis for distinguishing one department from another is that of *function*. In other words, all activities relating to agriculture are grouped in the Department of Agriculture, and all those relating primarily to health are grouped in the Department of Health. Furthermore, the departments are subdivided into lesser units, known as divisions and bureaus, on a sub-functional basis. For example, the Department of Agriculture has within it a Division of Marketing, which in turn is divided into bureaus of markets, market news, agricultural statistics, fruit and vegetable standards, and weights and measures. In general this represents an effort to group like activities requiring the skills to perform in the same administrative package. In many instances, though, organization can be explained by observing that all activities which serve a particular public or set of "customers" have been grouped together.

The present pattern of state administrative organization in California is the result of numerous reorganization efforts that began in 1918. Previously the state administrative organization was composed of hundreds of independent offices and units. Each unit competed with the others for funds, and there was often much overlapping of activities. It was an expensive and inefficient situation. Every governor since 1918 has caused some reorganization and several legislative interim committees have pursuaded the legislature to approve reorganization plans that grouped related activities together and produced a more rational organization.

Coordination

State administration has moved slowly from the loose collection of miscellaneous offices, bureaus, and boards that characterized it in 1900, to a more nearly coordinated organization with a chief executive—the governor—who could direct heads of the major units and produce administrative teamwork. Department heads are appointed by the governor and are responsible to him for the conduct of their departments. For example, the governor may instruct the director of the Department of Health and the director of the Department of Agriculture to work together to solve a common problem. Much of the governor's duties involves keeping himself informed about the progress of the state's administration. He does this partly by dealing directly with department heads, partly by conferring with a group of key administrators on an important problem that cuts across departmental lines, partly by meeting with the governor's council (a body organized by law and comprising most departmental heads), and partly with the aid of staff assistants in the governor's office and the Department of Finance. One of the large deficiencies still remaining in state administration, however, is coordination between the major administrative departments.

Boards and Commissions

Not all the state's administrative organization is as streamlined as previously described. Throughout the organization are to be found many boards and commissions composed of three, five, seven, or more members. What are the duties of such bodies? Some are to advise administrators. An example is the state communications advisory board. Many review applications for licenses to carry on a profession, trade or business. Examples of this are the Board of Medical Examiners and the Realty License Board. Others help establish standards and rules that are enforced by an administrative department or bureau. Examples of this type include the commission of housing and the apprenticeship council in the Department of Industrial Relations. Still other boards and commissions decide on claims for compensation or decide what rates may be charged for certain services. An example of the first is the industrial accident commission; one of the latter is the utilities commission. A body like the state highway commission has the highly important and difficult task of determining the routes for state highways. Often a highway that is to enter a metropolitan area like San Francisco-Oakland or Los Angeles stirs much political controversy over whether the route should pass through a residential area or a park, or near schools. Boards like the state Personnel Board combine several important administrative functions. This board determines rules for employment in the state service, hears appeals from employees whose rights may have been harmed, and directs the administration of the central personnel department.

A strong effort has been made in state administration to reduce the number of boards or commissions that are responsible for directing the work of a department or bureau. It is commonly agreed that the most appropriate functions of a board or commission are to advise top management to determine rules that shall guide administrative officers and to decide specific cases. Wherever possible, boards and commissions have been brought into some appropriate departmental framework. An example of this is found in the Department of Industrial Relations, where six boards are related to an equal number of administrative divisions for rule making and case hearing in specialized fields. A different type of situation is illustrated by the department of vocational and professional standards. A large number of separate boards were brought together within a general departmental framework so that certain administrative services required by each board could be provided by a common staff. A pool of qualified legal officers capable of conducting administrative hearings became available to each board from the departmental expert staff and relieved the individual board of responsibility for building a special group to serve its needs.

Liquor control is a recent example of an administrative task removed from a board's jurisdiction and placed under a single-headed department. Between 1933 and 1954 the function was directed by the Board of Equalization. Although the board employed a chief enforcement officer, each of the four elected board members took a hand in directing affairs within their district. The chaotic and allegedly corrupt conditions that resulted led the voters to approve a constitutional amendment changing this. Thereupon, the legislature created a Department of Alcoholic Beverage Control to administer and a separate appeals board to hear appeals from liquor license decisions. This organization follows the modern practice of separating administration and decision of appeals, and uses a board for the latter activity.

Fiscal Control

The Department of Finance has become the righthand staff unit to assist the governor in controlling the state's administrative bureaucracy. Under supervision of the director, civil servants in this department prepare the governor's budget, advise and assist the chief executive in answering legislative questions regarding fiscal matters, and help in coordinating the governor's finance programs. Once the budget is adopted by the legislature, it becomes the department's task to exercise certain controls over the spending by the departments.

It has long been a rule in American practice that an administrative officer may not undertake to spend more than the legislature appropriates for specific details of activities. There are occasions, however, when it becomes necessary to shift funds to meet urgent requirements. Certain transfers of funds can be accomplished if the department head can convince the director of finance that such a transfer is required and that funds may be legally used. The legislature also usually appropriates an emergency fund which the governor may allocate to departments to meet unforeseen situations that require more money than was specifically appropriated. The Department of Finance makes the investigation of claims for funds from the emergency fund.

A division of the Department of Finance makes studies of administrative organization and advises regarding management procedures in order to improve administrative performance. These studies are usually requested by the department concerned but the finance department may take the initiative to determine whether funds can be saved through reorganization or improved procedures.

Another type of budgetary control is exercised by control of purchases. Most of the state's purchasing (except that by the state highway division) is done by the division of purchases in the Department of Finance. Through standardization of purchases, large scale buying, and skillful administration, considerable money has been saved. Another division exercises control over printing work done for state agencies. A tremendous amount of printing is done regularly; and elimination of duplication and unnecessary printing work is a means of saving. Other controls pertain to personnel and payrolls. No department may employ a person unless a position has been approved by the legislature and funds have been appropriated to pay the salary. Review of the number of positions becomes a regular part of the work of the Department of Finance in preparing the budget estimates. When a position becomes vacant through resignation, transfer, or death of an employee, this department exercises financial control by demanding that the department in whose service the position is located justifies the refilling of the position. Although the state Personnel Board establishes salary scales for the various classes of positions in state service, salary setting is done in cooperation with the Department of Finance, which studies all proposals in terms of the state's ability to pay.

For many years the Department of Finance has enjoyed the confidence and respect of the legislature as well as of the governor. Through the exercise of fiscal control duties that have been granted periodically by the legislature, the department has become the one agency capable of exercising general management of the state's administration, subject to general policy direction by the governor. Gradually the administrative machinery has achieved more coordination. Resistance to supervision and coordination by the chief executive continues where an administrative agency is particularly close to an interested group that believes its particular program will not be highly favored by the executive. Therefore, the organizational pattern never remains completely static. Change is usually taking place at some point.

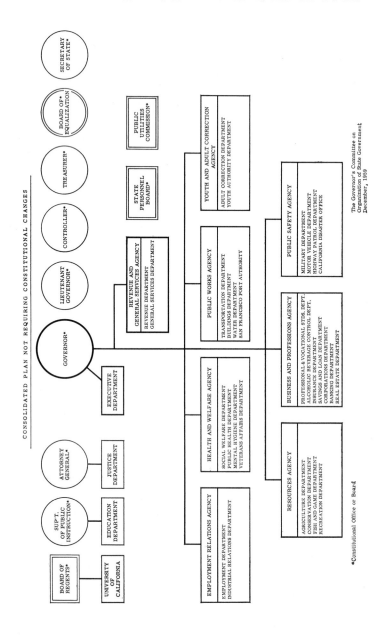

CONSOLIDATED PLAN NOT REQUIRING CONSTITUTIONAL CHANGES

BOARD OF REGENTS*

UNIVERSITY OF CALIFORNIA

SUP'T. OF PUBLIC INSTRUCTION*

EDUCATION DEPARTMENT

ATTORNEY GENERAL*

JUSTICE DEPARTMENT

GOVERNOR*

EXECUTIVE DEPARTMENT

LIEUTENANT GOVERNOR*

CONTROLLER*

TREASURER*

BOARD OF* EQUALIZATION

SECRETARY OF STATE*

REVENUE AND GENERAL SERVICES AGENCY
REVENUE DEPARTMENT
GENERAL SERVICES DEPARTMENT

STATE PERSONNEL BOARD*

PUBLIC UTILITIES COMMISSION*

EMPLOYMENT RELATIONS AGENCY
EMPLOYMENT DEPARTMENT
INDUSTRIAL RELATIONS DEPARTMENT

HEALTH AND WELFARE AGENCY
SOCIAL WELFARE DEPARTMENT
PUBLIC HEALTH DEPARTMENT
MENTAL HYGIENE DEPARTMENT
VETERANS AFFAIRS DEPARTMENT

PUBLIC WORKS AGENCY
TRANSPORTATION DEPARTMENT
BUILDINGS DEPARTMENT
WATER DEPARTMENT
SAN FRANCISCO PORT AUTHORITY

YOUTH AND ADULT CORRECTION AGENCY
ADULT CORRECTION DEPARTMENT
YOUTH AUTHORITY DEPARTMENT

RESOURCES AGENCY
AGRICULTURE DEPARTMENT
CONSERVATION DEPARTMENT
FISH AND GAME DEPARTMENT
RECREATION DEPARTMENT

BUSINESS AND PROFESSIONS AGENCY
PROFESSIONAL & VOCATIONAL STDS. DEPT.
ALCOHOLIC BEVERAGE CONTROL DEPT.
INSURANCE DEPARTMENT
SAVINGS AND LOAN DEPARTMENT
CORPORATIONS DEPARTMENT
BANKING DEPARTMENT
REAL ESTATE DEPARTMENT

PUBLIC SAFETY AGENCY
MILITARY DEPARTMENT
MOTOR VEHICLE DEPARTMENT
HIGHWAY PATROL DEPARTMENT
CALIFORNIA DISASTER OFFICE

*Constitutional Office or Board

The Governor's Committee on Organization of State Government
December, 1959

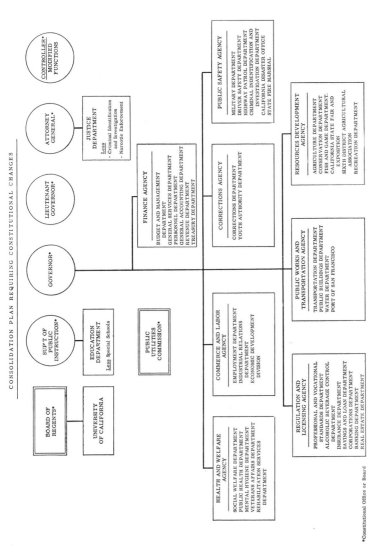

CONSOLIDATION PLAN REQUIRING CONSTITUTIONAL CHANGES

BOARD OF REGENTS*

UNIVERSITY OF CALIFORNIA

SUPT OF PUBLIC INSTRUCTION*

EDUCATION DEPARTMENT
Less Special Schools

PUBLIC UTILITIES COMMISSION*

GOVERNOR*

LIEUTENANT GOVERNOR*

ATTORNEY GENERAL*

JUSTICE DEPARTMENT
Less
- Criminal Identification and Investigation
- Narcotic Enforcement

CONTROLLER*
MODIFIED FUNCTIONS

FINANCE AGENCY
BUDGET AND MANAGEMENT DEPARTMENT
GENERAL SERVICES DEPARTMENT
PERSONNEL DEPARTMENT
GENERAL ACCOUNTING DEPARTMENT
REVENUE DEPARTMENT
TREASURY DEPARTMENT

PUBLIC SAFETY AGENCY
MILITARY DEPARTMENT
DRIVER SAFETY DEPARTMENT
HIGHWAY PATROL DEPARTMENT
CRIMINAL INDENTIFICATION AND INVESTIGATION DEPARTMENT
CALIFORNIA DISASTER OFFICE
STATE FIRE MARSHAL

CORRECTIONS AGENCY
CORRECTIONS DEPARTMENT
YOUTH AUTHORITY DEPARTMENT

RESOURCES DEVELOPMENT AGENCY
AGRICULTURE DEPARTMENT
CONSERVATION DEPARTMENT
FISH AND GAME DEPARTMENT
CALIFORNIA STATE FAIR AND EXPOSITION
SIXTH DISTRICT AGRICULTURAL ASSOCIATION
RECREATION DEPARTMENT

HEALTH AND WELFARE AGENCY
SOCIAL WELFARE DEPARTMENT
PUBLIC HEALTH DEPARTMENT
MENTAL HYGIENE DEPARTMENT
VETERANS AFFAIRS DEPARTMENT
REHABILITATION SERVICES DEPARTMENT

COMMERCE AND LABOR AGENCY
EMPLOYMENT DEPARTMENT
INDUSTRIAL RELATIONS DEPARTMENT
ECONOMIC DEVELOPMENT DIVISION

PUBLIC WORKS AND TRANSPORTATION AGENCY
TRANSPORTATION DEPARTMENT
PUBLIC BUILDINGS DEPARTMENT
WATER DEPARTMENT
PORT OF SAN FRANCISCO

REGULATION AND LICENSING AGENCY
PROFESSIONAL AND VOCATIONAL STANDARDS DEPARTMENT
ALCOHOLIC BEVERAGE CONTROL DEPARTMENT
INSURANCE DEPARTMENT
SAVINGS AND LOAN DEPARTMENT
CORPORATIONS DEPARTMENT
BANKING DEPARTMENT
REAL ESTATE DEPARTMENT

*Constitutional Office or Board

A committee appointed by Governor Brown recommended a plan for reorganizing the state administrative structure to make possible a greater degree of control of administration by the state's chief executive.

Reorganization

Soon after his inauguration in early 1959, Governor Brown appointed an organization advisory committee and asked it to prepare plans for improved structure and procedures. Six months later the committee's proposals were unveiled at a conference of senior administrative officers. To correct the existing fault of too many departments and independent agencies reporting directly to the governor, the committee proposed that virtually all units of the executive branch be grouped into eight great "agencies," headed by administrators. Under each agency were related departments and other units. The administrators of the agencies, together with the Lieutenant Governor, Superintendent of Public Instruction, Attorney General, and possibly one or two others, would constitute a governor's cabinet. It would be a body small enough to meet frequently with the governor and to provide him with advice on policy matters. Coordination would be achieved, according to the committee, through the work of agency administrators, whose main tasks would involve getting cooperation among their departments and units and representing them and their problems before the governor and the public. The agencies proposed, and the major departments under them are shown on the preceding charts.

The support of Governor Brown was not immediately forthcoming. The plan was far-reaching, involving drastic shifts of power and considerable alteration of constitutional offices. Gone or modified would be such traditional elective offices as Controller, Treasurer, Secretary of State, and the Board of Equalization. Abolition of these offices requires constitutional amendment, which is neither easy to propose nor ratify. The larger share of the plan, however, could be put into effect by statute and gubernatorial order. As this is written, piecemeal approach by other than constitutional means appears the more practical.

Further Reading

Bell, James R., *Coordinating California's Governmental Programs.* Berkeley: Bureau of Public Administration, University of California, 1959.

Bollens, John C., *Administrative Reorganization in the States Since 1939*. Berkeley: Bureau of Public Administration, University of California, 1949.

California, Legislature, Assembly Interim Committee on Governmental Reorganization, *First Partial Report*. Sacramento: State Printing Office, 1949.

——, ——, Assembly Interim Committee on Governmental Efficiency and Economy, *Partial Report of the Study of the Personnel Board and its Operations*. Sacramento: State Printing Office, 1949.

——, ——, Assembly Interim Committee on Government Organization, *Report*. Sacramento: State Printing Office, 1956.

——, ——, Joint Legislative Committee on Governmental Reorganization, *Management and Fiscal Control Functions of the California Department of Finance*. Sacramento: State Printing Office, 1955.

——, ——, State Department of Finance, *California State Government: A Guide to its Organization and Functions*. Sacramento: State Printing Office, 1958.

Hurt, Elsey, *California State Government*. 2 vols. Sacramento: State Printing Office, 1937-1940.

Nine | Courts and the

Judicial

Process

THE JUDICIAL POWER of California is vested
in a supreme court, district courts of appeal, superior courts,
municipal courts, and justice courts. In addition the senate sits
as a court for trying cases of impeachment.

THE JUDICIAL SYSTEM

The Supreme Court

The California Supreme Court has a chief justice and six associate justices. It may sit in bank, i.e., as a group, or the chief
justice may assign three associates to each of two departments.
Its headquarters are in San Francisco, and branches are maintained in Sacramento and Los Angeles.

Several changes were made in the judicial branch at the November, 1934 election. The most important was the abandonment of direct election of state justices and the substitution of a
compromise between election and appointment, which has been
called "self-perpetuating election."

This method of selection applies to justices of the Supreme
Court and the district courts of appeal. It may apply to superior
courts only in the counties that adopt the plan; counties
not adopting it continued to elect superior court judges by the
traditional competitive elections. Just before the close of his term

(twelve years is the full term) a judge may declare himself a candidate to succeed himself. His name then appears on the November ballot:

FOR ASSOCIATE JUSTICE OF THE SUPREME COURT

Shall B. Rey Schauer be elected to the office for the term prescribed by law?	YES
	NO

If a majority votes "yes," then the incumbent is elected to succeed himself. If a majority rejects the incumbent justice or the office falls vacant through death or other cause, the governor appoints a successor. The appointment is not effective, however, until passed upon by a commission on qualifications, composed of the chief justice, a presiding judge of the district courts of appeal, and the attorney general. Should the commission reject the governor's appointment, the executive may nominate another for the vacancy.

In 1940 the qualifications commission—in a decision that was considered by many to be politically-motivated—refused to confirm Governor Olson's appointment to the Supreme Court of Professor Max Radin, eminent jurist and member of the University of California law faculty. Although this action drew widespread criticism, accompanied by suggestions that the method of selection be changed, nothing was done at the time. In November, 1960, however, a constitutional amendment (SCA 14) will be voted upon which will, if approved, enlarge the qualifications commission from three to nine members. This proposal is supported by the state bar and the judicial council, on the grounds that broader representation is needed.

The Supreme Court has broad appellate jurisdiction, taking from the superior court cases in equity, cases in law involving real estate and taxes, and probate cases. Appeal is automatic if the death penalty is involved. In addition, the Supreme Court takes appeals from the district courts of appeal. It has power to issue writs of mandamus, certiorari, prohibition, habeas corpus, and other writs necessary for the exercise of appellate jurisdiction.

Regular sessions of the court are held in San Francisco, Sacramento, and Los Angeles.

District Courts of Appeal

Justices of the district courts of appeal are selected in the same manner as supreme court justices, and also serve for a term of twelve years. The legislature has exercised its power to create new appellate districts and has divided the state into four parts, each with its district court of appeal. Any court may then be split into divisions. The present distribution of counties by appellate districts is as follows:

> District I: San Francisco, Marin, Contra Costa, Alameda, San Mateo, Santa Clara, Santa Cruz, Monterey, and San Benito. Meets in San Francisco.
>
> District II: San Luis Obispo, Santa Barbara, Ventura, and Los Angeles. Meets in Los Angeles.
>
> District III: Del Norte, Siskiyou, Modoc, Humboldt, Mariposa, Madera, Merced, Tuolumne, Trinity, Shasta, Lassen, Tehama, Plumas, Mendocino, Lake, Colusa, Glenn, Butte, Sierra, Sutter, Yuba, Nevada, Sonoma, Napa, Yolo, Placer, Solano, Sacramento, El Dorado, San Joaquin, Amador, Calaveras, Stanislaus, Alpine, and Mono. Meets in Sacramento.
>
> District IV: Fresno, Tulare, Kings, Kern, Inyo, San Bernardino, Orange, Riverside, San Diego, and Imperial. Meets in Fresno, San Bernardino, and San Diego.

The first district has two divisions (each division comprises a "team" of justices that conducts the hearing of appeals); the second has three, the others have one. The Supreme Court may shift counties from one district to another. There are three justices in each division, and therefore twenty-one district courts of appeal justices at the present time.

Jurisdiction of the district courts of appeal is defined as appeals from the superior courts which do not go directly to the Supreme Court. Other cases may be transferred to the district courts of appeal from the Supreme Court by order of the high court. District courts of appeal also have jurisdiction, concurrently with the Supreme Court, to issue writs of habeas corpus, mandamus, prohibition and certiorari.

Superior Courts

The superior courts are the major trial courts in the California judicial system. One exists in each county of the state, or fifty-eight in all. The judges serve six-year terms. Unless the electorate of a county adopts the elective-appointive compromise used by the state courts (and none has to date), the judges are elected by the people without partisan designation at general elections. The number of judges varies with the size of the county and its court business. Many of the smaller counties have only one judge; Los Angeles has ninety.

Superior court civil jurisdiction is mainly original, including all probate and domestic relations cases and some tax cases. All juvenile cases go directly to the superior court, as do applications for certain remedies such as habeas corpus and injunctions. Criminal cases amounting to felonies and also some misdemeanors are within superior court authority. Appellate jurisdiction is limited to certain cases brought up from municipal and justice courts. The larger counties have separate appellate departments of their superior courts.

Inferior Court Reorganization

In November 1950 the electorate approved (2,307,328 to 552,-997) a constitutional amendment that provided for extensive reorganization of the inferior courts. This reform affected all courts below the superior court level. It provided for two types of lower courts: municipal courts for districts with a population of more than 40,000, and justice courts for districts with smaller populations. Provision was made for the election of judges by the people. Flexibility was secured by giving the legislature power to make such additional provisions as are needed. The new plan replaced the old chaotic system which had eight different kinds of courts, numbering 768 in all.

Municipal Courts

The new municipal courts—of which there are 207—actually represent a continuation and extension of courts which have borne that name and have been available to the larger cities with home-rule charters since the twenties. At the time of the adoption of the court-reform amendment, Los Angeles, San Francisco, Long Beach, Sacramento, San Diego, Pasadena, and Santa Monica already had municipal courts in operation. The 1951 legislature created twenty-nine additional municipal courts, replacing and consolidating township justice courts, city justice courts, inferior "municipal" courts, police courts, and "city" courts. Additional municipal courts may be established.

Municipal court jurisdiction covers civil cases involving amounts up to $3,000 and all misdemeanors except juvenile. Municipal courts have done much to relieve congestion in the superior courts of the counties in which they have been established. Extension of the municipal court system was justified on the grounds that it assured better-trained judges, paid more adequate salaries, and operated in well-equipped courtrooms.

Justice Courts

In areas where the population is below the 40,000 required for a municipal court, the justice court hears cases involving minor civil actions and misdemeanors. These courts serve the smaller cities and the rural areas. In the reorganization the quality of the judicial personnel and the conditions under which court work is done has been greatly improved. The state bar committee on inferior court structure hoped to replace all courts below the municipal level with a uniform "county court" and to ban non-lawyers from holding judgeships. Its recommendations did not prevail and laymen continue to sit as judges in about half of the 312 justice courts. This number of laymen is, however, rapidly declining.

JUDICIAL PROBLEMS AND PRACTICES

The Judicial Council

California has been a pioneer in the judicial council movement; when California established its council in 1926 it was the second state to create such an agency. A judicial council is a body set up to study a state's judicial system, compile judicial statistics, do judicial research, and recommend improvements. Forty-two states have now adopted some form of the judicial council. California's council is the only one authorized by constitutional amendment. Appropriations to this agency have been large enough to put its activities considerably ahead of those of other state councils.

The California Judicial Council is composed of eleven members: the chief justice, one associate justice of the Supreme Court, three justices of district courts of appeal, four judges of superior courts, one judge of a municipal court, and one judge of an inferior court. The chief justice is chairman and appoints the other members for two-year terms. A constitutional amendment has been proposed and will be voted upon at the November election of 1960, which would enlarge the judicial council from eleven to eighteen members. Senate Constitutional Amendment no. 14 would add one judge of a municipal court, appointed by the chief justice, four members of the State Bar, appointed by the board of governors, and two legislators, one from each house.

Major functions of the council fall under four headings: (1) it surveys the work of the courts, (2) it recommends to courts improvement in practices, (3) it proposes changes in the courts to governor and legislature, and (4) it adopts rules of practice and procedure for the courts, within the framework of existing law. As chairman of the council, the chief justice may assign any judge to another like court in order to relieve congestion. Judges are required to cooperate. The basic outline of judicial council power is found in the constitution, but other functions may be added by law.

The Grand Jury System

The grand jury is a body of nineteen citizens impaneled annually in each county in the state. The members are, for the most part, hand picked by the superior court judges of the county. Historically the primary function of the grand jury was to bring indictments against persons suspected of criminal acts. In California, however, as in many other states, the district attorneys may now bring persons to trial by an alternative procedure involving a preliminary hearing in an inferior court, followed by the filing of an "information" (a sworn statement) in the superior court. The great majority of all indictments are, in fact, brought in this manner rather than by grand jury action.

Grand juries are used most often when a case is weak or doubtful, when the matter is sensational in nature, as in murder or rape, when children or timid witnesses must be called, and when the case involves malfeasance in public office. One of the chief advantages of the grand jury proceeding is its secrecy, which helps protect the innocent against unfounded public accusations.

Because grand juries are concerned with only a small percentage of criminal indictments, most of their time is devoted to "watchdog" activities: looking into the conduct of public officials, the expenditure of public funds, and the functioning of local government, especially county government. The juries are seriously handicapped in this work because of their lack of expert staff help and their short terms of service (one year). Grand juries have, on occasion, been accused of irresponsible "fishing expeditions," and of engaging in unwarranted harassment of public officials. Others have rendered valuable service through their independent studies and investigations.

Other Features

Removal of a justice or judge from office may be secured through either impeachment or recall. The state assembly has the sole power of impeachment; that is, it may bring out the charges and accusations against a supreme, an appellate district, or a superior court judge. The senate *tries* cases of impeachment; a two-thirds vote of all elected members is necessary for conviction. The recall also applies to elective judgeships, including those filled by the new "self-perpetuating election" method. When a recall petition directed against a judge is properly filled out and signed by the requisite number of voters (12 per cent of the number voting at the last election), the electorate is given an opportunity to vote upon the question of whether or not he should be continued in office.

California makes provision for the voluntary retirement of its judges. When a supreme, appellate, or a superior court judge reaches the appropriate age, and has served the required number of years on the court, he may retire from active duty and receive yearly, for the remainder of his life, one-half of his last annual salary.

The proposed Senate Constitutional Amendment No. 14 would, if approved, empower the enlarged qualifications commission to remove a justice or judge of any court for willful misconduct or habitual failure to perform his duties, and to retire a justice or judge for "disability seriously interfering with the performance of his duties, which is, or is likely to become, of a permanent character."

Both the Supreme Court and the district courts of appeal publish records of their decisions. *California Reports* consists of reports of cases determined in the Supreme Court. The period 1850-1934 was covered by the first series (220 volumes); 1934 to date is included in the second series. *California Appellate Reports* contains reports of cases decided in the district courts of appeal. The first series includes the period 1850-1934; the second series, 1934 to date. California cases are also reported in the *Pacific Reporter*.

PROCEDURE

Civil Procedure

Civil suits arise from disputes between "persons" (individuals, corporations, cities, state agencies, etc.) over damages, contracts, and other non-criminal matters. The dispute is between the plaintiff, who brings the suit, and the defendant, against whom it is brought. The major steps follow:

1. A complaint is filed with the courts by the plaintiff, stating concisely the facts upon which the claim against the defendant is based.

2. The court issues a summons for the defendant and allows him ten days in which to answer the complaint.

3. The judge determines whether there is sufficient cause for action.

4. The trial begins before judge and jury, or before a judge alone if the parties agree to this. Ordinarily, trial juries have twelve members, but they may have less if the parties agree. (Cal. Const. Art. I, sec. 7.)

5. The attorneys for plaintiff and defendant present their cases.

6. The judge takes the case under consideration, if sitting without a jury, or instructs the jury. Under a 1934 constitutional amendment, the court is permitted not only to instruct as to law, but may also comment on evidence and testimony, and the creditability of witness. (Art. VI, sec. 19.)

7. Judgment is rendered by the court. A three-fourths vote is required for a jury verdict in a civil case.

8. Appeal may be made to a higher court on ground of procedural error, misdirection of the jury, and other errors which might result in a miscarriage of justice.

Criminal Procedure

Criminal cases involve acts against the state itself. The person accused is charged by the district attorney acting in the name of the people of California. The main outlines of the process follow:

1. An arrest is made by an officer or a citizen with or without a warrant.

2. The accused is brought before a judge for preliminary hearing to determine whether there is sufficient evidence to justify holding the accused or requiring bond. The accused is sometimes released on his own recognizance.

3. An indictment is issued either by a grand jury or on the basis of an information signed by the district attorney.

4. The accused before a trial court has five possible pleas: "guilty," "not guilty," "a former judgment of conviction or acquittal," "once in jeopardy," and "not guilty by reason of insanity." If he pleads guilty, he may be sentenced forthwith; if not guilty, the trial is granted. Unless the accused waives jury trial, a jury of twelve is impaneled.

5. The prosecutor and counsel for the accused present their cases.

6. The judge charges the jury. As in civil cases, he may instruct as to law and comment as to evidence and witnesses.

7. The jury deliberates and announces its verdict. A unanimous vote is required for conviction. If the verdict is "guilty," the judge pronounces sentence.

8. An appeal may be taken on the basis of mishandling law or evidence.

Further Reading

California, Judicial Council, *Report*. Sacramento: State Printing Office, biennial. Other Judicial Council publications include *Rules on Appeal, Rules for Superior Courts*, and *Inferior Court Reorganization*.

California, Legislature, Joint Judiciary Committee on Administration of Justice, *Partial Report . . . on the California Judiciary*. Sacramento: State Printing Office, 1959.

————, *Second Partial Report on the Operation of the Courts*. Sacramento: State Printing Office, 1959.

Holbrook, James G., *A Survey of the Metropolitan Trial Courts—Los Angeles Area*. Los Angeles: University of Southern California, 1956.

Kennedy, Harold W. and Briggs, James W., "Historical and Legal Aspects of the California Grand Jury System," *California Law Review* 43 (May, 1955), 251-267.

Smith, Malcolm, "Judicial Tenure in California," Unpublished Ph.D. thesis, Stanford University, 1951.

"Some Aspects of the California Grand Jury System," *Stanford Law Review* 8 (July 1956), 631-654.

State Bar of California, Committee to Survey the Inferior Court Structure of California, "The Township and City Courts of California," *Journal of the State Bar of California*, XX (September-October 1945), 293-345.

Stewart, Frank M., "Impeachment of Judge James H. Hardy, 1862," *Southern California Law Review*, 28 (December 1954), 61-69.

————, "Early California Impeachment Proceedings," *Pacific Historical Review*, XXIV (August 1955), 261-274.

————, "California's First Impeachment, 1857," *The Historical Society of Southern California Quarterly*, XXXIX (December 1957), 328-339.

Ten

Finance and

Personnel

CALIFORNIA'S STATE BUDGET has been running in the neighborhood of two billion dollars for some time. In Chapter Eight we saw some of the services that are purchased with that sum. The problem of financing the state and local government has been an ever pressing one. California's natural and business resources are great; therefore a high standard of living is possible. Its population expects a high quality of governmental service. At the same time, the policies governing the support of state and local government must meet the following questions: Which level of government should pay for which services of government? What should be the relative burdens of taxation? These continue to be the two basic questions for tax experts, the legislature, and the voters.

TAXATION AND FINANCE

State taxes in California are closely related to business activity and to the income and spending ability of the state's residents. The largest single source of state revenue comes from the state-wide retail sales tax that everyone pays when he buys something at a store or eats at a restaurant. Governor Brown estimated that 31.6 per cent of the revenue in the proposed state budget for 1959-60 came from that source. Taxes upon gasoline and motor vehicles provide nearly 22 per cent of the total revenue. Taxes upon banks and corporation franchises provide about 10 per cent, and taxes upon insurance premiums contribute another 2.5 per cent. The personal income tax brings in about 11 per cent, and taxes upon inheritances and gifts produce approximately 2 per cent. Taxes upon alcoholic beverages, tobacco and horse racing yield another 4.3 per cent of the total revenue; the remaining revenues needed to finance the state's expenses come from a variety of other smaller, nontax revenue sources and from reserve funds.

Counties, cities, school districts, and other special units of local government have been permitted to tax property and a few other items. After 1935 many cities began to levy sales taxes, and since 1956 counties also have such authority. Nevertheless, the tax resources of the local governments are more limited and are less productive than those enjoyed by the state. Consequently the state has agreed to contribute a substantial share of the money that it collects in state taxes to counties, cities, and school districts for the support of such local activities as schools, streets and roads, welfare, policing, health. Governor Brown estimated that 55 per cent of his total budget presented to the legislature in 1959 was for assistance to local governments—mostly payments fixed by the constitution and laws already approved by the voters. This is a somewhat surprising situation, because most taxpayers do not realize that they support such a large part of the cost of local governments through taxes paid to the state government.

STATE REVENUE

The Sales Tax

Since 1933 the state of California has levied a tax upon retail sales of commodities, normally at the rate of 3 per cent. Food purchases, other than meals at restaurants, have been exempt. Each retail merchant collects the tax from the purchasers, keeps records as required by the state Board of Equalization, and reports and pays over his collections to the board's enforcement staff. The board's staff check the returns and audit the merchants'

SOURCES AND USES OF STATE FUNDS
1959-60 FISCAL YEAR

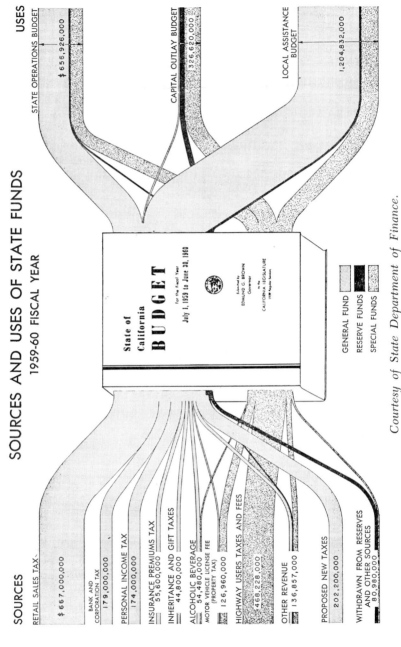

SOURCES

RETAIL SALES TAX
$667,000,000

BANK AND CORPORATION TAX
179,000,000

PERSONAL INCOME TAX
174,000,000

INSURANCE PREMIUMS TAX
55,600,000

INHERITANCE AND GIFT TAXES
44,800,000

ALCOHOLIC BEVERAGE
54,480,000

MOTOR VEHICLE LICENSE FEE (PROPERTY TAX)
126,960,000

HIGHWAY USERS TAXES AND FEES
468,228,000

OTHER REVENUE
136,857,000

PROPOSED NEW TAXES
202,200,000

WITHDRAWN FROM RESERVES AND OTHER SOURCES
80,980,000

USES

STATE OPERATIONS BUDGET
$656,926,000

CAPITAL OUTLAY BUDGET
326,620,000

LOCAL ASSISTANCE BUDGET
1,204,832,000

State of California
BUDGET
For the Fiscal Year
July 1, 1959 to June 30, 1960

Submitted by
EDMUND G. BROWN
Governor
to the
CALIFORNIA LEGISLATURE
1959 Regular Session

GENERAL FUND
RESERVE FUNDS
SPECIAL FUNDS

Courtesy of State Department of Finance.

statements. Actual collections from the sales tax amounted to $605,238,000 in 1957-58; and it was estimated that in 1959-60 the collection would rise to $667,000,000.

To protect California merchants from competition of goods being brought in tax-free from outside and to plug a considerable hole in possible tax income, the legislature established a 3 per cent tax upon purchases made outside California for use within the state. This is now known as the "use tax." Anyone who purchases a new car, takes delivery of it in Detroit, and drives it home to California finds that when he seeks to register it in California he is presented with a bill for the use tax upon the purchase price.

Motor-Vehicle Taxes

The owner of a motor vehicle pays a variety of *fees* and *taxes*. Each time he is required to renew his driver's license he must pay a small *fee*. These fees are mostly to pay the cost of registration and administering the regulations. When the vehicle owner obtains his license plates, he pays a *tax* based upon the estimated value of his car. This tax takes the place of any other tax that might be set by a county or city upon the property value of the car; hence it is known as the *in lieu tax*. Several years ago the counties and cities taxed automobiles as property, but the state has since been given exclusive authority to tax motor vehicles on the understanding that it will share the proceeds with the cities and counties.

A gasoline tax is collected on fuel used by vehicles that operate on the streets and highways. It is collected by the state from the original distributors, who in turn pass on the tax to the automobile users by including it in the price charged at the local service station.

The politics that shaped the development of the taxes upon motor-vehicle users produced a peculiar feature of present-day tax policies known as *earmarked revenues*. The thought underlying this is that if a particular group is singled out for taxation, the revenues from such taxes should be devoted exclusively to activities of concern to that group. Most taxes, such as those on property and on retail sales, are known as *general revenues* be-

TOTAL BUDGET DOLLARS
1959-60 FISCAL YEAR

REVENUES

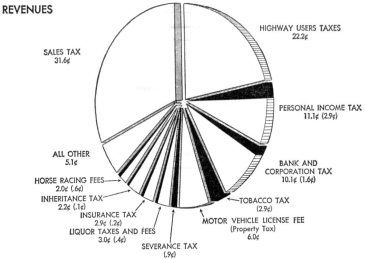

SALES TAX
31.6¢

HIGHWAY USERS TAXES
22.2¢

PERSONAL INCOME TAX
11.1¢ (2.9¢)

BANK AND
CORPORATION TAX
10.1¢ (1.6¢)

ALL OTHER
5.1¢

HORSE RACING FEES
2.0¢ (.6¢)

INHERITANCE TAX
2.2¢ (.1¢)

INSURANCE TAX
2.9¢ (.2¢)

LIQUOR TAXES AND FEES
3.0¢ (.4¢)

SEVERANCE TAX
(.9¢)

TOBACCO TAX
(2.9¢)

MOTOR VEHICLE LICENSE FEE
(Property Tax)
6.0¢

Dark areas indicate proposed new or increased taxes.
Figures are total of present and new taxes;
bracketed figures, new taxes only.

EXPENDITURES

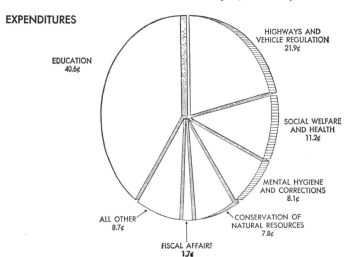

EDUCATION
40.6¢

HIGHWAYS AND
VEHICLE REGULATION
21.9¢

SOCIAL WELFARE
AND HEALTH
11.2¢

MENTAL HYGIENE
AND CORRECTIONS
8.1¢

CONSERVATION OF
NATURAL RESOURCES
7.8¢

ALL OTHER
8.7¢

FISCAL AFFAIRS
1.7¢

Courtesy of State Department of Finance.

GENERAL FUND BUDGET DOLLARS
1959-60 FISCAL YEAR

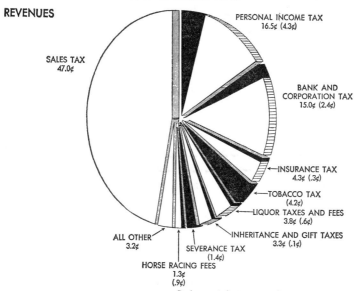

REVENUES

SALES TAX
47.0¢

PERSONAL INCOME TAX
16.5¢ (4.3¢)

BANK AND
CORPORATION TAX
15.0¢ (2.4¢)

◄—INSURANCE TAX
4.3¢ (.3¢)

◄—TOBACCO TAX
(4.2¢)

◄—LIQUOR TAXES AND FEES
3.8¢ (.6¢)

◄INHERITANCE AND GIFT TAXES
3.3¢ (.1¢)

ALL OTHER
3.2¢

SEVERANCE TAX
(1.4¢)

HORSE RACING FEES
1.3¢
(.9¢)

*Dark areas indicate proposed new or increased taxes.
Figures are total of present and new taxes;
bracketed figures, new taxes only.*

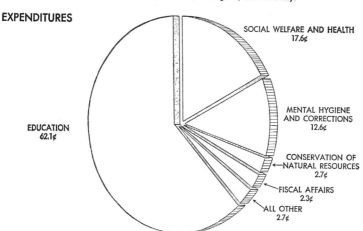

EXPENDITURES

SOCIAL WELFARE AND HEALTH
17.6¢

MENTAL HYGIENE
AND CORRECTIONS
12.6¢

CONSERVATION OF
◄—NATURAL RESOURCES
2.7¢

◄—FISCAL AFFAIRS
2.3¢

◄ALL OTHER
2.7¢

EDUCATION
62.1¢

Courtesy of State Department of Finance.

"earmarked revenues"

cause they support the general functions of government and are not earmarked for any special purpose. Taxes upon motor vehicles, however, have traditionally been earmarked for the support of construction and maintenance of state highways, major streets and roads, bridges, traffic signals, and other matters closely related to automobile traffic.

The great increase in the number of automobiles in California after World War II, and hence the increased need for street and highway facilities, resulted in a revision of the plan of motor-vehicle taxation at the 1947 special session of the legislature. The tax on gasoline and diesel fuel was raised to 4½ cents per gallon. Registration fees on automobiles and fees for drivers' licenses were raised. Charges upon commercial vehicles and trailers, based upon weight, were also raised. At the same time the apportionment of the money collected from motor-vehicle taxes was altered to give the counties approximately 1⅜ cents per gallon taxed, and the cities five-eighths of a cent per gallon taxed to be spent locally on streets and roads. Local governments had demanded a larger share of these taxes to enable them to keep pace with the increased traffic demands upon local streets and roads. However, the larger portion of these taxes continues to finance highway programs administered by the state highway division. In 1957-58 the motor-vehicle fuel taxes brought in $302,-671,000, and it was estimated that in 1959-60 they would produce $327,620,000.

The Personal Income Tax

California first began to levy a personal income tax in 1935. The plan of this tax follows the federal income-tax law closely, although the state's rates are considerably lower than the federal. All residents of California whose income is $2,000 or more a year are liable to pay a state income tax. In 1959, at the request of Governor Brown, the legislature increased the rates of this tax upon middle and larger incomes. In 1957-58 this tax produced $147,269,000 in revenue, and in 1959-60 a return of $234,000,000 was estimated.

Inheritance and Gift Taxes

An inheritance tax has been in force in this state since 1893, but in 1935 it was considerably revised and a modern schedule of rates was adopted. This tax is administered by the counties under state law because most of the legal work involved in clearing up an estate left at the death of the owner has to be done in the courts and in the county official record offices. Proceeds from the tax—less a percentage that the county retains to cover administration costs, and 5 per cent of net collections, which is devoted to teachers' pension funds—go into the general state treasury.

The gift tax, which was established in 1939, is related both to the income tax and to the inheritance tax. It is imposed upon transfers of property by gift and is intended to prevent evasion of the inheritance tax. The state controller administers this tax program. It was estimated that these two taxes would produce $46,800,000 in state revenue in 1959-60.

Business Taxes

Certain types of businesses have come to be taxed by the state on the basis of net income and consequently have been relieved of property taxes that might be levied upon them by local governments. The bank- and corporation-franchise tax is a good example of this. The tax levy is based upon net income, and all companies except insurance corporations and a few others must pay this. Banks that pay the franchise tax pay no other state or local tax. Insurance companies are subject to a separate type of tax whose provisions have been written into the state constitution. They are taxed upon their gross premium receipts collected in California. Any local property taxes which insurance companies pay upon property owned by them is deductible from the state tax on their gross premiums.

The corporate income tax enacted in 1937 was intended to reinforce the state franchise tax and to collect taxes from corporations that do business in California but which do not maintain facilities or plants here. Another relatively small tax that is usually listed in the financial estimates of the governor's budget is the private-car tax, which is paid by companies, other than railroads, that own tank, refrigerator, and sleeping cars. This particular tax was estimated as producing $1,875,000 in 1959-60. The other taxes on businesses were calculated to yield $212,600,000 in the same period.

Alcoholic Beverage Taxes

For many years California has been an important producer of wine grapes. When the federal and state prohibition laws were repealed in 1933, the voters of California agreed to vest in the state government the exclusive authority to regulate and tax the manufacture, distribution, and sale of intoxicating liquors. Wine, beer, and distilled spirits are taxed at rates set by the legislature. Licenses must be obtained by those who undertake to grow wine grapes, manufacture, distribute, or sell any alcoholic beverage, and fees of varying amounts are charged for these licenses. All enforcement relating to licensing is carried out by the state alcoholic beverage control department. Although the consumption of liquor adds to the cost of local policing, cities and counties are not permitted to license retail liquor sellers. Therefore the state divides the revenue from liquor licenses among the counties and cities in proportion to collections, and retains for state revenue purposes those taxes levied upon the liquor manufactured. Estimated liquor-license fees in 1959-60 amounted to $12,030,000; the estimated alcoholic beverage taxes were $51,656,000 for the same year.

Horse Racing and Pari-mutuel Taxes

Horse racing and pari-mutuel betting on the races has been permitted in California since 1933. For twenty years previous to that, horse-racing betting had been prohibited by popular vote. A part of the policy adopted in 1933 provided for a tax upon the money handled by the pari-mutuel pools, and part of the proceeds was to be devoted to the improvement of horse breeding. A large portion of revenue from the tax is deposited in a special state fair and exposition fund, from which considerable sums are allocated to the state fair at Sacramento and to various county and agricultural district fairs throughout the state. The California Polytechnic School at San Luis Obispo and the University of California are given fixed percentages of the revenues for research and teaching in agriculture and animal husbandry. In 1959-60 total taxes and fees on horse racing were estimated to bring in $42,095,000.

Revenue for General and Special Funds

Most of the taxes discussed above, except the motor-vehicle taxes, go into what is known as the state's *general fund*, from which the general expenses of the state government are appropriated. There are many other sources of revenue, however, and some of them are collected for special purposes and therefore must be kept separate from the state's *general fund*. For example, the state leases some tidelands along the coast where oil has been discovered. Revenue derived from the leases and from royalties on oil produced is placed in a *special fund* to be used for the purchase and development of beaches and parks. A different type of example is found in the *fees* collected by the Department of Professional and Vocational Standards for licenses issued to beauty operators, morticians, and members of many other professions and trades. These fees go into a special fund to defray the cost of the regulation and licensing. Yet another type of money income to the state that must be handled for a special purpose is that collected by deductions from the payrolls of industrial workers for *unemployment insurance*. This money is placed in a special fund that is administered by the Department of Employment in accordance with state and federal laws to compensate unemployed persons while seeking reemployment.

When one asks, "Is the California state budget balanced?" he is really asking whether the revenue that can legally be put into the *general fund* is sufficient to pay for the estimated costs of activities that may be charged to that fund. Money from the special funds may not normally be used to balance the general fund. Hence, the student may be bewildered when a tax analyst reports that state income is not sufficient and that more taxes must be levied, when some of the special funds actually have fat surpluses. This is not necessarily an improper situation, because money that has been collected for specific purposes cannot be spent otherwise.

COUNTY FINANCE

Receipts

The two major sources of county-government income are taxes on property and grants from the state and federal governments —which jointly yield 87 per cent of total county revenues. State grants to counties include shares of the state-collected liquor-license fees, gasoline taxes, and taxes upon motor vehicles. County road work is very largely financed by grants from the state. Other, minor types of state assistance include aid to juvenile homes and camps, apportionments to help pay the salaries of county veterans' service officers and county agricultural commissioners, and reimbursements for the administration of adoptions and care of children.

Federal aid to county governments is concentrated chiefly upon social welfare; 90 per cent goes to support that function, the remainder being devoted to highways, health, and forest protection. Most federal-aid money is paid to the state for the support of programs that are being carried on by county governments, and is passed on to the counties by the state departments charged with supervising the work—for example, the Department of Social Welfare and the Department of Public Health.

Although the property tax has declined in relative importance as a source of county-government finance, it remains the largest source collected locally by the county. Now that state law permits counties to enact sales-tax ordinances, an important new source is available. A county sales tax may be collected in the portions of the county outside incorporated cities and within any city that does not have its own sales tax. The legislature prohibits duplication or pyramiding of county and city sales taxes, although sharing arrangements are permitted under the Bradley-Burns Uniform Local Sales and Use Tax Law (the city-county total tax rate must equal one per cent of the sales price). Other sources of county income are fees, charges for special services, fines and penalties, and licenses and permits. In many of the larger counties these sources provide considerable sums of money, although in terms of percentage of the total amount of county income they are not large.

Expenditures

The social welfare function easily stands first among the objects of county governmental expenditures, accounting for just over 50 per cent of the total. Counties also spend money on general county administration, 14 per cent; streets and roads, 10 per cent; protection to persons and property, 9 per cent; health and sanitation, 4 per cent; probation and juvenile work, 3 per cent; and the remaining county functions, 10 per cent.

Bonded Indebtedness

A county may borrow money by selling bonds that are to be repaid over a period of time out of the general tax revenues of the county. However, the exercise of this activity is considerably limited by the state constitution and laws. No county can go into debt beyond an amount equal to 5 per cent of the total value of property assessed for tax purposes in the county. Furthermore, a county may incur a bond debt only if two-thirds of the voters who cast their ballots on the proposition approve. For many years county voters have been rather reluctant to approve bond debts, even when there has been general agreement that the county needed to construct a new hospital, juvenile hall, or similar public building. Today the chief purpose of county borrowing is to finance construction of important county structures.

MUNICIPAL FINANCE

Receipts

Municipal revenues come from a much wider range of sources than those of counties. The property tax is the most important single source (36 per cent), but significant amounts of money are also obtained from sales taxes, licenses and permits, fines and penalties, property sale or rentals, fees and service charges, parking-meter collections, and grants from the state and federal governments. All these sources yielded more than three-fourths of a billion dollars in 1958 for the cities of California. In addition to the regular governmental revenues, municipal utilities and public service enterprises took in one-third of a billion dollars in 1958—roughly equal to expenditures on these functions.

Although the value of taxable property in the cities has steadily increased since 1939, the property tax no longer plays the outstanding role in city taxation that it did in former years. This can be explained partly by the fact that state law and many city charters set a relatively low maximum limit for tax rates upon property, and as the costs of city government rose the cities were forced to develop other sources of revenue. As they were successful in doing this, the property tax declined in relative importance. The tax-limitation law prohibits cities that do not have a local charter from setting a property tax rate for general government purposes in excess of $1.00 per $100 of assessed value of property. A majority vote of the citizens may approve a higher rate. Several exceptions have been provided, permitting a city council to finance certain functions by special taxes over and above the general rate. These include tax levies for employee pension or retirement payments, construction of flood-control works and sewage facilities, maintenance of libraries, museums, hospitals, and veterans' centers, provision for municipal musical programs, and city advertising. Most cities have a property-tax rate approximately equal to the maximum allowed, and a considerable number have special taxes in addition.

Sales taxes represent the most significant recent development in California municipal finance. By 1959, 300 cities had enacted a sales tax under the Bradley-Burns tax law. Most of the cities are levying at a rate of 1.00 per cent of the sale price, and they contract with the state to collect the local tax. Business license taxes are also widely used in this state for city financing.

Grants from Other Governments

State grants are an important source of revenue for cities, amounting to an estimated $99,175,000 in 1959-60. These come chiefly from taxes upon motor vehicles and gasoline, and from liquor-license fees. They support street construction, policing, and general government. Smaller amounts of state assistance, or combinations of state and federal aid, are available for the support of city health programs. Federal aid was available also in previous years for the construction and extension of airports. By and large, however, in this state federal aid has played a smaller role in city finance than it has in county revenues.

Expenditures

Cities spent approximately $1,160,000,000 in 1957-58. Approximately $809,000,000 came from taxes and grants-in-aid. Of this latter sum, slightly more than 30 per cent was spent for the protection of persons and property—police and fire departments and related activities. Street expenditures amounted to over 15 per cent of city costs, interest and debt payments to 11 per cent, general city governmental costs 10 per cent, and recreation over 8 per cent. Sanitation, charities, libraries, health and miscellaneous activities accounted for the remainder. In addition to these governmental expenditures, cities spent $350 million on municipal utilities and public service activities in 1958, almost all of which came from the revenues of such enterprises.

Bond Debts

Cities are limited by law in borrowing money through bond issues. Those operating under the general state laws are prohibited from borrowing a total sum in excess of 15 per cent of the total value of property assessed for tax purposes within the city. Those operating under municipal charters have set various rates for themselves. In all cities a bond issue must be approved by a vote of two-thirds of those voting at the election. This referendum requirement has often deterred cities from going into debt; in most the bond debt is well below the legal limit. Bonds are used chiefly to finance the construction of municipal sewers, a city hall, library, or other municipal buildings. Many bond issues have financed municipal water systems or electric developments.

Tax Assessment and Exemptions

Assessment

Property is assessed in order to discover its value for tax purposes. In practice the assessed value is considerably lower than the sale value. Assessment of general property (land and buildings) has been the responsibility of city and county governments since government was organized in this state. Property of utility companies, such as electric companies, gas companies, and railroads, is assessed for tax purposes by the state Board of Equalization.

The county assessor, an elected county official, determines the assessed value of property within the county for county, school-district, and other special-district purposes. Any incorporated city may make its own assessment within its city limits. Some cities have an elected assessor; many give this responsibility to the city clerk. Approximately half the cities throughout the state make a contract with the county government to have the county tax assessor furnish them with the assessment figures that he prepares for the county; with these figures as a basis, the city councils set the tax rate for their cities. This saves duplication between the city and the county, because the county assessor must value property inside cities as well as in unincorporated areas for county purposes.

After the assessor has done his work of calculating the value of pieces of property, the owner of the property may appeal to a body known as a board of equalization if he believes that his property has been given too high a valuation in comparison with other, similar properties. The county board of supervisors acts as a board of equalization; the city council may do likewise for city assessments. The work of the state Board of Equalization is to make sure that the valuation of property in the various counties is uniform—that there is no great discrepancy between counties. This body has done much work in recent years in advising and guiding county assessors in improving valuation work.

Tax Exemptions

California has subsidized and encouraged several groups by granting exemption from property taxes. Between 1850 and 1879 it was the legislature that gave exemptions to private schools, churches, orphanages, and even some business concerns. The present constitution, when it was adopted in 1879, prohibited the legislature from doing this, yet the voters of California have approved several amendments granting exemptions to many groups. Churches, colleges, and other public-service organizations have been exempt from paying property taxes on property that they use for religious, educational, or charitable purposes. Cemeteries are also given exemption. Veterans of all wars are given exemption on the first $1,000 value of their homes if the total value does not exceed $5,000. Although there are no accurate figures to show how much property has been taken out of the taxable resources of cities, counties, and school districts by such exemption, it is generally known that the amount is large. It should be noted that these exemptions apply only to local property taxes, although they are granted by the state. One view is that if the state continues to give exemptions, it should reimburse the various local governments for their losses of revenue.

State-owned property is not subject to local property taxes; likewise, county buildings located within a city are not taxable. Where a city owns property outside its boundaries it may be subject to taxes by other governments. For example, both Los Angeles and San Francisco own waterworks and land in other counties and must pay taxes on that property. The City of Los Angeles Water and Power Department is the biggest taxpayer in Inyo and Mono counties.

Property owned by the federal government is not subject to taxation by any local government. Development of large military bases and training areas in California has removed vast acreages from county taxation, although in most instances such land did not bring in much revenue previously because it was low-value mountain or desert acreage. A more significant exemption, perhaps, exists in federal buildings, warehouses, and establishments. Several counties and school districts have been hard hit by a

1959 California Supreme Court ruling that materials used by aircraft plants and others in defense equipment for the Federal Government are exempt from local property taxes. When the national forest program was established in the early 1900's, those lands were withdrawn from local taxation. In several California mountain counties 25 to 70 per cent of the total area is within national forests. The national government, however, shares with these counties the revenue brought in by timber cutting and makes other reimbursements.

PERSONNEL

California's governments have a good reputation throughout the nation for the quality of their employees and for the modern character of governmental personnel administration. The governments in this state are among the largest employers in the nation; consequently personnel programs are important. A large percentage of employees have been brought under the merit system. Some of the larger governments in the state were the first to adopt a civil service program. San Francisco adopted it in 1900; the City of Los Angeles followed in 1903; Los Angeles County did so in 1913. The state adopted a limited system in 1913 by statute. Approximately two-thirds of the cities in California having 10,000 or more population have civil service systems.

State Personnel Board

A number of groups interested in establishing a strong, modern personnel program for the state pooled their ideas in a constitutional amendment that was adopted in 1934. To ensure reasonable stability of the management of the system and independence from much of the election politics, the amendment created a five-member state Personnel Board having overlapping ten-year terms. Board members are appointed by the governor subject to confirmation by the senate. Inasmuch as few California governors have served longer than four years, it was thought that normally no governor would have the opportunity to appoint a majority of the personnel board and so come to dominate that body. Board members serve part time; they normally meet every two weeks for a two-day session. They select an executive officer, who himself comes under civil service, to administer the program under board policies. A staff of personnel technicians, directed by the executive officer, carries out the work of the board in accordance with its rules.

The Personnel Board now plays an important role in the state's administration. It directs the recruitment and examination of employees, determines the classification of positions, determines promotion policies, conducts training programs to improve the quality of employees' work, and holds hearings when requested if an employee is dismissed, suspended, or otherwise severely disciplined. Finally the board determines the rates of pay for workers in each classification in the civil service. The salary-setting activity of the board brings it into close relationship with the legislature, which must, in the last analysis, provide the money. In setting salary scales the board must be careful not to exceed a total sum for wages and salaries that seems reasonable to the legislature.

Civil Service Coverage

Not all state employees were placed in the civil service by the 1934 amendment. Certain officers and employees were exempt from what is termed the *classified service*, and thereby are exempt from the rules of the Personnel Board. These include elective officers, officers appointed by the governor or attorney general, attachés of the courts, employees of the legislature, one deputy to each elected officer, employees of the University of California and of the Public Utility Commission, and employees of agencies financed in part or wholly by federal funds. Unless a position falls specifically in one of these categories, however, it comes within the classified service and is subject to the rules of the board.

The State's Civil Servants

The term "classified service" arises partly from the fact that the Personnel Board is required to classify all positions under civil service and to establish uniform rates of pay. The theory of classification is that positions shall be defined in terms of the degree of skill or knowledge called for and the amount of responsibility involved in the work. Positions requiring similar skill and responsibility are grouped together to form a *class*. This theory is a basic one in governmental personnel administration in the United States.

Recruitment and examinations are conducted to fill vacancies within a class rather than for single isolated positions. The classification idea is also important in setting salaries. Positions requiring equal skill and carrying equal responsibility should draw equal compensation. Salary rates can then be set for a class of positions and can be related to the salary scale of other classes that require other degrees of skill and responsibility.

Promotion in the public service involves moving to a higher class of position, one that requires greater skill and usually more responsibility and receives higher compensation. Thus classification of positions is a basic operation in an orderly personnel system.

Although the bulk of the employees in a large employment system such as that of the state of California are clerical workers, the variety of functions performed by the state government creates employment for almost every type of skill, profession, and occupation. Machinists, nurses, psychiatrists, librarians, accountants, dentists, real estate appraisers, entomologists, veterinarians, biochemists, geologists, and a long list of others are employed by the state.

Recruitment and Selection

The general public is probably more aware of the recruitment and examination work of the Personnel Board's staff than of its other activities. By means of bulletins, newspaper advertising, radio, correspondence with schools, and exhibits in public places, the board advertises for candidates for state jobs. The bulletins give a sketch of the requirements (education and experience) for the position, the type of work to be performed, the salary scale, and other information regarding employment policies. Of necessity much of the work of the board's technical staff is taken up with preparing examinations. The law requires that the examinations must be competitive and must rate the comparative abilities of the candidates to hold the position sought. When examinations have been scored, an eligible list is prepared ranking the candidates in order of their grades (the final grade of a candidate includes the added points given a war veteran). A department must then fill any vacancy it has from among the three highest candidates on the eligible list. A new employee serves a trial period of not more than a year, after which, if he serves satisfactorily, he can be dismissed only upon specific charges. Positions may be abolished, however, and the employee may be laid off if there is no longer a need for him.

Retirement of Public Employees

An important part of any career system of employment is the provision for retirement after long service. California set up a retirement system for its state employees in 1931, a system which has proved helpful in attracting employees to the state service. It is financed by appropriations from state tax funds and by deductions of a fixed percentage of employees' salaries. The funds so accumulated are managed by a retirement system board which also passes upon the eligibility of employees to retire in accordance with established rules.

In 1939, the legislature authorized cities, counties, and various other local governmental units to contract with the state employees' retirement board to join the state system. A large number of local governments have availed themselves of this opportunity. Employees of the University of California and of the state colleges have also been brought within the state retirement system. Thus the state employees' retirement board has come to serve a majority of the state- and local-government employees in California. In 1955 it was made possible for the state and local retirement systems to merge with the federal old age and survivors' insurance program.

LOCAL GOVERNMENT PERSONNEL

County Civil Service

A few of the larger counties, such as Los Angeles, Alameda, San Diego, Sacramento, Santa Clara, and San Mateo, were among the first to adopt civil service or a personnel program. They did so by means of a county charter which was adopted by the voters of the county. In 1939 other counties were given the legal authority to adopt personnel programs for all of their employees or for any group of them. A county civil service ordinance must be submitted to the voters of the county before it can be put into operation. Provisions to govern the dismissal, suspension, or demotion of county employees were set forth in the state legislation and were to be included in county civil service ordinances. Any county is authorized to prohibit its employees from engaging in political activity, and to establish a retirement program for county employees.

Los Angeles was the second county in the nation to adopt civil service. Its charter places all county employees in the classified service, except elective officials and a small number of assistants to the district attorney, sheriff, and assessor. The county Civil Service Commission in this county also administers the personnel program for the Flood Control District, the Air Pollution Control District, and fire-protection districts. It also contracts with fifteen cities within the county to give examinations and conduct other personnel duties for them.

Most of the county civil service systems are administered by commissions composed of three or five persons appointed by the board of supervisors to determine rules and policies, to hold hearings in cases involving discharge or suspension of employees, and to supervise the work of their technical staff. A few counties have an organized personnel system operating under a personnel officer who is responsible to the board of supervisors. Also most of the counties that have appointed a chief administrative officer or county manager give that officer responsibility to recommend salary rates and advise the Board of Supervisors on many matters closely related to personnel management.

More than half the counties of the state, however, do not have organized personnel programs. County employees take an active part in the election campaigns for county officers, and changes are made, at least in the higher-paid positions, where there is a substantial change in the membership of the board. Department heads are often expected to clear their appointments with members of the board of supervisors. Employees of county welfare departments, however, come under an organized personnel program that is administered by the state in accordance with a merit system laid down by federal social security laws. This is because county welfare departments administer aid programs financed by state and federal money.

City Civil Service

Cities like Los Angeles, with 30,000 employees, and San Francisco, with 15,100, are among the big governmental employers. Every city, with its police and fire forces and a street department, will have a roster of from thirty to several hundred on its payroll. Even the new city of Lakewood, which contracts with Los Angeles County for almost all of its city work, finds it necessary to have a few staff members to conduct the city's business under city council direction. As was seen with counties, those municipalities that have been permitted to have a home-rule city charter have been among the first to establish a civil service program. General state law municipalities were later permitted to adopt civil service, and many have done so. Most cities have followed the usual pattern of appointing a citizens' commission to determine personnel policies and rules, and employing a technical staff to give examinations and perform other duties of a central personnel office. Several city-manager cities have placed the responsibility for personnel management upon the manager. In Berkeley, for example, the manager appoints a personnel officer who is advised by a personnel commission. In Pasadena the manager is responsible, and he appoints a personnel officer to carry out his policies and assist him generally. In Santa Monica the manager appoints a personnel director subject to the approval of the personnel board which is appointed by the council. A city manager or an administrative officer must of necessity concern himself with many matters relating to personnel if he is to direct the city's administration. Most managers appoint department heads and other key officers without reference to civil service, although the rank and file of employees may be selected from civil service eligible lists.

Any city, county, or district may make a contract with the state Personnel Board, a county, a city, or a private firm to give examinations, classify positions, and train employees. The state Personnel Board has a special staff that serves local governments. Most of the cities served are small ones that do not find it economical to employ their own personnel technicians, but who desire to use a modern personnel system.

Recruitment to municipal civil service positions is generally restricted to persons already residing in the city, although a number of cities have waived this residence requirement and have sought the best-qualified person they could find to fill such important posts as city health officer, city planning director, police chief, or city engineer. As standards of education and training are raised for the key positions, cities find it necessary to look outside their own city limits for well-qualified persons. Entrance into city service is generally at the beginning level, however, and promotion within the various departments permits the long-time employee to rise to higher-paid and more responsible jobs. Employment is fairly stable in most cities in California, although police departments in a number of the smaller places suffer disruption and a turnover when there is a change in the membership of the city council.

Further Reading

Finance

California, Legislature, Assembly Interim Committee on Government Organization, *The Need for a Department of Revenue in California*. Sacramento: State Printing Office, 1955.

California, Legislature, Joint Fact-Finding Committee on Highways, Streets and Bridges, *An Analysis of Taxation for Highway Purposes in California, 1895-1946*. Sacramento: State Printing Office, 1946.

California, Legislature, Senate Interim Committee on State and Local Taxation, *Report*. Sacramento: State Printing Office, 1955.

California, Legislative Analyst, *Analysis of the Budget Bill.* Sacramento: State Printing Office, annual.

Crouch, W. W., J. E. Swanson, W. R. Bigger, and J. A. Algie, *Finance and Taxation.* Los Angeles: Haynes Foundation, 1954.

Kitchen, James D., *Administration of Municipal Sales Taxes in California.* Los Angeles: University of California, Bureau of Governmental Research, 1949.

Lee, Eugene C., *State Equalization of Local Assessments.* Berkeley: University of California, Bureau of Public Administration, 1953.

McCarty, John F., *A Survey of State Taxes.* Berkeley: University of California, Bureau of Public Administration, 1955.

Stockwell, Marvel M., *Studies in California Taxation, 1910-1935.* Publications of the University of California at Los Angeles in Social Sciences, VII. Berkeley: University of California, 1939.

Personnel

California, Legislature, Assembly Interim Committee on Governmental Efficiency and Economy, *State Salary Policies and Practices.* Sacramento: State Printing Office, 1953.

California, Legislature, Senate Interim Committee on Civil Service, *Final Report.* Sacramento: State Printing Office, 1953.

California, State Personnel Board, *Biennial Reports.* Sacramento: State Printing Office.

California Taxpayers' Association, *Personnel Administration, Selected California Counties, 1953-54.* Los Angeles, 1954.

Jones, Helen L., *Personnel Management (Metropolitan Los Angeles: A Study in Integration,* Vol. X). Los Angeles: Haynes Foundation, 1953.

League of California Cities, *A Suggested Personnel System.* Berkeley, 1953.

National Civil Service League, *Whither the Merit System?* New York, 1945.

Olson, Emery E., "A Personnel Board in Action," *Public Personnel Review,* 7 (October, 1946), 200-208.

Eleven

County Government

THE DESIRABILITY of having county governments was recognized in the Constitution of 1849. Acknowledgment of their necessity was rooted in the conviction that the state government should not attempt to supply all of its public services from one central location. Rather, the constitution framers decided that political subdivisions of the state should be formed to aid in rendering certain functions of statewide importance promptly and efficiently to people in local areas. The constitution therefore specified the election of numerous judicial officials, the board of supervisors, clerk, coroner, district attorney, and sheriff, and instructed the state legislature to create as many counties as were needed. In the following year the legislature carved the entire territory of the state into twenty-seven counties. Thus were born in California not only the governmental institution of counties but also their early functional and organizational patterns.

STATE-COUNTY RELATIONS

Functionally, counties for many years were almost exclusively aides to the state government. Their activities were then mainly judicial work, property recording and assessment, election administration, tax collection, law enforcement, and road construction and maintenance. Only in more recent years have functions of a different nature been added, such as public welfare programs, flood control, water conservation, parks and recreation, and agricultural services. Out of this expansion of activities, counties have become both administrative subdivisions of the state government and units of local government. Organizationally, separately elected officials were required from the beginning to be in charge of many individual services. This structural characteristic still persists in most counties.

Excluding a limited number of state constitutional requirements, counties were for sixty-two years entirely subject to actions of the state legislature. During the initial thirty years, the period of the first state constitution which was replaced in 1879, many laws applying to the duties of particular officers in all counties were passed as well as an exceedingly large amount of legislation pertaining to one or a few counties.

The legislative power to enact special or local laws affecting county elections and activities was eliminated in the new constitution of 1879. Furthermore, the legislature was instructed to create a uniform system of county government throughout the state. With the passage of the new constitution, the state government was limited to the enactment of general laws in its regulation of local governments. A further important change materialized in 1911, when the county home-rule amendment became part of the state constitution, thus making all counties eligible to have their own charters upon approval of the local electorate. Subsequently all counties have operated under either general-law or charter organization.

AREAS

The areas of all fifty-eight counties became stationary shortly before county home rule became available. Although no county boundaries have been altered for more than fifty years, there were many changes before 1900. Sometimes this resulted from the establishment of new settlements as the population increased, and the demands of the residents for quicker and better county services than could be furnished from a distant county seat. At other times such changes grew out of political deals in the legislature in which a modification in county territory was made in exchange for support of another legislative proposal. With some frequency, therefore, the legislature readjusted territorial lines and formed new counties out of part of the area of one or more existing counties. In addition, some county seats were transferred from one community to another and several new county names supplanted original designations. The last county, Imperial, was created in 1907 by taking part of the land of San Diego County. Three years later a state constitutional amendment was passed, making more difficult the future division of counties to organize new ones. Since the formation of Imperial County the total has been fifty-eight counties, including the one city-county of San Francisco. The latter, which is a consolidated county and city, was created through a special legislative act passed in 1856. A section in the constitution of 1879, permitting the merger of a county with cities within its territory, has so far not been used, in part because of the difficult nature of the voter approval procedure.

Differing Characteristics

The areas of counties are seemingly permanent for the foreseeable future. Only occasionally, as in Riverside County in 1955 and San Bernardino County in 1959, are there outcries of support for dividing a county, but such efforts are generally sporadic and short-lived. Currently there is no widespread interest in either further divisions or consolidations. In addition, retention of the existing arrangement is fostered by the plan of state senate representation, which is founded on counties. The characteristics of the areas occupied by counties range widely and have a direct effect upon the nature and intensity of the services supplied. Even in amount of territory covered there are strong contrasts. At one extreme, San Bernardino County, the largest territorially in the United States, covers more than 20,000 square miles. At the other, the city and county of San Francisco embraces only 42 square miles, and Santa Cruz County, the smallest regular county, has 435 square miles. There are broad differences, too, in the topography and economy of many of them, which in turn affect their financial resources. Furthermore, the size of the resident population varies greatly among counties. One of them in the Sierra Nevada, Alpine County, has a population of 400, which constitutes a smaller number than lived there in 1900. On the other hand, Los Angeles County has nearly six million inhabitants, and the floodtide of migration is continuing.

Such differing characteristics bring on variations in the types and levels of demands for services, the ability to finance them, and the operational or administrative methods employed. In other words, as a result of their presence the problems encountered are not the same for all county governments. Whatever the individual differences that exist, counties are generally continuing to grow in number of services provided directly to people. Most of today's counties are engaged in far more activities than any counties of a hundred or even fifty years ago.

SERVICES TO THE PEOPLE

In turning to representative examples of county governmental functions, it is to be emphasized that not all county services are supplied to the public on a county-wide basis. Some, such as public welfare programs, probation, testing of weights and measures, and recording of documents and vital information, are exclusively provided by the county government throughout the entire territory of the county. They are furnished both to city dwellers and to persons living in the county outside of cities. Some others, such as police and fire protection, are furnished by the county government only to people not living within cities; city inhabitants obtain them from their city government. Still others are handled by the county government for non-city people and may be performed for city dwellers if the city government contracts with the county. Included are tax assessment and collection, public health, and recreation. A final group consists of services needed solely in the agricultural or rural county sections. Illustrations are animal inspection and forest and wildlife protection.

Charities and Corrections

By far the largest amount of money expended by county governments is devoted to a series of services collectively known as charities and corrections. It consists of social-welfare programs, county hospital and physician activities, housing for the aged, and probation work. The principal social-welfare services of counties involve four programs. Each is concerned with help, generally in the form of money, to a different group. The first program is aid to the needy aged. The second is aid to the needy blind and to partially self-supporting blind residents. The third is aid to needy children under eighteen years of age who require assistance because of abandonment or loss or incapacitation of parents. The fourth is general relief, consisting largely of assistance given to indigents outside of institutions. It includes cash payments, distribution of commodities, and provision of services needed.

The national and state governments provide grants of considerable size in support of the counties rendering services in the first three programs. Only the general relief program is financed entirely by counties. The programs are administered by either the county board of supervisors or the board of public welfare, acting through welfare departments which have been established in all counties in the state. Activities in the first three programs receive additional supervision by national and state government agencies. Approximately 500,000 people receive aid under the various social-welfare programs.

County hospital and physician services for the care of the indigent are another important part of the charities and corrections service group. More than 25,000 hospital beds are provided for indigent and part-pay patients. The facilities receive regular inspection by the state Department of Social Welfare which also reviews plans for changes. Furthermore, all counties provide for the housing of needy aged, and many maintain separate homes for them.

Adult and juvenile probation form the final, significant phase of the numerous charities and corrections services supplied by counties. A major objective of adult probation is to have trained officers supply guidance to offenders most likely to respond to treatment outside of penal institutions. The offenders are given a conditional suspension of their prison sentence by the court during the probation period. If their response is affirmative, the sentence suspension becomes permanent. Sometimes juvenile probation involves similar work. At other times it consists of activities concerning children who have not committed an offense. In these instances the probation officer investigates cases about children allegedly neglected or abused, whose homes are unfit, or whose welfare is otherwise in doubt. If necessary, they are given court protection and casework services through the county probation department. This department also investigates the commitment of feeble-minded persons, handles money paid by court order to support a ward of the court, and manages the county's juvenile hall or detention home. Broad discrepancies exist between counties in probation staffs, facilities, and equipment.

Roads and Bridges

Road and bridge construction and maintenance are further important services of county government. The state government is now responsible for building and repairing the main highways, but the counties maintain roads totaling 67,000 miles. This is almost two-thirds of all road and street mileage kept up by state and local governments in California. Most of the money used by counties for these functions is supplied by the state government. For many years the administration of county roads was actually performed by each member of the board of supervisors acting as road commissioner for his district. Sizable variations in the adequacy of roads and the standards of construction and maintenance then existed.*

State legislation enacted in 1947 required the consolidation of all county road activities into a single department. All counties have completed the mandatory consolidation, and most of the road commissioners are now registered engineers. In a few cases, however, the consolidation is only nominal. This legislation also

---

* State Legislature, Joint Fact-finding Committee on Highways, Streets, and Bridges, *Engineering Facts and a Future Program* (Sacramento: State Printing Office, 1946), p. 27.

required the selection of a primary county road system on which part of the state money must be spent. Some counties have carefully selected their primary systems, but others have simply designated one-half of their maintained mileage as primary.

Protective Activities

County governments supply numerous services that are protections to persons and property. These include law enforcement and jail maintenance, the recording of documents and information, the inspection of weights and measures, the furnishing of agricultural aids and livestock inspection, and fire protection. County law enforcement is carried out by the sheriff's department in the non-city sections of the county. The departmental personnel preserve the peace, investigate public offenses, and arrest offenders. The sheriff also maintains the county jail and has numerous duties pertaining to civil and criminal proceedings, including summoning jurors and executing court orders.

The county provides for the recording and preservation of documents and information designed to safeguard the personal and property interests of individuals. Two county officials, the clerk and the recorder, have recording responsibilities. The clerk keeps records of voter registration, elections, naturalization, marriages, and persons professionally engaged in public-health work. The recorder registers land titles, transfers, and encumbrances, as well as wills, births, and deaths.

Other protective services are also supplied. The county sealer of weights and measures periodically inspects and tests scales, weights, and other measuring instruments utilized in selling goods publicly. The county agricultural commissioner inspects and assists in protecting orchards and crops from infestation, and works toward eliminating plant and animal pests. Furthermore, in cooperation with the state and national governments, counties provide protection against forest, brush, and grass fires in rural areas.

Justice and Elections

Major work is performed by counties in the basic public services of the administering of justice and the conduct of elections.

In the former, for example, the county supplies clerical and recording services and personnel to both the superior and lower courts. Then, too, the district attorney prosecutes cases of public offenses and has powers of investigation. The county operates an election system which is used in selecting national, state, and county officials and in some instances city and special-district officers. The responsibility for its honest and efficient operation rests generally upon the county clerk and, in several larger counties, upon a special registrar of voters. The county clerk or the registrar of voters and his deputies are the only officers who can register people for voting. City and district clerks utilize the county registration records to identify people desiring to vote in their elections.

A Variety of Other Services

Counties provide numerous health and sanitation services to non-city people, and frequently to city residents through contracts with individual city governments. Included here is the provision by counties of almost 7,000 hospital beds for tuberculosis control. Through the county superintendents of schools, they supply assistance and specialized services that would otherwise be available exclusively to students in the larger and wealthier school districts. Many county library systems are in operation, frequently circulating books through small distribution centers or bookmobiles. Surveying and map-making services are available through the office of the surveyor. The coroner of the county government investigates deaths suspected to have resulted from unnatural causes. The public administrator handles the estates of people who have died without a will and without known heirs. These various functions represent the most frequent county governmental services. There are numerous others which are provided less frequently—airports, beaches, parks, playgrounds, camping and picnic grounds, and sewage, garbage, and rubbish disposal. Obviously, therefore, counties are important governments providing a broad range of activities which are significant to many people. Moreover, the scope of county services to both city and non-city inhabitants is expanding.

General Government Functions

Brief mention should be made of several county governmental operations without which the previously considered public services will be rendered either less efficiently or not at all. They are called general government functions. Taxes must be collected to help pay for the functions. The county tax collector takes in property and county license taxes. All county money is deposited with the treasurer. Money is received into the treasury only upon certificate of the auditor, and expenditures of county funds are similarly made solely upon his warrant. In these ways, he is able to keep account of all money entering and leaving the treasury. The value of property for taxation purposes is determined by the assessor. The clerk, in addition to his other duties, acts personally or has a deputy serve as record keeper to the board of supervisors. Sometimes there exists a civil service commission to establish recruitment and employment rules for county personnel. Frequently, too, a planning commission and its staff are active in subdivision and land-use control. And most fundamental of all operations are the decisions of the five-member board of supervisors which controls county finances and legislates county policy.

ORGANIZING FOR ACTION: GENERAL-LAW COUNTIES

Like many other endeavors involving numerous people, counties must have a structural arrangement in order to carry out their activities. Forty-seven counties, or almost four out of every five, have an organization based directly upon the uniform system of county government created by the legislature. Because of their great dependence upon state legislative decisions which are applicable to the organization of all of them, they are known as general-law counties. In instituting this system more than eighty years ago, California followed the plan of older states and provided for the election of each officer performing important functions and of some exercising minor ones. As social and economic conditions and public needs have changed, certain original offices have been eliminated and several that have been retained have been combined. However, the original basic plan has not been substantially altered.

Many Elected Officials

The most prominent feature of the organization of general-law counties is the election of many officials. Although some required offices and boards must be filled by appointment or by officials serving ex officio, numerous offices must be elective in general-law counties in accordance with state constitutional and legislative provisions. These include the board of supervisors, assessor, auditor, clerk, coroner, district attorney, public administrator, recorder, sheriff, superintendent of schools, surveyor, tax collector and ex officio license collector, and treasurer. Each of these many officials has his own separate sphere of activity—or petty kingdom, to use the term of numerous critics of this type of organization. Each of them is responsible only to the voters and not to a legislative body or a single chief executive. General-law counties thus operate under an organizational system that is much more disintegrated than that of either the state government or most city governments. Formal unified direction can be exerted principally through the annual budget-making power of the board of supervisors. Because of its nature, however, the authority can be utilized only intermittently. Then, too, although the board can question the need for increases in salaries, personnel, equipment, and supplies, it is not empowered to order changes in procedure that might reduce the justification for various requests. Informally, of course, personality or political factors may facilitate increased coordination of activities, and sometimes conscientious officials voluntarily cooperate.

The organization of general-law counties makes necessary the use of a long ballot in county elections. A lengthy list of officeholders and candidates seeking to unseat the incumbents generally confronts the voters. This situation occurs every four years at the same election as that for governor and several other state and national officers. As in all local elections, those for county positions are nonpartisan in the sense that the names of the candidates appear without political party label. This has been the continuing practice in the state since 1913, although unsuc-

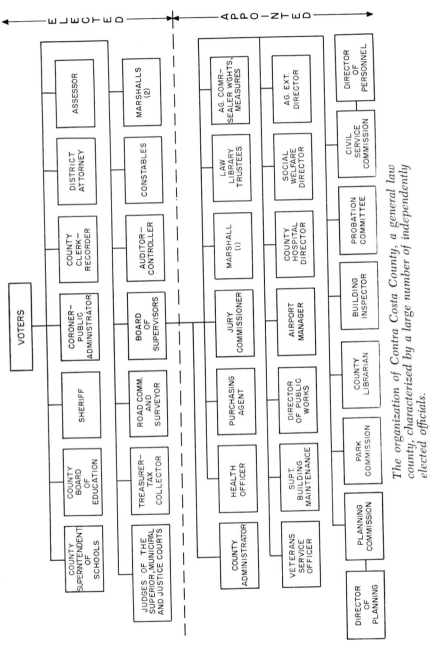

The organization of Contra Costa County, a general law county, characterized by a large number of independently elected officials.

226

cessful attempts were made during the 1955 and 1959 state legislative sessions to convert county and municipal elections to a
partisan basis. Usually the incumbents in administrative posts
who run for re-election are successful in their candidacy. Many
have served for several consecutive terms, and some have been
re-elected continuously for twenty or more years.

Criticisms

The lack of central direction, control, and responsibility, the
election of administrators, and the heavy burden placed on the
voters are criticized as being unfortunate results of the diffused
organizational structure. The state legislature has taken an increasing interest in this problem. In 1959 a bill was passed which
allows the board of supervisors in general-law counties with a
population in excess of 220,000, with the approval of the electorate, to replace the elected county auditor with an appointed
director of finance. The same legislature considered but did not
pass a bill which would have given the supervisors, after receiving voter approval, the power to (1) appoint most of the positions currently filled by election and (2) create the appointive
office of county executive.

Office Consolidations

Partial rather than substantial reorganization has been taking
place over the years in general-law counties. Five developments
have contributed toward this movement. The first is the authority
of the board of supervisors in all or many counties to pass ordinances consolidating numerous offices into one or more of
twenty combinations. Of the positions involved, only those of
the agricultural commissioner and the sealer of weights and measures are appointive rather than elective. Therefore, broad use of
this power can substantially reduce the number of elective officials and increasingly concentrate responsibility among fewer
persons who can be more easily held accountable by the voters.
Three of the optional mergers each concern the duties of three
officers. They are (1) auditor, clerk, and recorder, (2) assessor,
tax collector, and treasurer, and (3) recorder, tax collector, and

treasurer. Each of the other seventeen alternatives listed below integrates two offices. The office in the left-hand column may be combined with the office, or any of the offices, appearing opposite it in the right-hand column.

Agricultural commissioner	Sealer of weights and measures
Assessor	Tax collector or treasurer
Auditor	Clerk or recorder
Clerk	Auditor, public administrator, recorder, or tax collector
Coroner	District attorney, public administrator, or sheriff
District attorney	Coroner or public administrator
Public administrator	Clerk, coroner, district attorney, sheriff, or treasurer
Recorder	Auditor, clerk, or treasurer
Sealer of weights and measures	Agricultural commissioner
Sheriff	Coroner, public administrator, or tax collector
Tax collector	Assessor, clerk, sheriff, or treasurer
Treasurer	Assessor, public administrator, recorder, or tax collector

After being integrated, these offices may later be separated by supervisorial ordinance, or be reconsolidated in any of the other allowable combinations. This happens occasionally. Recently, for example, Amador County separated—within a period of three years—the merged positions of sheriff and tax collector and joined the previously separate offices of tax collector and treasurer. Persons filling the combined positions perform the duties and receive the compensation of the offices involved.

How extensively is the comprehensive authorization being utilized? Every one of the forty-seven general-law counties has at least one combination in operation; and, in all, well over one hundred office mergers are in effect. Sixteen of the twenty possible combinations are in use. Furthermore, the unification of three or more offices has materialized in more than one-half of the counties. In general, however, the development is most widespread in the less populous counties, substantially because of the part-time nature of many offices which have a heavier volume of public business elsewhere. As an illustration, Modoc County, with fewer than 10,000 residents, has five combinations of offices. On the other hand, very few of the general-law counties with more than 30,000 population—and these make up well over one-half of the total—have effected more than three combinations.

The most frequent consolidations involve the offices of coroner and public administrator. About three-fifths of the counties have done this. Other offices often combined are treasurer and tax collector, agricultural commissioner and sealer of weights and measures, and sheriff and coroner. No counties have utilized the triple consolidation of assessor, tax collector, and treasurer or the dual mergers involving the assessor and treasurer, the clerk and public administrator, and the clerk and tax collector. Even though its extensive use has been, for the most part, limited to the more sparsely populated counties, the development constitutes a direct reduction in the number of elected county officials and an important step toward increased concentration of authority and responsibility.

Assigning New Functions to Supervisors

The second development bringing on change in the organization of general-law counties is the result of new functions that have been undertaken. Authorization to perform many additional services has been granted to counties, especially since 1930. Some of these powers have been vested in existing independent offices and others have been conferred upon newly established offices or boards. Many times, however, the administration of new functions has been allotted to employees appointed by the board of supervisors rather than to independently elected officials. Often the supervisorial board decides whether the function will be exercised by the county. In large part, therefore, the increase in functions has meant an increase in supervisorial power and consequently a greater degree of administrative integration and coordination in county activities under the board of supervisors.

Staff Services and Salary Control

The third development has involved the introduction of staff services as aids to the board of supervisors in carrying out its responsibilities. The two most important are modern budgetary practices and centralized purchasing. Now in use in numerous general-law counties, they contribute to increased concentration of authority and control.

Supervisorial control of most county salaries is the fourth development. Although the board of supervisors had the power of determining the budget amounts of all county departments from the beginning, it was not equipped to challenge particular requests until uniform budgetary procedures were installed. Even then, independently elected officials were substantially free in their operations because the legislature determined the salaries of these officers and their subordinates. It was not until 1933 that the state legislative power over county salaries was restricted. The boards of supervisors were then authorized to fix the compensation of all county officers and employees except their own salaries and those of the auditor, district attorney, and members of grand and trial juries. Most of the exceptions were made to guarantee the independence of certain county activities in financial, legal, and investigatory matters. The power to determine salaries of county school superintendents was subsequently returned to the legislature through a constitutional amendment in 1946.

The Administrative Officer Development

The fifth development important to the partial reorganization of general-law counties is now in a period of rapid growth. It is the appointment by the board of supervisors of a full-time person to assist the board in the performance of some of its duties. This person is most often legally identified as the administrative officer or county administrator, although in a few counties he is called administrative assistant and in one, county executive officer. Most of them come from one of two work backgrounds. Many were the administrative head or an employee of a department in the same county. Many others were the administrative officer or staff aide to one in another county.

The creation of this type of post does not mean a transfer of authority from the board of supervisors. Such a delegation is legally forbidden in general-law counties. Rather, the board assigns to the administrative officer certain duties which continue to be its final responsibility. The duties are performed by him at the discretion of the board and under its direction. He is therefore a full-time assistant, holding his post at the pleasure of the board, which is part-time in its county activities. He is in no legal sense a county manager, a matter to be discussed later in connection with charter counties.

The legal bases—ordinances or resolutions—of the boards of supervisors creating these positions vary considerably in the exact activities which are allotted. In practice, however, the duties are much the same. Generally, therefore, the administrative officer aids the board in preparing the annual budget or recommends a proposed budget to the board. He oversees the operation of the adopted budget, principally to make certain that departments function within the amounts granted to them. He directs a centralized purchasing service. He conducts research into administrative practices and personnel policies, presenting suggestions designed to improve efficiency and cooperation. He represents the county in contacts with other governments. He undertakes particular assignments requested of him by the board of supervisors.

The practice of appointing an administrative officer is expanding rapidly after a hesitant start. In 1946, Kern County became the first general-law county to utilize the idea, but no others followed this example during the closing years of the decade. Since 1950, however, there have been many adoptions throughout the state in counties both large and small, rural and urban. A total of twenty-five general-law counties have become part of this significant movement, a majority of them since 1955.

The rapid rise in popularity of the idea can be traced mainly to the growing work burden of the board of supervisors. This in turn is the result of the continued increase in services demanded by county residents. The degree of success experienced by an administrative officer is substantially determined by his relations with the board of supervisors and the other county officials. Formally the county organization still remains largely disconnected because the elective status of numerous county officials remains undisturbed. Nevertheless, through offering help, direction, and cooperation the administrative officer is in some counties making noticeable contributions toward improved performance of services to the public.

ORGANIZING FOR ACTION: CHARTER COUNTIES

The second or charter type of organization is in operation in ten counties, less than one-fifth of the total. In 1911 the county home-rule amendment was added to the state constitution. In this way California became the first state in which authority was granted to counties to operate under a charter containing a locally conceived and approved plan of government. Charter counties, however, are not completely free from certain general state laws and state constitutional sections. They may endow themselves with some extension of functions, but the additions must not be in conflict with general state laws relating to activities they perform as administrative subdivisions of the state. Furthermore, although the exact extent of charter-county functions has not been determined by the courts, it is apparently much more restricted than that of charter cities in the state.

Significance of Charter Power

The greatest significance of the charter or home-rule power is that any county, regardless of population, can substantially reshape the organization under which it has been functioning as a general-law county. In addition, the authorization permits consideration of local conditions which cannot be included in general state legislation. Reorganization can be extremely thorough. For example, under the constitutional grant, a charter can be prepared making all county officers the appointees of the board of supervisors, who are the only elected officials. One appointee of the board can be a full-time professional administrator or executive responsible to the board for overseeing, directing, and coordinating all county activities. This governmental form contrasts markedly with the diffused organization of general-law counties. On the other hand, it parallels the council-manager system, the type most often adopted in recent years by cities in California and throughout the United States. San Bernardino County adopted a charter in 1912 in which only the board of supervisors was elected. But this structural arrangement never got a chance to be tried. An amendment reconverting all of the previously elected officials to their former status was approved three years later before the charter became effective.

Mandatory and Optional Provisions

The county home-rule section of the state constitution requires that certain matters must be included in a county charter. A board of supervisors of at least three members must be elected and their compensation stipulated. The appointment or election of numerous county officials must be established by the charter or the board of supervisors. The powers, duties, and method of removal of supervisors and other county officers must be specified. The consolidation and segregation of offices and the filling of vacancies must be determined. These are among the most important matters that must be incorporated in a charter. Many others may be included at the option of the charter drafters. Thus it can be seen that the state constitution simply sets a broad framework for the organization that is determined by local charter drafters.

Charter Activities

Adoption of a county charter involves several steps. Three or more of the supervisors passing an ordinance or 15 per cent of the qualified county voters signing petitions constitute a sufficient action to initiate the election of fifteen persons charged with drawing up a charter. They have one year (the time was extended from a limit of 180 days with the passage of a 1956 state constitutional amendment) to decide upon the contents of the charter. The finished document is submitted to the county voters at a special election and must receive a majority of the votes cast to be approved. The charter is then transmitted to the state legislature for its approval without amendment or alteration. Legally the legislature may disapprove the proposal, but it has never done so. The charter can be subsequently amended through majority popular vote. It can also be annulled by a two-thirds vote at a special election. So far, however, no county has rescinded its charter and returned to operating exclusively under the general state laws.

Interest in obtaining county charters has been intermittent. The greatest amount of activity occurred immediately after the passage of the home-rule amendment and in the depression years of the 1930's. Ten have been approved and have gone into effect, and sixteen have been rejected. The ten counties and the effective dates of their charters are:

Los Angeles (1913)	Fresno (1933)
San Bernardino (1913)	Sacramento (1933)
Butte (1917)	San Diego (1933)
Tehama (1917)	San Mateo (1933)
Alameda (1927)	Santa Clara (1951)

Sacramento, San Diego (twice), and Santa Clara counties had earlier charter defeats. In addition, a charter approved in 1948 in Santa Clara County was later declared unconstitutional because of faulty official publication. An election effort has been made in only a single county to supplant the original charter with a second one. This occurred in 1935, when a new charter was disapproved by the electorate of Butte County. Unsuccessful attempts to obtain charters have been made in ten other counties. They are Napa (1917), Santa Barbara (1917), Stanislaus (1930), Mendocino (1932), Kern (1935), San Luis Obispo (1935), Siskiyou (1947, 1948), Merced (1950), Riverside (1958), and Marin (1958). Installation of the administrative officer idea in numerous general-law counties has reduced charter interest in many of them.

Charters are largely in use in the most populous counties in the state. Of the ten having them, only Tehama and Butte counties possess small populations. Conversely, all but four of the counties with more than 250,000 people operate under charters. The exceptions are Contra Costa, Kern, Orange, and Riverside.

Important Changes

What important differences have resulted from adopting a county charter? Two major distinctions have materialized in some charter counties, but the two have not always occurred in the same counties. The most basic change is the appointment by the board of supervisors or their agents of numerous officials who are elected in general-law counties. This places greater authority and responsibility for efficient performance of county activities upon the supervisors. It also does away with the traditional long county ballot and permits the voters to concentrate their attention on electing and holding accountable a few major officials. Three counties have made extensive changes of this sort, and a fourth has converted several previously elected officers to appointive status.

The most comprehensive alterations have taken place in Los Angeles County. There the only elective officials are the board of supervisors, assessor, district attorney, and sheriff. The list of elected officials, with one addition for each of them, is the same for two other counties, Santa Clara and Sacramento. The county superintendent of schools is elected in Santa Clara County and the auditor is elected in Sacramento County. All three of these counties therefore represent very substantial deviations from the large number of officials elected in general-law counties. The alterations in San Diego County are much less thorough. Three officials elected in general-law counties—the auditor, county superintendent of schools, and surveyor—are appointed in San Diego County. However, eight officials other than the five members of the board of supervisors are elected. The other six charter counties have generally followed the general-law county pattern of electing many officials.

The second principal distinction is the appointment by the board of supervisors of a county manager or county executive who has the direct authority under the charter to supervise and control the activities of the county government. He is responsible to the board for the quality and the efficiency of county services and may be removed by it at any time. The county-manager system is functioning in three charter counties. Sacramento

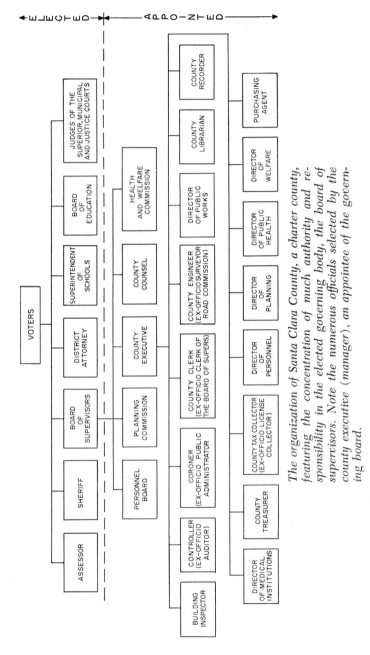

The organization of Santa Clara County, a charter county, featuring the concentration of much authority and responsibility in the elected governing body, the board of supervisors. Note the numerous officials selected by the county executive (manager), an appointee of the governing board.

County has operated under the plan since 1933, Santa Clara County since 1951, and San Mateo County initially from 1933 to 1938 and again since 1951. At the time of appointment, the county managers were occupying jobs as assistant chief administrative officer of San Diego County, county counsel and former acting county executive of Santa Clara County, and county manager in Charleston County, South Carolina.

There is an important legal difference between administrative officers, discussed earlier, and county managers. The former act for the board of supervisors and are largely confined to recommending. On the other hand, county managers have direct authority to act on matters outlined in the charter. Thus, for example, unlike administrative officers, county managers can appoint and remove numerous county officials and employees.

Although some counties have incorporated a reduction in elected officials or a county-manager system or both into their charters, most charter counties have installed neither of these changes. In other words, most charter counties are very similar to general-law counties in having many elected officers and no county manager. However, many charter counties have become a part of the administrative-officer movement that has also involved numerous general-law counties. Thus, by ordinance or resolution of the board of supervisors six charter counties have administrative officers. They are (with the starting dates of operation in parentheses): Los Angeles (1938), San Diego (1947), Butte (1947), San Bernardino (1948), Fresno (1949-50, 1952), and Alameda (1950). The duties and previous work experience of the men holding these posts is quite similar to those of administrative officers in general-law counties.

THE CITY AND COUNTY OF SAN FRANCISCO

San Francisco merits separate consideration, since it is the only city-county in the state and one of the few in the United States. By special legislative act in 1856 the San Francisco city limits were enlarged and the new area was separated from the remainder of the county, which became San Mateo County. A consolidated city-county, whose single government provided both city and county functions for its residents, thus came into existence. The first local charter was adopted in 1898 and was repeatedly amended. It was replaced by a second charter which has been in operation since 1932.

The current charter represents a blending of the terms of county and city government. The governing board is called the board of supervisors. It contains eleven members, six more than serve on the supervisorial board of any other county in California and more nearly resembling the size of some city councils. Every two years five or six supervisors are elected at large to four-year terms. The board chairman, legally known as the president, is selected from among the members for a two-year period. The mayor, possessing a title used in most cities in the United States, is elected for four years. He has important appointive powers, including the selection of a chief administrative officer, a designation used in numerous counties and cities in the state.

Exclusive of the superior and municipal court judges, the elective officers consist of the mayor, the supervisors, and the heads of six executive departments—assessor, city attorney, district attorney, public defender, sheriff, and treasurer. The various officers are elected for four-year terms at three successive annual elections. The board of supervisors is confined to legislative functions and has been divested of administrative duties. They have been assigned to the mayor and his appointees, especially the chief administrative officer and the controller, and to elected department heads.

Responsibility for the operations of city-county government in San Francisco is therefore divided among the mayor, the chief administrative officer, and six elected department heads. Although the mayor is independently elected, possesses the veto power, and appoints various department heads, he has less authority than the mayors of numerous cities in other parts of the United States. For example, he selects the chief administrative officer when a vacancy exists in the position, but he does not have the power of removal. Removal can be accomplished only through a two-thirds vote of the board of supervisors or through recall by the voters after six months or more in office. The chief administrative officer directs ten departments and passes upon their budget estimates. Neither removal method has ever been attempted. The first incumbent held the post for ten years until his death, and the second one served seventeen years until his retirement. In contrast, the third person to occupy the position resigned after seven months.

Further Reading

Bollens, John C., and Stanley Scott, *Local Government in California.* Berkeley: University of California Press, 1951.

California, Legislature, Assembly Interim Committee on Municipal and County Government, *Modernization of Noncharter County Law.* Sacramento: State Printing Office, 1959.

County Supervisors' Association of California, *County Government in California.* Sacramento, rev. ed., 1958.

————, *County Government 1959.* Sacramento, 1959.

News Letter, published periodically at Sacramento by the County Supervisors' Association of California.

Twelve

City Government

CITY GOVERNMENTS have always been regarded as fundamental parts of the governmental system of California. Since the first days of statehood large numbers of people have lived in close proximity and faced difficulty in working out some common problems on a private basis. In response to these situations city governmental machinery was early formulated as a collective public means of locally attacking problems and providing services to residents of such areas. Over the years the necessity of having these governments has increased. Continuing public demands have brought on a growth in numbers and levels of city governmental functions. In addition, much of the heavy population increase of the state has occurred in cities. Approximately seven of every ten Californians are at present city dwellers.

STATE-CITY RELATIONS

During the period of the first state constitution from 1849 to 1879 city governments were largely controlled by the state government. Some cities functioned entirely under individual state laws passed at various times, but most of them in addition to such acts operated under special charters conferred by the state legislature. A special charter consisted of a series of grants and restrictions relating to a specific city. Typical powers often given in these charters were to make ordinances and determine penalties for violations, prevent and remove nuisances, license and regulate various kinds of businesses, construct and maintain public buildings and areas, regulate building construction, provide for city elections, borrow money, incur indebtedness, and levy a limited amount of taxes.*

Early State Interference

Although functions authorized in special legislative charters were grants of local self-government, actual interference by the state legislature in local affairs was widespread. Charters were often amended, superseded, or repealed. Then, too, state laws were frequently passed which substantially intervened in the activities of individual cities. Only occasionally were the desires of city officials or residents considered before such state actions went into effect.

The many kinds of state interference with municipal affairs before 1879 can be grouped generally into three classes. Meddling in the financial affairs of specific cities was most prevalent. Municipalities were ordered to pay individual claims, transfer money in city funds, and issue bonds without obtaining prior approval of the local voters. They were also frequently compelled to pay certain salary amounts to city officers, spend money or levy taxes for particular purposes, sell city-owned property, and receive city warrants or other claims in payment of city taxes. A second state legislative approach was to establish special boards or commissions whose representatives were not selected by officials or residents of the city. These boards were empowered to regulate various matters of local concern, such as fire protection, municipal waterworks, parks, and streets. In the third type of intrusion the state ostensibly enabled the city to act on certain matters. This was the most deceptive form of interference, since the California supreme court early held that many of these laws would be interpreted as being compulsory. Thus, state laws pur-

---

* The evolution of cities toward a greater degree of local determination is traced in detail by John C. Peppin in four articles in the *California Law Review*, November, 1941; March, 1942; December, 1944; and December, 1946.

porting to be permissive were actually mandatory and directed cities to assume additional functions.

The scope of state intervention in local matters had been substantially reduced even before restrictions were placed in the new Constitution of 1879. By this time the California supreme court had completely abandoned the doctrine of absolute legislative supremacy over cities. For example, in the four years immediately preceding the constitutional convention of 1879, the court announced three implied limitations on state legislative power over city activities: (1) no interference with city affairs by mandatory state legislation, since such action violated the inherent right of local self-government; (2) no legislatively authorized claims against cities for municipal purposes without the consent of those to be taxed for such payment; and (3) no creation by the state legislature of claims which were not for municipal purposes against the funds or property of cities.

Changes in the Present Constitution

The framers of the constitution in 1879 incorporated in Article XI of the document several provisions specifically curtailing state legislative power over municipal affairs. The most important new sections prohibited the state legislature from passing special legislation and special charters, provided for the incorporation of cities under general state laws, and empowered any city of not less than 100,000 residents to construct its own charter. Through inclusion of this last provision, California became the second state (following the pioneering example of Missouri four years before) in which the city charter power became available. The right was broadened in 1892 to permit any city of more than 3,500 inhabitants to have a local charter. Subsequently, through constitutional amendments in 1896 and 1914, cities possessing charters were given considerably more freedom from state legislative control of their municipal affairs.

CREATING A CITY

When there is sufficient local interest and support, it is relatively easy for an area to be incorporated as a city. But several major requirements must be met in the legal process of incorporation. The area must contain at least 500 inhabitants, or 500 registered voters in counties with a population of 2 million or more, and must not already be a city or a part of one. The petition for incorporation as a city must be signed by at least 25 per cent of the landowners holding at least 25 per cent of the total land value. The county board of supervisors must find the petition to be valid and sufficient in such matters as the number of signatures and the boundary description. The board must also hold a hearing on the proposition, after which it may decrease but not increase the area by altering the boundaries which have been proposed. The incorporation proposal must receive a majority of the votes cast at a special election by the voters residing within the boundaries of the proposed city.

The hearing before the county board is sometimes a heated affair. One in Riverside County recently resulted in a strong dispute as to whether an area, in which some people favored incorporation largely so that draw poker could be established, actually had 500 residents. The unsuccessful claim was made that a number of individuals were living in the community only temporarily and were actually transients. The incorporation election may also be bitterly contested. Usually the advocates urge that becoming a city will bring more adequate service and local determination and control, while the opponents are fearful of higher taxes and unnecessary regulation. A city can disincorporate and return to the status of being an unincorporated area in the county. In the state history of California, however, this has occurred only eleven times.

The Decline in Incorporations

The greatest growth in the number of areas incorporating and becoming cities occurred between 1900 and 1920. During these two decades 137 cities came into legal existence. This was seventeen more than were established in the fifty-year period beginning in 1850; and in the years since 1920 the number of areas becoming cities (100) still has not equaled the total incorporations in the preceding twenty years. Many new cities have been created in recent years, including Del Mar (San Diego County),

Pacifica (San Mateo), Union City (Alameda), and Rosemead (Los Angeles). On the other hand, there have been more than a few rejections of such proposals by local residents. The defeats are most often found in areas where the fears of more taxes and increased regulation are prevalent and where the county is providing intensified urban services or enough of them are being obtained from special-district governments.

Cities are highly concentrated in a few sections of the state. In four counties there are no active cities, and in each of ten others (excluding the city-county of San Francisco) there is only one. By contrast, nine of the fifty-eight counties, Los Angeles, Orange, Santa Clara, San Mateo, Fresno, Alameda, Riverside, Contra Costa, and San Bernardino (listed in descending order of number of cities) have more than 50 per cent of the total of 358 cities in the state.

DIFFERENCES IN CITIES

Geographical Proximity

Many cities differ broadly in one or several basic features. These variations have importance because they frequently bear directly upon the nature and extent of services provided to people by individual city governments. Among others, there are wide variations in the geographical proximity and relationships of city governments as well as in their area, population, economic base, and social characteristics. Some cities are isolated communities largely unaffected by other cities; others are either the central city or a suburb of a central city situated in the midst of many neighboring cities. The service patterns of these central and suburban cities are influenced by interrelationships growing out of their geographical nearness. As an illustration, suburban cities frequently spend less per capita, partly because their residents have easy access to such facilities as recreational and park areas and equipment located within and financed by the central city. An important trend has developed in the administration of services by a number of the newer cities within large urban areas. Many of these cities, particularly in

Los Angeles County, have entered into contracts by which the county government provides most of the needed municipal services on a cost basis.

Area and Population

In area, cities encompass from one-fifth of a square mile to more than 455 square miles. The largest, Los Angeles, covers more territory than Santa Cruz County. More than one-half of the cities contain less than three square miles. A city embracing a large area has far more difficult problems in providing services such as fire and police protection and sewage disposal than does one that is territorially small. In population, cities range from less than 200 to more than 2,000,000. More than one-half of them have less than 10,000 people. In cities of small population services are noticeably fewer than in their larger counterparts. This difference is especially apparent among cities under 8,000 population in California. Many of them make only negligible expenditures for libraries, sanitation, sewers, and fire and police protection.

Economic and Social Characteristics

Cities also vary as to the predominant basis of their economic life. California has representatives of all these types: industrial city, retail trade center, manufacturing locality, education center, wholesale trade center, resort or retirement locale, government center, diversified city with manufacturing employment first and retail trade second, and diversified city with retail trade first and manufacturing important. A city's economic basis is related both to the nature of the public demands for services and the financial ability of the city government to undertake certain functions. Furthermore, the social characteristics of cities differ. Consequently, crime and delinquency rates vary among cities, causing the city governments in which such rates are high to intensify their protective and preventive activities. As a result of divergences in these matters as well as others, individual city governments differ in the number, types, and intensity of the services they perform. This is important to remember because much of the sampling of major city governmental services which fol-

Protection of children on busy streets is a problem confronting all cities. Courtesy City of Pomona.

lows must of necessity be presented without taking such differences into account.

CITY GOVERNMENTAL FUNCTIONS

Protective Services

Protection to persons and property consumes a large amount of city governmental money. Excluding debt service and public-service enterprises (such as municipally owned water systems), about one of every three city-government dollars goes for law-enforcement activities, fire fighting and fire prevention, and building, plumbing, and electrical inspection. As the principal law-enforcement unit of the city, the police department undertakes patrolling to prevent and discover crimes, responds to emergency calls, and regulates traffic. Numerous police departments, especially in the more populous cities, also engage in detective

This culvert built during the dry summer months is designed to carry large run-offs during the rainy season. Courtesy, City of Pomona.

work and in juvenile delinquency control programs. However, many have fewer activities because of limited departmental manpower. In more than one-third of the cities of California the entire police department consists of ten persons or less. At the other extreme, Los Angeles has more than 6,200 and San Francisco in excess of 1,800 police employees. The chief of police is generally appointed by either the city council or the city man-

Municipal recreation programs have become big business as cities move to provide leisure time activities for old and young alike. Courtesy, City of Pomona.

ager. Only occasionally is he chosen by a police commission or elected directly by the people. Santa Clara is an example of the elective practice.

Fire prevention is increasingly being recognized as an important complement to fire fighting. The personnel of a fire department may be full-time and paid, entirely volunteer, or a combination of the two. Cities of less than 10,000 people rely heavily on volunteer firemen, and cities under 5,000 depend primarily on them. Since much of the work time of firemen is spent in stand-by duty, they spend more time than other city employees at their work location. Usually this is from sixty-seven to seventy-two hours each week. The fire chief is generally chosen in the same manner as the police chief. One city, Sunnyvale, has combined its police and fire operations into a single department of public safety. Some other cities, such as Lakewood, utilize county fire and police services on a contractual basis.

Public Works

Although taking less total money than protection to persons and property, public-works functions absorb a sizable proportion of the city dollars. The most frequent activities of this type are improving and maintaining streets, providing sewers and sanitation, and collecting and disposing of refuse. About two-thirds of the total public-works funds are spent on street improvement and maintenance alone. Although adequate methods of sewage collection are common, disposal practices have not kept pace. Water pollution and other nuisances have therefore become frequent, and sewage disposal has become a matter of increased concern for city officials and state legislators. Refuse collection is largely a city-government function in southern California. In the northern half of the state the individual householder generally pays a charge to a private scavenger. Whether collection is public or private, the most prevalent disposal procedure of open burning is increasingly meeting disfavor from city and county governments which possess the power of regulating the practice within their boundaries. This is because open burning contributes to air pollution, a problem of growing significance in heavily populated areas.

Other public-works functions performed less frequently are airport construction and operation, off-street parking facilities, and urban renewal and redevelopment. Urban renewal and redevelopment projects are receiving growing attention in a number of California cities, and there has been increasing participation in federally sponsored programs. Various kinds of building inspection are performed by the city public works agency or other city departments.

Recreation, Health, and Education

Many cities are also active in providing recreational opportunities. Playgrounds, swimming pools, and parks are common city services, although they are not always adequate. In addition, day camps, hobby groups, and exhibits have become frequent in numerous cities, especially those of large population. Furthermore, in terms of total number of city residents served, public-health activities represent an important series of city governmental functions. Most cities contract with the county government for such services; but since most of the relatively few maintaining their own health departments are heavily populated, about one-half of all city people are served largely by city health departments.

In addition, city governments sometimes render important educational functions. They are, however, largely limited to library activities, for all public education below the college level (as well as some in the first two collegiate years) is carried on by independent school districts. All the large cities have their own libraries, but many of the smaller ones are served by the county library system.

Public-Service Enterprises

There is another important group of activities in which many city governments engage. Known as municipally owned public-service enterprises, they have two prominent characteristics which, considered together, distinguish them from most other city activities. First, they are financed by direct, separate charges on the user. Second, they are functions which are provided in some areas by private companies.* These operations consist of waterworks, electric-light plants, wharves, docks and landings, gas plants, and mass-transit systems.

Waterworks are the most significant in terms of the number of cities involved and consumers served. Furthermore, about one-third of all expenditures for public-service enterprises are devoted

---

* These features are also present in a limited number of other functions undertaken by some city governments, such as airports and off-street parking facilities, which are not classified as public-service enterprises.

to this activity, performed by 197 cities. Most waterworks were obtained in the early part of the current century, but municipal ownership in this field is continuing to expand. For example, twelve additional cities have acquired water systems since 1950. City-owned electric plants also constitute an important public-service enterprise, although only twenty-three cities own such facilities. Their total expenditures represent about one-half of all outlays in this category of city functions. This is attributable in large part to the extensiveness of the operations of the city of Los Angeles. Practically all of these plants were obtained by city

Professionalization of municipal police services is progressing rapidly as the officer trained in the classroom and on the pistol range replaces his volunteer counterpart of early years. Courtesy, City of Pomona.

governments from thirty-five to seventy-five years ago. The latest acquisition was in 1932.

Each of the other public-service enterprises is performed by only a handful of city governments, ranging in number from five to twelve. However, the volume of activity of some individual operations involving wharves, docks, and landings (Los Angeles, Long Beach, and Oakland) and gas supply (Long Beach) is highly impressive. Most acquisitions of mass transit systems by city governments have been relatively recent developments: more than one-half of the cities in the transit business have entered the field since 1940. Furthermore, some other cities have been seriously discussing similar endeavors.

General Government Functions

Considerable city governmental money must also be spent on activities that make possible direct public services or aid in their more competent performance. They are known as general govern-

To help preserve high value central business districts cities are moving ahead rapidly in the field of off-street parking. Courtesy, City of Pomona.

ment functions. Thus, unless the city contracts with the county on a service-charge basis, it must assess property and collect taxes. It must supply personnel, materials, and facilities for city elections when they are held separately. It must provide the space and some of the staff for municipal courts. Public monies must be deposited in a safe place, and this usually involves a city official, the treasurer. Funds must be audited, records kept, supplies and equipment purchased, budgets prepared and adopted, and laws passed. Furthermore, most city governments have a civil service system which fosters the recruitment and retention of qualified employees. Then, too, many cities have planning agencies to prepare guides and rules for the promotion of orderly, intelligent community development.

THE GENERAL-LAW TYPE OF CITY ORGANIZATION

Evolution and Number

With only two exceptions, California cities are at present organized and operating under either general state laws or individual local charters.° In compliance with a mandate in the new state constitution, the legislature in 1883 adopted the Municipal Corporations Act. The act and its amendments, subsequently made part of the *Government Code,* grouped all cities subject to general state legislation into several classes according to population. It then provided the governmental organization and grant of powers for all cities falling within each class. Gradually all cities other than some in the fifth and sixth classes adopted local charters, thereby removing themselves from the effects of general state laws pertaining to municipal affairs. As a consequence, by 1950 all cities operating under general state laws were either fifth-class or sixth-class cities. The matter was soon

---

° Special-charter cities existing when further adoption of such charters was prohibited in the Constitution of 1879 were permitted at their discretion to continue to operate under their old charters. Alviso and Gilroy in Santa Clara County are the only cities now actively operating under pre-1879 special charters. Like all cities, they are protected from additional special legislation. As this book went to press, Gilroy voters were about to cast ballots at an election on a locally-drawn charter.

further simplified. In 1953 the last two fifth-class cities changed their status, Santa Ana by adopting a local charter and Woodland by transferring to the sixth class. Thus, for the first time in seventy years all general-law cities were of one class, the sixth class. In fact, therefore, sixth-class cities and general-law cities became synonymous terms. Legal recognition of this actual condition came in the 1955 state legislative session when the legal title of sixth-class cities was changed to general-law cities.* More importantly, this development means that the state legislature can enact laws relative to structure and functions that are applicable to all cities not possessing charters. All new cities must begin their corporate existence as general-law cities.

General-law cities, numbering 289, represent 80 per cent of the total. All of them combined, however, contain only approximately 30 per cent of all of the city inhabitants in the state. They range in population from Amador in Amador County, with 151, to Downey in Los Angeles County, with 97,656.

Structural and Financial Features

What are the major characteristics of a general-law city? Its government is vested in a five-member council, clerk, treasurer, chief of police, and such other officials as the council decides are necessary. The council must be elected for terms of four years. The mayor is selected from its membership or may be elected to the post by the voters. The clerk and the treasurer are also elected unless a proposal to make them appointees of the council is approved by the electorate. The chief of police and other officers are appointed by the council. The office of city manager or chief administrative officer may be created and filled by the council. Structurally, therefore, cities functioning under the general state laws must organize within an established framework which permits some flexibility.

Financially, general-law cities are subject to an important restriction. Excluding taxation for certain specific purposes, the annual property tax may not be more than $1.00 for each $100 of assessed valuation unless a majority popular vote favors exceeding the limit. Although the state legislature has conferred a

---

* Cal. Stats. 1955, Chapter 624.

considerable range of powers on these cities, in general only functions specifically authorized in the state laws may be undertaken by them. The only functional area in which they possess broad freedom of action is in exercising the police power, most notably in protective and nuisance-eliminating activities. Furthermore, the general state laws frequently specify the exact procedure which must be followed in carrying out authorized functions.

THE CHARTER TYPE OF CITY ORGANIZATION

Sixty-seven, or almost one-fifth, of the cities operate under locally formulated and locally approved charters. Almost all of the larger cities function under a charter organization. All cities with a population of more than 100,000 have charters as do one-half of all cities between 30,000 and 100,000 in size. Although charter cities constitute a minority in the state, they contain a large majority of the total city population. They extend in population from Dairy Valley, with 3,454, to Los Angeles, with 2,397,000, both in Los Angeles County.

Obtaining a Charter

Any California city containing more than 3,500 people may adopt its own charter by following the procedure set forth in the state constitution. This process is initiated through an election upon the questions of drafting a charter and choosing a board of fifteen freeholders. The election may be called either by a two-thirds vote of the city council or by a petition signed by 15 per cent of the qualified electors of the city. If a majority of the voters favor drafting a charter, the fifteen freeholder candidates receiving the greatest number of votes at the same election are given the responsibility of drafting a charter within a period of one year. An optional method, which is seldom used, is to have a charter framed by the city council or its representatives.

A majority vote in favor of the charter is required for local ratification. The charter is then submitted to the state legislature at its next session, where it must receive a majority vote in both houses. In practice, such approval has been automatic, for no charter devoid of legal flaws has yet failed to get legislative ratification. After local sanction and state legislative approval, the charter is filed with the secretary of state. Charter amendments may be proposed by the city council or by a petition containing signatures of 15 per cent of the city voters. They also must be approved by a majority of the city voters and by the state legislature.

Significance

Freeholder charters illustrate the doctrine of home rule for cities. Briefly stated, it is the power given to cities by state constitutional provisions to frame and adopt their own charters and to have supremacy in municipal affairs. The reasoning behind the doctrine of municipal home rule is that each city is a natural social and economic unit having its individual problems of self-government. It is held that citizens of individual cities are therefore in a better position than the state legislature to decide what organization and functions they need.

Several conclusions about freeholder charters embodying the doctrine of municipal home rule can be made on the basis of the numerous decisions by the courts of California. First, when ratified by the state legislature a freeholder charter becomes the law of the legislature and automatically repeals any inconsistent general statutes dealing with the municipal affairs of the particular charter city. Second, a charter city is independent of the state laws dealing with municipal affairs, and its charter prevails over the general law whenever there is a conflict. However, general state laws operate within charter cities in matters of state-wide policy and in municipal matters not covered by the charter.

Third, the vital question of what is a municipal affair is reserved to judicial interpretation. There has never been a comprehensive definition of "municipal affairs" in California. As questions have arisen about specific municipal activities, separate court decisions have been necessary. Determination of what are and what are not municipal affairs is therefore a slow process of judicial inclusion and exclusion. Some matters which have been judged to be municipal affairs are the compensation and pensions of city employees, the election and removal of municipal officers, provision for certain public utilities, prosecutions for violations of the city charter and municipal ordinances, street widening and maintenance, bridge construction and repair, and rate regulation of a public corporation within city limits. Other matters have been determined to be state affairs and not under the jurisdiction of charter cities. They include the organization and control of school districts, dispositions of fines for misdemeanors in violation of state laws, organization and annexation of territory, and streets declared to be secondary highways.

Through placing certain matters in a charter, a city can organize and operate differently than under the general state laws in several important ways. It can take into account specific local conditions that cannot be included in general legislation. It can establish the kind of government, both as to organization and function, that the residents want. It can shape its administrative structure according to the prevailing local viewpoint.

Three lines of administrative change are indicative. The size of the council can be increased. For example, Los Angeles and Palo Alto have fifteen councilmen and Merced, seven. The mayor can be elected independently of the council and given separate appointing, budgetary, and veto powers. Independent election or separate powers of the mayor or both are features of such charters as those in Berkeley, Los Angeles, Modesto, Napa, San Diego, San Francisco, San Rafael, and Vallejo. The elective or appointive status of officials in general-law cities can be converted. The much more frequent appointment of the clerk and treasurer in charter cities than in general-law ones is illustrative. The elected city attorneys under the Pomona and Compton charters are also examples.

Furthermore, a city charter enables a community to perform a very broad scope of functions in the field of municipal affairs so long as the relevant state constitutional and national legislative provisions are not violated. It frees a city from many of the procedural requirements contained in general state laws. It authorizes a city to utilize tax sources not available to general-law cities. It permits a city to set a higher property-tax limit or to choose to establish none at all. In brief, a city charter provides a means for a city to formulate a set of basic rules of governance reflective of local needs and desires and to alter them as local conditions change. Sensitivity to the people of a locality constitutes a prominent benefit that a city can obtain from the use of a charter.

CALIFORNIA LOCAL-CHARTER CITIES

City	Population	Effective date of first and present charter
Alameda	70,642	1907, 1937
Albany	17,590	1927
Alhambra	53,558	1915
Arcadia	37,271	1951
Bakersfield	54,381	1915
Berkeley	121,900	1895, 1909
Burbank	90,966	1927
Chico	15,263	1923
Chula Vista	35,557	1949
Compton	63,877	1925
Culver City	31,370	1947
Dairy Valley	3,454	1959
Eureka	28,011	1895, 1959
Fresno	123,238	1901, 1957
Glendale	114,460	1921
Grass Valley	5,859	1893, 1952
Hayward	65,100	1956
Huntington Beach	10,067	1937
Inglewood	61,001	1927
Long Beach	324,822	1907, 1921
Los Angeles	2,397,000	1889, 1925
Marysville	7,826	1919
Merced	20,394	1949
Modesto	38,200	1911, 1951
Monterey	21,840	1911, 1925
Mountain View	26,143	1952
Napa	19,793	1893, 1915
Needles	4,776	1958
Newport Beach	23,500	1955
Oakland	405,200	1889, 1911
Oroville	7,025	1933
Pacific Grove	10,741	1927, 1955
Palo Alto	48,003	1909
Pasadena	123,000	1901
Petaluma	12,595	1911, 1947
Piedmont	10,639	1923
Pomona	62,138	1911

CALIFORNIA LOCAL-CHARTER CITIES

City	Population	Effective date of first and present charter
Porterville	8,018	1927
Redondo Beach	41,723	1935, 1949
Redwood City	43,700	1929
Richmond	102,944	1909
Riverside	84,000	1907, 1953
Roseville	11,685	1935, 1955
Sacramento	170,949	1893, 1921
Salinas	25,100	1903, 1919
San Bernardino	90,200	1905
San Diego	501,851	1889, 1931
San Francisco	775,357	1898, 1931
San Jose	160,719	1897, 1915
San Leandro	64,649	1933, 1949
San Luis Obispo	19,000	1911, 1955
San Mateo	65,999	1923
San Rafael	16,526	1913
Santa Ana	76,300	1953
Santa Barbara	55,675	1899, 1927
Santa Clara	43,281	1927, 1951
Santa Cruz	22,794	1907, 1948
Santa Monica	87,200	1907, 1947
Santa Rosa	29,980	1903, 1923
Stockton	82,507	1889, 1923
Sunnyvale	41,867	1949
Torrance	93,372	1947
Tulare	13,322	1923
Vallejo	68,183	1899, 1946
Ventura	25,985	1931, 1933
Visalia	14,551	1923
Watsonville	13,700	1903
Whittier	34,100	1955

A substantial number of the eligible cities have made use of the charter right during the period in which it has been available at the more-than-3,500 population level. Two trends, unknown to the county-charter movement, are particularly noticeable. Almost one-half of the charter cities have replaced a first charter with a second, and some, such as Riverside, have had three charters. There has also been a considerable number of adoptions of new city charters in the post-World War II years. In contrast, no county has ever supplanted its original charter, and Santa Clara County is the only county to have put a charter into operation since 1933.

Reasons for Moderate Use

Despite the impressive record of adoptions of city charters, well over two-thirds of the cities which are eligible because their populations are in excess of 3,500 do not have them. Some, such as National City, have framed such documents which have been rejected by the voters. But most of them have never had a charter formulated by an elected board of freeholders or by the city council or its appointed representatives.

There are several reasons why many cities do not take advantage of the privilege. One is widespread satisfaction with many of the general laws under which noncharter cities function. These laws are extensive and discretionary on various matters and have not generally been altered detrimentally by the state legislature in recent years. This satisfaction with the general laws is reflected in the fact that in almost all recently incorporated areas that contain more than 3,500 people, including a number in excess of 50,000 population, there has been no concerted effort to utilize the home-rule charter power.

A second reason is local inertia. It is often difficult to excite the citizenry of a community about the values of drawing up a charter fitted to local circumstances so long as city operations seemingly function in a reasonably efficient and economical manner. Of course, public lack of interest in governmental affairs is not confined to city charters or to local government alone. It is certainly fostered in terms of city charters through the absence of dissatisfaction with the general state laws. In other words, substantial modification by the legislature of important provisions relating to general law cities would likely bring forth a prompt, widespread interest in local charters.

A third reason is the belief of some groups and individuals in certain cities that some charter provisions might differ importantly from parts of the general state legislation which they favor. A good case in point is support for the one dollar property-tax rate in effect in general law cities. Such a stipulation can be written into a charter, but the limit can also be raised or entirely removed. Supporters of this tax limit are therefore often opponents of the drafting of a city charter.

A fourth reason is a fear by some people that particular sections inserted in the charter may later be declared illegal by the courts, with resultant confusion or disruption of city governmental activities. This feeling arises because the field of municipal affairs in which charter cities can freely operate has not yet been completely determined by the judiciary.

In the light of these four reasons, it seems probable that city charter adoptions will continue, but not at a very rapid pace.

FORMS OF CITY GOVERNMENT: MAYOR-COUNCIL

Within the guides set forth in the general state laws or charters, cities establish their particular structural arrangements through which public services are presented. These are known as forms of government, and two types (mayor-council and council-manager) are in operation in general law and charter cities and a third (commission) is available to cities that have local charters.

The mayor-council system is the oldest and most prevalent. Its principal features are an executive or presiding officer (the mayor), a legislative body (the council) of five to fifteen members, elected at large or from wards and responsible for enacting local laws, and varying numbers of elected or appointed department heads and administrative or advisory boards. Mayors are elevated to the post by a vote of the council from its own membership or are elected directly by the voters. There are three variations of the mayor-council form, largely distinguishable by the method of selection and the nature of the duties of the mayor. None of them, however, assures sustained administrative leadership.

Three Variations

Under one variation the mayor is selected from among the council membership by majority vote and is merely the presiding officer at council meetings. He has no separate power of appointing administrative personnel, preparing the budget, or vetoing acts of the council. In matters of personnel, budgeting, and legislating, he acts as a member of the council, possessing the same degree of legal authority as each other member. The position is often rotated on an annual basis.

A second variation, passed by the legislature in 1959, permits the independent election of the mayor in a general-law city, provided this arrangement is approved by the voters. However, a mayor selected in this manner has no additional legal powers beyond what he would have if he were chosen by the council.

A few charter cities utilize a third variation of the mayor-council form. Usually independently elected, the mayor possesses considerable separate administrative and legislative responsibilities. The most prominent examples of this approach in California are found in Los Angeles and San Francisco, although neither mayor has powers equal to those assigned in some mayor-council cities in other states.

In Los Angeles the mayor is independently elected for four years, submits a proposed budget, makes recommendations to the council, can veto bills, and has responsibility for general supervision of most city departments. However, a part-time, five-member board directly supervises and makes rules for each administrative department. The board members serve staggered terms, and consequently no incoming mayor can appoint a majority to the board during a single term of office. Furthermore, he must receive council approval of board appointments and removals.

In San Francisco the mayor is separately elected for a term of four years. He possesses the budgetary, message, veto, and appointing powers, but actually controls only a part of the executive operations of the city-county. For example, he appoints but has no power to remove the chief administrative officer who directs the operations of ten city departments. The latter official serves indefinitely until he resigns, dies, or is removed by two-thirds vote of the governing board or recall action of the voters. Thus, unless a vacancy occurs in the office, the mayor cannot make an appointment.

FORMS OF CITY GOVERNMENT: COMMISSION

The commission plan, the second oldest form of city government, has become a matter of history in the state. Under this system, commissioners, usually five in number, are popularly elected. Together they serve as the legislative body and individually as heads of administrative departments; there is no separate executive. Sacramento, the first commission city in the United States, adopted the plan in 1863 and replaced it thirty years later. After the plan was revived and popularized nationally through its use in Galveston, Texas, and Des Moines, Iowa, in the early years of the present century, many communities in California became commission cities. The popularity of the plan rose until 1917, but subsequently there have been many abolitions and very few adoptions. Its quick decline is attributable to the diffusion of administrative responsibility among five commissioners and the lack of a single, unifying executive. All too frequently it was discovered that commission government meant little coordination of activities, much duplication of effort, and frequent conflict between department heads who had not been elected for their administrative qualifications.

The Last Example

In 1947 the state legislature eliminated the form from the possibilities for general-law cities. In the same year, Santa Monica and Vallejo adopted new noncommission charters. This left Fresno the lone city operating under the commission plan. No other charter city has exhibited recent interest in adopting this governmental form.* An effort to replace the commission charter was decisively defeated in Fresno in 1954, but another attempt three years later succeeded.

---

* In various less populous general-law cities, councilmen act as part-time advisers to departments. They are not, however, department heads within the meaning of the commission form of government. Any exercise of administrative authority by councilmen acting individually is illegally assumed.

FORMS OF CITY GOVERNMENT: COUNCIL-MANAGER

Fastest-growing of the three city governmental forms is the council-manager plan and a variation termed the chief administrative officer system. Under the council-manager form the elected city council makes policy decisions which are enacted into ordinances, approves the budget, and appoints and may remove the city manager, who directs the administrative operations of the city government. Neither the mayor, who is generally appointed by the council from among its own members, nor the council is to interfere with the manager in his administrative duties. The council is to deal with administration only through the manager, whose actions are subject to councilmanic review.

The city manager possesses a grant of administrative authority through sections of the charter or the ordinance installing the plan. He supervises all parts of the government. He sees that all laws and ordinances, including franchises and permits, are enforced, making use of court action if necessary. He appoints, disciplines, and removes, according to civil service regulations and other local laws, department heads and subordinate employees. He prepares the annual budget for consideration by the council and sees that it is carried out after adoption. He advises the governing body on financial conditions and needs. He makes reports and recommendations to the council at its request or as he judges desirable. He controls or makes purchases. He performs other responsibilities assigned by the charter, if one exists, or through council action.

The theory of this plan of government is that the manager is chosen on the basis of his training and experience in public administration. This recommendation is followed by city councils in making most appointments. The predominant previous work experience of most managers in the state has been as a department head, department employee, assistant to a manager, or manager of a local government, generally in a city other than the one they are now serving.

In the thirty years following the first adoption in Inglewood in

1914, the council-manager plan generally had a steady growth.*
In the subsequent years of the post-World War II period, the
numerical gain in council-manager cities has been spectacular.
The total in 1960 was 184, more than four times the number of
fifteen years before.

An Offshoot

The chief administrative officer system, a variation of the council-manager plan, is of more recent origin and has also experienced a quick growth. Its first use in the nation in what is now
its most usual form was in Montebello in Los Angeles County in
1945. It differs from the council-manager operation in that the
chief administrative officer advises the council on administrative
activities. The CAO, unlike the manager, does not possess a
grant of administrative authority. Instead, the council has the
authority and acts favorably or negatively on his suggestions. His
job is thus similar to that of the chief administrative officer in
county government. A modification of the council-manager form
and therefore representing partial rather than complete central
administrative management, the chief administrative officer system was operating in forty-two cities in 1960. A number of cities,
recent examples of which are Concord, Escondido, and Ocean-
side, have converted from the chief administrative officer to the
manager arrangement.

A Widespread Development

The rapid acceptance of this third city governmental form in
terms of both managers and chief administrative officers is the
most significant recent development in California city government. A large majority of the cities of more than 10,000 population have either a city manager or a chief administrative officer.
More than nine-tenths of the city population lives in communities
functioning under this governmental form.

---

* Inglewood abolished the plan after one year, but later reinstated it
after a long interval. Glendale, which also installed the form in 1914, has
been a council-manager city longer than any other community in the state.

This third form of city government is the only one in which an individual chosen on the basis of administrative qualifications and experience has the responsibility for directing the day-to-day governmental operations. In most cities its results have been highly significant, particularly in getting work done promptly and ably. The principal criticisms that have been made are the high turnover of persons holding the positions and the decrease in the political leadership of elected officials. In most cities, however, the benefits are judged to outweigh the deficiencies. More than 90 per cent of the cities which have ever installed a manager or chief administrative officer continue to prefer the form to any other that is available.

Further Reading

Bollens, John C., *Appointed Executive Local Government*. Los Angeles: Haynes Foundation, 1952.

————, *The Problem of Government in the San Francisco Bay Region*. Berkeley: University of California, Bureau of Public Administration, 1948.

California, Legislature, Assembly Interim Committee on Municipal and County Government, *Incorporation Practices*. Sacramento: State Printing Office, 1959.

Council of State Governments, *The States and the Metropolitan Problem*. Chicago, 1956.

Crouch, Winston W., *Intergovernmental Relations (Metropolitan Los Angeles: A Study in Integration*, Monograph No. 15). Los Angeles: Haynes Foundation, 1955.

Ferguson, Jenniellen W., *City Council Organization and Procedures in Los Angeles County*. Los Angeles: University of California, Bureau of Governmental Research, 1955.

Ross, Polly R., "A Municipal Charter Guide for California." Unpublished Master's thesis, Stanford University, 1947.

Scott, Stanley and Lewis Keller, *Annexation? Incorporation? A Guide for Community Action* (3rd ed.) Berkeley: University of California, Bureau of Public Administration, 1959.

Western City, monthly periodical of the League of California Cities and five other similar far western organizations; published in Los Angeles.

Wilcox, Robert F., "The Administration of Law Enforcement in Metropolitan Los Angeles." Unpublished Ph.D. dissertation, Stanford University, 1937.

Thirteen

Special Districts

CALIFORNIA'S SPECIAL DISTRICTS form a third "branch" of the state's local governmental system, rivaling the cities and counties in importance. In many areas the districts—which number more than four thousand—form an almost invisible layer of government, and local residents usually have little knowledge of their activities. This is true despite the fact that citizens are significantly affected by district operations, service charges, and tax levies.

The districts come in many varieties. Each type normally specializes in only one function, but all the districts, taken together, provide a wide range of services. They administer the public-school system, supply water for domestic and irrigation purposes, build roads and bridges, provide for sewage and garbage disposal, generate and distribute electricity, conduct air pollution control programs, and maintain fire-protection facilities, to name a few of the more important activities.

Indeed, the services that may be provided by special districts include practically the full array of city and county functions and others in addition. This does not mean that districts are handling all these functions on a statewide basis. Public education is the only major service that is provided at the local level solely by districts. Most of the other functions are undertaken by such units only as occasion demands, and as an alternative to city or county administration.

A majority of the districts are separate units of local government, and have substantial fiscal and administrative independ-

NUMBER OF ACTIVE LOCAL GOVERNMENT TAXING UNITS
IN CALIFORNIA, BY SELECTED YEARS*

	Year			Numerical Change
	1935	1941	1959	1935-1959
Special districts	4,838	4,394	4,717	−121
School				
Elementary	2,951	2,539	1,374	−1,577
High	297	264	233	−64
Unified	—	40	109	+109
Junior college	18	14	29	+11
College	—	—	2	+2
Acquisition and improvement— county and municipal	262	106	6	−256
Airport	—	—	2	+2
Air pollution control (San Francisco Bay area district only)	—	—	1	+1
Bridge	1	1	2	+1
Cemetery	133	184	249	+116
Community services	—	—	59	+59
Conservation—soil	—	2	42	+42
Conservation—river or water	6	10	19	+13
County service area	—	—	40	+40
Drainage	15	17	29	+14
Fire protection	194	256	452	+258
Flood control	3	6	112	+109
Garbage	3	5	14	+11
Highway—joint	10	12	10	—
Hospital	—	—	57	+57
Improvement	259	143	68	−191
Irrigation	95	104	115	+20
Levee	9	10	11	+2
Library	20	10	12	−8
Lighting	259	280	454	+195
Maintenance				
General or maintenance	—	—	26	+26
Drain or storm drain	—	5	25	+25
Lighting	59	59	181	+122
Road	—	—	8	+8

* Sources: State Board of Equalization, Valuation Division, *Summary of Revenue Districts, 1959* (Sacramento, 1955), and earlier reports; State Controller, *Annual Report of Financial Transactions Concerning Irrigation Districts of California, 1958* (Sacramento, 1959).

NUMBER OF ACTIVE LOCAL GOVERNMENT TAXING UNITS IN CALIFORNIA, BY SELECTED YEARS[*]

	Year			Numerical Change
	1935	1941	1959	1935-1959
Sewer	—	49	91	+91
Water	—	—	11	+11
Memorial	—	—	22	+22
Mosquito and pest abatement	24	27	60	+36
Park, recreation and parkway	2	9	92	+90
Parking	—	—	24	+24
Police	4	5	14	+10
Port and harbor	2	4	11	+9
Protection and storm water	8	6	10	+2
Road—permanent	7	7	10	+3
Sanitary	51	79	120	+69
Sanitation	10	16	124	+114
Sewer	48	7	4	−44
Transit	—	—	2	+2
Utility—municipal	3	6	4	+1
Utility—public	16	29	68	+52
Water and waterworks	68	78	292	+224
Miscellaneous (local health, reclamation, and separation of grade)	1	5	17	+16
Cities (excluding one city-county)	280	284	358	+78
Counties (including one city-county)	58	58	58	—

ence of other governments. Many others are governed by the county board of supervisors or city council ex officio.[*] California's 4,717 special districts outnumber its 358 cities and 58 counties by twelve to one. They are also important financially. In fiscal year 1958, the districts spent a total of $2.15 billions—including construction expenditures supported by bond sales. This is 100 per

---

[*] For the purposes of this chapter, a broader and less rigorous definition of the terms "special district" is employed than that utilized by the U. S. Bureau of the Census. Thus the Census would not count as separate units any districts which are controlled by a city or county governing body, ex officio, or which otherwise do not possess "substantial autonomy." The authors have no quarrel with the Census definition, and depart from it only because the primary sources of information for this chapter, the State Controller and the State Board of Equalization, base their count on a different definition.

cent more than county disbursements, and 37 per cent more than total city expenditures—again, including bond construction expenditures. California uses the special-district device more often than most states, being second only to Illinois in the total number of independent districts, excluding school districts (nearly half of Illinois' districts are for one purpose only—drainage).

School districts account for most—about four-fifths—of general fund expenditures by districts in California. The remainder is largely spent by water supply and utility, irrigation, hospital, flood control, fire protection, and sewerage and sanitation districts. Forty other types spend only about 2 per cent of the total.

Organization Procedures and Governing Boards

The nature of a special district is usually determined by the state act under which it is organized. Ordinarily these laws carefully outline the kinds of areas that may be formed into a district, the procedures required for organization, the functions and powers, and the selection and composition of the governing body. Methods of annexing area to the district and of dissolving the district are usually provided.

Normally the first step in district organization is the circulation of a petition which must be signed by a specified number of qualified residents of the area to be included. After approval by the local governing body (in most instances the county board of supervisors), the proposal is generally submitted to a vote in the area concerned. A number of laws permit the district to be established by action of the local governing body alone, but most require an election. With a few exceptions, all the resident qualified electors may vote. A simple majority is usually sufficient to establish the district. The local governing body then passes a resolution bringing the district into legal existence.

Districts are governed by either (1) an independent elective board, chosen at large or from subdivisions of the district; (2) an appointive board, generally chosen by the governing body which supervised establishment of the district; (3) an ex officio board, which consists of the county board of supervisors or the city council; or (4) a board composed of selected members of the governing bodies of local governments located within the district. Numerous urban districts and most county-wide districts are governed by the county board of supervisors. Maintenance, local assessment, and improvement districts are administered by the city council or county board of supervisors. The large metropolitan and regional districts, which usually cross many local boundary lines, are governed by independent elective or appointive boards. Three to five-member boards are most frequent. In some large districts the size of the governing body depends on the number of participating local governments and the populations involved.

Four Major Kinds of Districts

Special districts may be grouped into four principal classes.

1. Small districts are organized within unincorporated communities to provide *municipal-type* services for urban areas that have no city government. The activities of such districts include most of the services provided by cities.

2. Metropolitan or regional districts, such as the Metropolitan Water District of Southern California and the Bay Area Air Pollution Control District, are created to handle *areawide problems.*

3. School districts are the best-known and most numerous type and have the local responsibility for maintaining *public schools* throughout the state.

4. Agricultural districts serve the *rural areas,* their chief functions being irrigation, soil conservation, drainage, and reclamation.

Districts Providing Municipal-Type Services

Much of California's recent rapid growth has occurred in areas adjacent to, but outside, the limits of cities. Large urban populations have sprung up in county areas. In the absence of any clear state policy that "what is urban shall be municipal," many of these communities have chosen to remain unincorporated and create large numbers of special districts to supply their most urgently needed public services. The process of district organization has been piecemeal, and the result has been a crazy quilt of units in the urban unincorporated areas, each district providing a single service, and each levying a separate property tax.

Most of these urban districts are small in area, their boundaries approximating those of the unincorporated communities served. They are found throughout the state, but the largest numbers are in counties having the greatest suburban growth. Los Angeles, Contra Costa, Sacramento, Orange, and Santa Clara counties contain approximately one-third of all such districts.

Their important functions are fire protection, street lighting, and sanitation. Other major district activities include cemetery maintenance, mosquito abatement, public-health work, hospital construction, airport construction, police protection, and water supply. The most numerous districts are lighting and lighting maintenance, fire protection, water, cemetery, sanitary and sanitation, and sewer maintenance. Taken together, these six types account for more than two-thirds of all the districts organized primarily to provide municipal-type services in unincorporated urban areas.

Factors Causing the Establishment of Districts

The primary reason for the formation of special districts in urban areas is the desire to obtain municipal-type services without having to create or annex to a city government. Residents of urban areas in need of municipal services may shun annexation or incorporation as carrying with it the danger of higher taxes. They may feel that a special district will supply their needs more cheaply than a city.

Unincorporated communities may avoid annexation to an adjacent city because residents fear a loss of community "identity." Resistance to change also leads unincorporated communities to choose the less drastic course of special-district formation rather than incorporation or annexation. Often many of the residents of newly developed areas have moved there to escape the confines of the nearby city. They cling to the "rural" character of their new homes, despite the fact that the areas have become highly developed communities. Non-city status is viewed as more "rural" than city status, although the area may already have become obviously urban.

Government, Organization, and Annexation

Many of the districts in unincorporated urban areas are governed by specially created bodies, either independently elected or appointed by the county board of supervisors. Others are governed directly by the county board of supervisors. The district governing body has authority to select all employees, to approve and pay bills, to authorize expenditures, and usually to request inclusion in the county budget of a property tax for district purposes. The directors or trustees generally take no part in actual district operation, although in some cases they perform clerical and inspectional duties. Most districts whose activities require full-time supervision are administered by a secretary, superintendent, or caretaker, who is appointed by and responsible to the board of directors.

District organization procedure follows the usual steps of petition by residents, review of the petition by the county board of supervisors, and an election in the area. This procedure is sometimes modified to allow initiation by a city or county governing body instead of through a petition, or approval by one or more local governing bodies instead of through an election. Annexation of new territory requires the consent of the district governing body and, usually, approval by residents of the area to be annexed.

Problems of Urban Special Districts

Districts have been organized to supply services that are most urgently needed in urban, unincorporated communities. Normally in any one community this process takes place over some period of time, a different district being created for each new service. The usual result is a stack of overlapping special districts, each providing a separate service and each levying its own tax. Such a governmental pattern is complicated, difficult to coordinate, and expensive. And even if the districts are able to cooperate, they lack certain municipal powers. Most important of all, districts do not have the power to plan and regulate land uses through zoning. The financial structure of districts is also more restricted than that of municipalities. Districts must rely heavily on the property tax for revenue, whereas cities have numerous other sources, including certain state subventions for which districts are not eligible.

The substitution of special districts for city government is probably advantageous in communities that are not heavily urbanized, are growing slowly, and need only one or two services. But the excessive use of special districts in urban areas has brought on a crisis in California local government.

An attempt to meet the problem of single-purpose districts was made in 1951 through the passage of the Community Services District Act, under which a single district can handle one or more of some eight different services. The community-service district represents an effort at improvement, but it has not been put into general use.

Although they are intended to be agencies of democratic local control, districts present many problems in this regard. A majority of the districts are governed by boards of directors elected locally from within the district. But the election returns tell a story of citizen unawareness, for many of the scheduled elections are never held, because of the absence of contests. When elections are held, the proportion of actual voters is extremely small in comparison with participation in other elections.

The districts that are governed directly by the county boards of supervisors also present serious problems of local representation and control. Most district activities are urban in nature and are limited in scope to the local community served, whereas the county as an area-wide unit of government does not always give adequate representation to the local interests of urban communities.

If the problem of local representation raised by county control of districts is ignored, however, it appears probable that county supervision is an improvement from a purely administrative point of view. The small scale of most district operations makes it difficult to obtain the advantages of large-scale purchasing, centralized bookkeeping, and personnel systems. Similarly, because of the limited need within a single district, equipment may stand idle when closer cooperation with nearby areas would result in fuller utilization. The contractual exchange of services between districts, between cities and districts, and between counties and districts represents a significant attempt to meet these problems. But one effective approach to problems of small-scale operation is integrated county-wide administration of all district affairs.

METROPOLITAN AND REGIONAL DISTRICTS

Special districts are useful devices for administering certain functions that cannot be handled effectively by individual cities and counties. The creation of a metropolitan or regional district represents a method of adjusting governmental boundaries to coincide with the areas affected by large-scale problems. The functions administered through such districts include water and electricity supply, operation of regional parks, air-pollution control, rapid transit, flood control, public-health administration, sewage treatment and disposal, the management of port and harbor facilities, and bridge construction. Included among California's metropolitan and regional districts are such agencies as the Metropolitan Water District of Southern California, the Golden Gate Bridge and Highway District, the Sacramento Municipal Utility District, the San Joaquin County Local Health District, and the Bay Area Air Pollution Control District.

Formation and Governing Body

The formation requirements for metropolitan districts are usually less stringent than for other types. Also, more discretion and power in the initiation and organization of several of these districts is given to the cities and counties that are to be included. A county sanitation district may be established by a simple resolution of the county board of supervisors, unless there is a protest from 2 per cent of the voters, in which case an election must be held. Formation of a metropolitan water district is initiated by resolution of any city council, and is established by an election in all municipalities whose councils have approved the resolution. Formation of a municipal utility district may be started by resolutions of one-half of the public agencies that are to be included. A metropolitan fire-protection district may be originated by any city council or county board of supervisors and approved by the governing bodies of other cities or counties to be included.

California's metropolitan and regional districts have employed four different approaches in the selection of a governing body. (1) When the area to be served contains a number of local governmental units, each of which has an interest in the district's function, the governing board of the metropolitan district may be composed of representatives of the governing bodies of the member units. The Metropolitan Water District of Southern California, the San Francisco Bay Area Rapid Transit District, and Bay Area Air Pollution Control District illustrate this type of organization.

(2) When the area of need and the area of a single county coincide reasonably well, the county board of supervisors may serve as the ex officio district governing board. This is the arrangement in the Los Angeles County Air Pollution Control District and the Los Angeles County Flood Control District. County administration of district activities is particularly appropriate when the problem involved, such as flood control, is of concern to both rural and urban areas.

(3) Sometimes district board members are elected directly by popular vote, as in the East Bay Regional Park District and the Sacramento Municipal Utility District. There is, however, considerable opposition to the direct election of regional and metropolitan district officials.

(4) Occasionally board members are appointed by the governor, as is true of the Los Angeles Metropolitan Transit Authority.

Supervision and Finance

Most of these districts are completely independent of direct county controls, and their boards have the necessary powers for budgeting, assessment, and tax collection. There is also little state supervision, other than permissive control over dam construction, bridge construction, and sanitary-system installation.

All metropolitan and regional districts have the power to levy a general property tax, but they vary in the extent to which this source is used. The Metropolitan Water District of Southern California receives nearly 80 per cent of its income from the property tax, and the Los Angeles County Flood Control District depends solely upon this source. The East Bay Municipal Utility District, the Sacramento Municipal Utility District, and the Golden Gate Bridge and Highway District rely primarily upon service charges and toll fees. Although metropolitan and regional districts are relatively small in number, the volume of their operations is very large, and they budget well over one-half of all non-school district expenditures in California.

Merits of Metropolitan Districts

The chief advantage offered by these districts is their ability to cross established local governmental boundaries. They provide a governmental unit whose territory coincides with the area requiring service. They provide for unified, area-wide planning of a function. They pool the resources of governments that separately might be unable to finance an expensive project. They utilize more effective and economical procedures in management, budgeting, purchasing, and personnel.

Possible Weaknesses

The creation of a metropolitan district means the addition of a new governmental unit in metropolitan areas that have too many governments. This weakness could be overcome by using one multiple-purpose metropolitan district in each area, to which could be assigned all problems that are metropolitan in scope. Thus, to the extent that it represents the integration of functions that were previously distributed among several different jurisdictions, such a district would actually reduce the dispersion of authority.

This is Pardee Dam, the main source of water supply of the East Bay Municipal Utility District, an important metropolitan district operating in the East Bay sector of the San Francisco Bay area.

Separate election of the governing board of some metropolitan districts is another weakness. Election has the effect of setting up an independent agency to handle functions that are closely related to the activities of the existing cities and counties. This increases the difficulties of coordination and may bring on major unresolved conflicts over public policy. In order to prevent such conflict and ensure the general local governments a direct voice in district affairs, most of the enabling laws now provide for representation of the local units on the metropolitan district boards and avoid the method of direct election.

Twin aqueducts from Pardee Reservoir in the Sierra foothills form 94-mile water lifeline to more than 1,100,000 consumers served by the East Bay Municipal Utility District.

SCHOOL DISTRICTS

School districts are virtually the exclusive providers of public education below the collegiate level. They are exceedingly numerous, constituting 37 per cent of all California's special districts, and are found throughout the state. Practically every foot of ground in California is within a school district. Not only are school districts more numerous and extensive in coverage than other districts, but they also spend more money—83 per cent of all district expenditures.

Organization and Governing Body

A number of different kinds of school districts are in operation. In most instances, separate districts function at the elementary,

high-school, junior-college, and college educational levels. There
are some unified districts providing both elementary and high-
school education, and occasionally junior-college training. These
unified districts, which are growing in number, are most common in urban sections. In 1959 the distribution of separate districts operating at the various educational levels, and of unified
districts, was as follows:

Elementary	1,374
High	233
Unified	109
Junior college	29
College	2

Within the general classifications of elementary and high-
school districts, there are several different types. Among elementary districts there are city, regular, joint, union, and joint union
districts. Among high-school districts there are city, union, joint
union, and county districts. For the most part differences between
these various types are of minor importance, and relate to the
method by which the district was formed or to the governmental
situation within which it operates.

Most school districts are governed by locally elected boards of
trustees, but the boards of education in charter cities may be
either elected or appointed depending on the charter provisions.
The school-district tax is actually levied by the county board of
supervisors. However, since the supervisors must levy a tax sufficient to fulfill the requirements of the district budget, the effective taxing power resides in the district board. With certain exceptions, tax levies that exceed established statutory limits require a favorable vote of district residents for approval. The exact
limits depend upon the number of levels of education offered
within the district. The school boards may issue bonds only after
a two-thirds favorable popular vote. At the elementary, high
school, and junior college levels of operation, the total value of
all bonds issued for construction purposes may not exceed 5 per
cent of the assessed valuation within the district.

County and State Supervision and Assistance

The county superintendent's office has developed significantly
as an agency providing the local districts with assistance and

specialized services that would otherwise be available only in the larger and wealthier districts. Public education is a state function, and although the responsibility for immediate management has been largely delegated to the local districts, the state through its Department of Education exercises important supervisory powers. State activities in public education include the provision of elementary textbooks, approval of high-school textbooks, regulation of professional educational credentials and certificates, approval of high-school and junior-college courses of study, and adoption of rules and regulations for the government of public schools. Financial assistance given through the state aid program is a major source of local district revenues.

School-District Finance and the State Aid Program

Major sources of California school-district revenue are the local property tax and funds provided by the state aid program. Small additional sums are supplied by fees, sales, and federal grants. In fiscal year 1958, school operating expenses, including bond interest and retirement costs, amounted to $1,334,000,000. Most of the revenues necessary to pay operating expenses were derived from district property taxes and from state aid. Capital-outlay expenditures were $416,000,000 in the fiscal year of 1958, and were supported largely by the sale of local bonds and by state loans. The total of all school expenditures in 1958 amounted to one and three-quarter billion dollars.

State financial assistance to local school districts is provided through a number of separate funds, each distributed on a different basis. The total of state aid in fiscal year 1958 mounted to $535 million for current expenses, plus about $85 million in capital-outlay loans and grants.

1. Basic state aid provides $125 per average daily attendance of pupils within the district, with a minimum of $2,400 for any eligible district.

2. State equalization aid is distributed in order to enable all districts to maintain a "foundation program" calling, in general, for annual district expenditures of $234 per average daily attendance in elementary districts, $324 in high-school districts, and $424 in junior-college districts.

3. Special aid is also given for the attendance of adults receiving educational services.

4. Within limits, the state pays the excess cost of educating and transporting physically handicapped and mentally retarded students.

5. The state assists in paying regular student transportation costs.

6. Within limits, the state reimburses school districts for the excess cost of maintaining automobile driver education programs, up to $35 per pupil instructed.

7. The county school service fund supports a number of activities through which the counties assist their school districts. The primary source of income for this fund is state aid.

8. A very important aspect of the state's aid to school districts has been the financial assistance given to help construct new facilities. Since 1947, building aid funds totaling nearly $800 million have been provided in the form of state loans and grants.

One of the most pressing problems in the California school-aid program has not yet been solved. A conflict arises between the need to guarantee the availability of an adequate educational program in all districts, and the need to avoid the continued existence of unnecessary districts that are too small to provide adequate education. This conflict has not been resolved, for the state aid program has helped to bolster uneconomic districts, but it has not given all of them adequate educational programs.

School-District Reorganization

California school-district structure has two major organizational faults. The first is that most California school districts are too small for effective administration. These inadequate districts predominate in rural areas, and their presence usually means increased per-pupil costs and lower educational standards. The second major defect in organization is the separation of the elementary and high-school levels of education into different districts. This contributes to the excessive number and small size of districts, and obstructs the administration of an integrated educational program. Although these fundamental defects have long been recognized, California has only recently attempted a comprehensive reorganization.

In 1945 the legislature created the State Commission on School Districts to supervise a statewide survey aimed at planning effective district unification or reorganization. The commission appointed five regional commissions, which in turn designated local areas of study and chose local survey committees. In 1949 the duties of the state commission were assumed by the state Board of Education, the regional and local survey committees were allowed to lapse, and a county committee was provided in every county except San Francisco. The county committees are now appointed by representatives of the local school districts, and are responsible for investigating school-district reorganization needs. Other phases of the reorganization program are being continued with little change.

The reorganization program has been directed largely toward the unification of existing high school districts with the elementary districts included in their boundaries. At its present rate of progress, the reorganization program will bring about many improvements in time. Since it began in 1945 there has been a 37 per cent decrease in the number of elementary districts, a 10 per cent decrease in high-school districts, and a 142 per cent increase in unified districts.

AGRICULTURAL DISTRICTS

The most important agricultural districts are concerned with irrigation, reclamation, drainage, and soil conservation. They are all rural in nature. Certain other districts (fire protection and police protection, for example) may provide services for rural populations, but these are not strictly agricultural needs.

The Irrigation District

The irrigation district is the best-known and most important example of the agricultural district. Beginning with the Wright Act of 1887, the first law under which any important organization took place, the irrigation district has developed from an uncertain endeavor into a financially stable and powerful governmental unit. The earliest districts to be organized encountered difficulty because they were formed without sufficient consideration of water supply, agricultural potentialities, and financial ability. Most of them were active for only a few years.

A new crop of districts sprung up during World War I and the 1920's, when high prices and population growth restored confidence. These districts were considerably more successful than their predecessors, but they, in turn, met a crucial test during the depression of the 1930's. After a period of severe stress, most of them came through, with the help of the state and federal governments. The current over-all condition of irrigation districts is excellent.

The Functions of Irrigation Districts

By far the most important function of irrigation districts is the procurement and distribution of water for agricultural uses. This usually involves making arrangements for the water supply and constructing and operating canals and distribution systems, and frequently includes operating pumping lifts. The district must also apportion water among its members and provide drainage to facilitate irrigation work. Most water-procurement operations of irrigation districts are necessarily small. Where large regional developments are necessary to insure the water supply, as is common in the Central Valley, the irrigation districts must depend upon a state or national agency.

Irrigation districts may also purchase or generate electric power and provide for its transmission and sale. Only a few districts utilize this function, but the magnitude of their operations is considerable. Electric-power sales constitute over 30 per cent of all irrigation-district receipts. The importance of district irrigation activities is reflected in the acreage involved. The total area of all districts is approximately 4,500,000 acres, or more than 7,000 square miles, of which about one-half is irrigated crop land.*

---

* State Controller, *Annual Report of Financial Transactions Concerning Irrigation Districts of California, Calendar Year 1958* (Sacramento: State Printing Office, 1959).

District Relations with Other Governments

Except for the requirements of its formation procedure, the irrigation district is independent of the county. State regulation of irrigation districts begins with the stipulation that the state engineer make a feasibiliy report upon each projected district before the proposal for its formation is brought to a vote. This report includes a thorough investigation of the district's financial, agricultural, and engineering practicability. If the state engineer reports unfavorably, a three-fourths majority at an election is required to organize the district. Through informal relationships the state engineer stops many incipient districts before they have reached the petition stage. Then too, if some alteration of plans would increase the feasibility of the proposed district, the state engineer will advise local leaders to make such changes. Irrigation-district bond issues must be approved by the District Securities Commission, and expenditures from approved bond sales must be made under commission supervision. Direct relations between irrigation districts and the Federal Government have been established through Bureau of Reclamation operations as a major supplier of water in the Central Valley and the Imperial Valley:

> The construction of the Central Valley Project by agencies of the Federal Government and the development of the irrigation potentialities of the Colorado River have had a marked effect on the California irrigation district movement during the past decade. The availability of new sources of water has prompted 15 districts to execute contracts with the Bureau of Reclamation and the U. S. Department of the Interior for supplemental water supplies and, in some instances, for distribution systems. . . . Execution of these contracts has created a wide range of problems of intergovernmental relations, administrative, economic, and legal°

Soil-Conservation Districts

Most of the soil-conservation districts have been formed since 1941 primarily as a result of efforts by the United States Depart-

---

° Assembly Interim Committee on Conservation, Planning and Public Works, *Irrigation District Movement in California: A Summary* (Sacramento: State Printing Office, 1955), p. 9.

ment of Agriculture. The districts are governed by five elected directors, and their function is the furtherance of soil-conservation activities within their areas. Their formation is supervised, and their work assisted, by the State Soil Conservation Commission. They cooperate closely with the national government in stimulating individual farmers to adopt soil-conservation practices. Important activities of the districts include the construction of improvements, such as terraces for soil conservation, and the regulation of cropping and range practices, subject to approval by landowners at an election.

❁ ❁ ❁

Vitality is the prevailing characteristic of local government in California. Cities and counties, the two local units that were most significant in the early years, continue to be important. They have recently been joined in large numbers by a third type of local government, the special-purpose district. All three units are active and influential. Although they are by no means perfect, the local governments of California have, on the whole, a highly respectable record, especially when compared with the other states. Nevertheless, there is still much room for progress; there is also no doubt that California has the potential of developing a sound, progressive, and flexible system of local government. The full attainment of such a goal should be a matter of concern to both private citizens and public officials in a state faced with the constant challenge of adjustment to the pressures of an increasing population.

Further Reading

Bollens, John C., *Special District Governments in the United States.* Berkeley and Los Angeles: University of California Press, 1957.

California, Assembly Interim Committee on Conservation, Planning and Public Works, *Adapting Government to Metropolitan Needs: A Review of Organizational Devices,* by Stanley Scott and others. Sacramento, 1957.

————, *Irrigation District Movement in California.* Sacramento, 1955.

————, *A Metropolitan Multipurpose District for California.* Sacramento, 1959.

————, Commission on School Districts, *The Process of Optional Reorganization of School Districts.* Sacramento, 1947.

California Commission on Public School Administration, *A Pattern for School Administration in California.* Sacramento: State Department of Education, 1955.

California Department of Education, *Financing Small Elementary Schools and Small High Schools in California.* Sacramento, 1955.

————, *Study of Local School Units in California.* Sacramento, 1937.

Strayer, George D., *A Design for the Administration of Public Education, with Particular Reference to California.* Stanford: Stanford University Press, 1955.

Fourteen

Metropolitan Areas

DURING THE PERIOD since World War II a
wide range of problems involving heavily urbanized areas has
received growing public attention in California as well as in many
other states. These metropolitan problems originate in a whole
series of developments affecting a large part of the total population of the United States and the other countries of the world.

WHY METROPOLITAN PROBLEMS?

One major cause of metropolitan problems is growing pains.
The population is constantly expanding beyond the capacity of
the available public facilities, as well as beyond the boundaries
of the local governmental units established to provide these
necessary facilities and public controls. Thus the failure of local
governmental boundaries to adjust to a rapidly increasing population is an important source of these problems—but by no means
the only one. Urbanized areas that once were separate and distinct have grown together and coalesced, while the legal limits
of the governmental units have changed less rapidly. Great metropolitan complexes with a high degree of internal economic interdependence have been created, yet they are divided govern-
mentally.

The Los Angeles County-Orange County metropolitan area is
a case in point. This area, which is practically a solid mass of

urbanization, is governed by two counties, 84 cities, 161 school districts, and 531 other special districts and taxing jurisdictions, making a total of 778 governmental units. Local government in the San Francisco Bay area is even more dispersed, with 9 counties, 81 cities, 304 school districts, and 573 other special districts—totaling 976 governmental units.

Another important cause of metropolitan problems is found in the increased mobility of urban people. The automobile and the freeway make it possible for people to crisscross governmental boundaries for work, shopping, and social activities. The old boundaries, therefore, no longer contain self-sufficient populations. The economic interdependence of various parts of a metropolitan area is not paralleled by linkages or close interrelationships among governments functioning in the area.

Still another source of metropolitan problems lies in the increased standard of living and greater leisure time which characterize post-war America, and especially California. Under these conditions, urban residents expect more satisfactions from life under urban conditions than they did in times past. Consequently, much greater demands are made upon governmental and nongovernmental service agencies than was true 25 or 50 years ago. In the private sector of the economy these increased demands are fulfilled reasonably well—at least for a major portion of the population—by new automobiles, television sets, comfortable homes, refrigerators, supermarkets, and the other sources of consumer goods.

The public sector of the economy has served the needs of urban populations less adequately. The schools are crowded and their results are being questioned. Streets are congested and parking spaces are hard to find. Public transportation is one of the great service failures in metropolitan areas. Air pollution is another serious problem. Urban development is sprawling and open space is disappearing. Recreation areas and facilities are inadequate. Metropolitan communities are confronted by slums, juvenile delinquency, mental illness, family breakdown, racial discrimination, and other social problems.

Man's ability to control and manipulate his environment is very great. The necessary technical skill is available to clean the air and water of pollution, build adequate freeways, develop transportation systems, and eliminate slums. Psychologists and sociologists know a great deal about the causes of social maladjustment, juvenile delinquency, and mental illness. But these skills are not being utilized to the extent that they could be. Many metropolitan problems are of this nature: the technical knowledge and resources necessary to effect solutions are available, but public decisions to organize and apply them have not been made.

There are many reasons why accomplishment has lagged behind ability in dealing with metropolitan problems. Financial difficulties may stand in the way. Political and ideological conflicts may be the obstacle, or a lack of consensus among the affected groups may prevent action. Sometimes, delay has resulted from public unawareness that certain technical solutions are feasible. An important reason for the failure to make public decisions on metropolitan area problems, however, is the absence of a decision-making body—the lack of an area-wide forum for sustained study and public discussion of major problems confronting the metropolitan community.

The key words here are study and discussion—careful study, and organized, regular discussion that can get somewhere and have a lasting effect. A great deal of discussion takes place now —on the part of city councils and county boards of supervisors, chambers of commerce, school boards, welfare councils, state legislative committees, organizations such as the Commonwealth Club and Town Hall, service clubs, voters' leagues, and many others. But there is no method of focusing the results of these scattered discussions for review and consideration by a permanent, representative, area-wide forum.

The Role of Government in the Metropolitan Area

The problems of metropolitan areas are by no means the exclusive province of local government. The state and national governments are also concerned in a multitude of ways. For example, the federal social welfare, urban renewal and public housing programs represent important attempts to deal with problems besetting the metropolitan areas. The state government's freeway building program and the financial assistance given for city street construction mean that the state plays an important role in developing the street and arterial systems in metropolitan areas. Through its division of Bay toll crossings, the state acts as the bridge-building agency for the San Francisco Bay area. The statewide but regionally decentralized water pollution control program becomes, in the metropolitan areas, essentially a metropolitan control program. The state Department of Public Health is playing an increasingly significant role in the study of air pollution control programs, and particularly those relating to mobile sources, such as automobile exhausts, which may prove difficult for the metropolitan air pollution control districts to handle unaided. The state's Feather River Project is largely a program to develop new water sources for the southern California metropolitan areas. These are only a few examples of the many ways in which the state and federal governments are deeply concerned with urban needs.

Despite the extent of federal and state involvement in these problems, however, local government is normally expected to take the primary responsibility for the actual administration of services, facilities and controls in metropolitan areas. Or, if existing local governments appear to be inadequate, a locally-based regional district or authority may be created to do the job. The American philosophy of local government and home rule, stressing the use of community-based governmental organizations whenever possible, is the ideological foundation for this emphasis. Because of the resulting central role of local government in any discussion of metropolitan problems, it is appropriate to survey the existing local governmental patterns in selected California metropolitan areas.

The Patterns of Local Government in Selected Metropolitan Areas

There are three basic governmental patterns found in the major metropolitan areas of California: (1) the Los Angeles pattern with one dominant county and a multitude of cities; (2) the San Francisco Bay area pattern with a multiplicity of counties, as well as a large number of cities, and (3) the single-county pattern found in San Diego, Sacramento, Fresno, Kern, Santa Barbara, and other counties where there is one major central city and very few other municipalities.

Metropolitan Los Angeles*

Within its single county, a good deal of governmental integration has taken place in the Los Angeles metropolitan area gradually over a period of about 40 years.

(1) Many local functions have been transferred in whole or in part from cities to the county. One of the earliest functional transfers occurred in 1907 when Los Angeles County took over property tax assessment and collection from the city of LaVerne. At present every city within the county receives some service from the county, and nineteen get most of their municipal services from the county under contract (the Lakewood Plan).

(2) Los Angeles County provides many municipal-type services in the unincorporated urban area, either directly or through special districts. Among the services so provided are fire protection and sewers (through districts), police protection, building inspection, streets and highways, planning and zoning, and recreation facilities.

(3) Formal and informal agreements have done much to reduce administrative difficulties and facilitate day-to-day cooperation among the many different governments operating in close proximity. Examples of these arrangements are the agreements for mutual aid in fighting fires and for cooperation in meeting law enforcement problems.

(4) Los Angeles County and certain specially created metropolitan districts have assumed a number of area-wide functions. The Los Angeles County Air Pollution Control District, the Los Angeles County Flood Control District, and the Los Angeles County Regional Planning Commission are all area-wide agencies

---

* This discussion is limited to Los Angeles County, although growth has been so great that Orange County is now, in reality, an integral part of the Los Angeles metropolitan area, and several other counties are significantly affected.

controlled by the county government in an ex officio capacity. The county sanitation districts of Los Angeles County form a distinct entity, although the county participates in their administration. The Los Angeles Metropolitan Transit Authority includes the whole county and is controlled by a seven-man board appointed by the governor. The Metropolitan Water District of Southern California is a truly regional government, extending far beyond the boundaries of Los Angeles County.

(5) A final and extremely important integrating factor has been the growth of the city of Los Angeles itself. With a population of 2,300,000 and an area of 455 square miles, Los Angeles has, by the very fact of its existence, helped to unify the metropolitan area in a governmental sense. Certainly the governmental structure of the area would be vastly different if the city of Los Angeles were broken into 20 or 30 cities of 50,000 to 100,000 each.

The San Francisco Bay Area

The most important single feature distinguishing the pattern of government in the San Francisco Bay area is the existence of nine separate county governments, and absence of a single dominating unit. For this reason, the San Francisco Bay area has not been able to depend on the county government to provide a framework for some degree of metropolitan integration, as has Los Angeles. Also, the central city of San Francisco is not the dominant feature—at least in terms of population and geography—that the city of Los Angeles is in the southern metropolis. Whereas the city of Los Angeles has 40 per cent of the county's total population and 11 per cent of its land area, San Francisco has only 23 per cent of the population and less than 1 per cent of the land area.

This relative dispersion of governmental authority has had two important consequences for the San Francisco Bay area. First, the area is simply not as well organized as the Los Angeles area. Second, the San Francisco Bay area has been forced to devise other techniques in attempting to solve its metropolitan problems—it has not been able to depend on a single encompassing county or on a gargantuan central city. As a result, it has done a good deal of experimentation with metropolitan special districts. The most important of these are the East Bay Municipal Utility District, the East Bay Regional Park District, the Golden Gate Bridge and Highway District, the Bay Area Air Pollution Control District, the Alameda-Contra Costa Transit District, and the San Francisco Bay Area Rapid Transit District. Each of these districts provides service to an area of from two to six counties.

Because the Bay Area Air Pollution Control District is being viewed as something of a prototype for metropolitan district structure in the Bay area, it will be useful to take a closer look at the district's pattern of organization. The governing board consists of two representatives from each county within which the district is active—six counties at present. One member of each pair is a county supervisor, chosen by the county board of supervisors. The other representative is a city mayor or councilman chosen by a "city selection committee" made up of all the mayors within the county.

The district's governing board constitutes, in effect, a "federation" of the participating cities and counties, six of the board members representing the counties, and six representing the cities. The district is thus headed by an indirectly elected policy-making board, giving the local governments some voice in the administration of district affairs. This was done, in part, because the cities and counties were considered to have a vital interest in air pollution control, and because it was believed their direct participation would help to insure better coordination between the district and the local governments.

The concept of a "federated" district, including representation of the participating local governments, is not unique to the Bay Area Air Pollution Control District, but is actually quite widespread. Both the Metropolitan Water District of Southern California and the County Sanitation Districts of Los Angeles County embody the principle, as does the Golden Gate Bridge and Highway District, the newly created San Francisco Bay Area Rapid Transit District, and many other districts of various types. It was the use of this principle in the Bay Area Air Pollution Control District, however, which focused attention on this pattern as a possible basis for effective metropolitan governmental bodies both in the Bay area and elsewhere in California.

Other California Metropolitan Areas

The San Diego, Sacramento, Fresno, Bakersfield, and Stockton urban regions are single-county metropolitan areas. They have relatively few municipalities, other than the dominant central city, and, except for San Diego County, they possess extensive unincorporated urban fringe areas adjacent to the central city. The San Diego metropolitan area has only six small suburban municipalities in the immediate vicinity of the central city. The latter, located in the southwest portion of the county, has approximately three-fourths of the metropolitan population, and more than four-fifths of the incorporated territory. There is one important complication, however, which will probably be of increasing significance and for which there will be no easy solution. An international boundary—the border between the United States and Mexico—passes through the San Diego metropolitan area. A rapidly growing population currently estimated at between 150,000 and 200,000 live on the Mexican side, in the state of Baja California, but are clearly being drawn more and more into the economy of the larger metropolitan area. In another way, however, the San Diego area appears to be well ahead of the other single-county metropolitan areas. This results from a strong annexation policy by the central city which has been highly successful in recent years.

The Sacramento metropolitan area has only one other municipality in the vicinity of the central city. Lying east and northeast of the city of Sacramento are extensive urban unincorporated areas which are much larger than the city itself, in both population and in area. The problems arising from this situation have prompted several years of study and investigation, culminating in a report with recommendations made by the Metropolitan Government Committee in June, 1959. The report contained three basic points: First, it recommended against an earlier proposal for full city-county consolidation. Second, it urged a program of large-scale annexation to the city of Sacramento, with the goal of bringing into the city as soon as possible all those areas which will be urbanized by the year 1980. Third, the report called for functional consolidations between the city of Sacramento and Sacramento County, placing selected area-wide functions under single administration.

The governmental situation in the Fresno metropolitan area is quite similar to that of metropolitan Sacramento. Early in 1959, both the city and the county agreed to support a metropolitan survey along the lines of that conducted in Sacramento, but smaller in scale. This survey will result in a report with recommendations.

THE LEGISLATURE LOOKS AT METROPOLITAN AREAS

Six recent California legislative committee reports have dealt with the general problem of government in metropolitan areas. The first reviewed different approaches which have been employed in attempting to handle metropolitan problems, including regional planning commissions, single or multi-purpose districts and authorities, and comprehensive governmental reorganization, but made no specific recommendations.*

Two companion reports published in 1959 dealt specifically with the question of using metropolitan multi-purpose districts to solve existing problems.† As an outgrowth of these reports, a bill was introduced in the 1959 session of the state Legislature to make possible the creation of metropolitan multi-purpose districts by local action. The bill (AB 1896) was considered in committee but was reassigned for further study during the 1959-61 interim.

A fourth legislative committee report, also published in 1959, reviewed the various alternatives for metropolitan government. The report did not present a specific recommendation, but alerted the Legislature to recent trends, and to the probability that early legislative action of some kind would be necessary:‡

There is a definite trend toward increased recognition that a number of the services presently provided by numerous cities

---

* California Legislature, Assembly Interim Committee on Conservation, Planning and Public Works, *Adapting Government to Metropolitan Needs: A Review of Organizational Devices* (1957).

† California Legislature. Assembly Interim Committee on Conservation, Planning and Public Works, *Metropolitan Government in California.* (1959); and *A Metropolitan Multipurpose District for California* (1959).

‡ California Legislature. Assembly Interim Committee on Municipal and County Government, *Concepts in Metropolitan Government* (1959), p. 24.

and special districts in metropolitan areas in the State of California could be better provided by a single centralized government. It would seem that some time in the not too distant future one or more of the areas presently studying or discussing metropolitan problems, such as Los Angeles, Sacramento, Fresno, and Santa Clara, will present a plan for metropolitan government to the Legislature to effect their study recommendations.

A prime factor for the Legislature to determine is, should each area be authorized to adopt a specific, tailormade plan for their area or should a single flexible plan be developed for the use of all areas in the state? . . .

The Senate Interim Committee on Metropolitan Areas issued a report in June, 1959 to the effect that further study of its assigned subject would be required. The committee laid special emphasis on the importance of the state's role:*

At the present writing, state participation would appear to be indicated, first, in an appraisal of the adequacy of our present systems of local government. A second step would be the enactment of permissive legislation authorizing the creation of metropolitan units that will be adequate as to functions, financial ability, and control by the people who reside in the areas affected. Related to this, a third step would be the adoption of methods to be used in putting the metropolitan units into operation.

Major Legislative Proposals—1959 Session

Five proposals of state-wide interest were introduced at the 1959 session of the California Legislature to establish, or permit the establishment of, various kinds of metropolitan districts and authorities. Three of the bills were held over for interim committee study during 1959-61: AB 1896, which would permit the creation of metropolitan multi-purpose districts, AB 919, which would allow metropolitan municipal service authorities to be set up, and AB 2477, which would enable metropolitan fire protection authorities to be established. All three of these proposals, as amended, embody systems of representation adapted from that of the Bay Area Air Pollution Control District. Senate Bill 576

---

* *Senate Journal,* June 8, 1959, p. 3397.

created a Golden Gate Authority Commission to study further the possibility of establishing a single port, airport and bridge authority in the San Francisco Bay area. Senate Bill 644 created the eight-county San Joaquin Valley Air Pollution Control District, based on the Bay area district's pattern. Activation of the San Joaquin Valley district depends upon gaining a favorable popular vote in the area at the November 1960 election.

THE GOVERNOR'S COMMISSION

In March, 1959, Governor Brown appointed a state Commission on Metropolitan Area Problems and charged it with the task of studying the problems and recommending solutions. Certain problem areas were marked out for special consideration by the commission, including transportation, freeways, streets and rails; housing, redevelopment and land use planning; the prevention of air pollution and water contamination; maximum economy in public services; and the structure of government in metropolitan areas.

CONCLUSION—THE IMPORTANCE OF FURTHER STUDY

The following remarks of Coleman Woodbury, director of urban studies, University of Wisconsin, constitute an excellent statement about the importance of metropolitan area problems and the need for further study:[*]

> Of the traditional three levels of government in the United States, local government contributes most to the quality of our civilization and its day-to-day life. . . . I submit that local public agencies, in educating our children and some adults, protecting the public health and safety, maintaining peace and order, providing most of our facilities for noncommercial recreation, making more nearly tolerable the frictions and costs of urban circulation, influencing markedly the amenities and satisfactions of our residential areas, guiding the intricate processes by which newcomers to urban areas . . . learn to adjust to new conditions and responsibilities, and providing opportunities for

---

[*] *Public Administration Review* (Autumn, 1958), p. 339-40.

direct participation in public affairs, play a more significant role in determining the *quality* of our increasingly urban civilization.

In what we do about metropolitan communities and their problems, therefore, the stakes are high—very high. They fully justify all the attention, funds, and brain power they now attract —and much more besides.

Further Reading

Berkeley, Office of the City Manager, *A Report to the Berkeley City Council on Metropolitan Government*, by John D. Phillips. Berkeley, 1958.

Bigger, Richard D. and others, *Metropolitan Coast: San Diego and Orange Counties, California*. Los Angeles: University of California at Los Angeles, Bureau of Governmental Research, 1958.

Bollens, John C., *The Problem of Government in the San Francisco Bay Region*. Berkeley: University of California, Bureau of Public Administration, 1948.

California, Legislature, Assembly Interim Committee on Conservation, Planning and Public Works, *Adapting Government to Metropolitan Needs—A Review of Organizational Devices*, by Stanley Scott and others. Sacramento, 1957.

————, *Metropolitan Government in California—A Background Study with Recommendations*, by Pacific Planning and Research. Sacramento, 1959.

————, *A Metropolitan Multipurpose District for California—Report of the Subcommittee on Planning*. Sacramento, 1959.

California Legislature, Interim Committee on Municipal and County Government, *Concepts in Metropolitan Government*. Sacramento, 1959.

Cottrell, Edwin A. and Helen L. Jones, *The Metropolis—Is Integration Possible?* Los Angeles: Haynes Foundation, 1955.

Council of State Governments, *The States and the Metropolitan Problem—A Report to the Governor's Conference*. John C. Bollens, study director. Chicago, 1956.

Los Angeles Chamber of Commerce, State and Local Government Committee, *Proceedings—Metropolitan Government Symposium, April 8, 1958*. Los Angeles, 1958.

Public Administration Service, *The Government of Metropolitan Sacramento*. Chicago, 1957.

Sacramento Metropolitan Government Committee, *Governmental Reorganization for Metropolitan Sacramento*. Sacramento, 1959.

Index